W9-BFL-172

Crime Prevention at a Crossroads

Edited by Steven P. Lab
Bowling Green State University

North East Multi-Regional Training
-Instructors' Library-
355 Smoke Tree Plaza
North Aurora, IL 60542

ACJS Series Editor, Joycelyn M. Pollock

Academy of Criminal Justice Sciences
Northern Kentucky University
402 Nunn Hall
Highland Heights, KY 41076

Anderson Publishing Co.
Criminal Justice Division
P.O. Box 1576
Cincinnati, OH 45201-1576

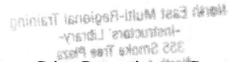
North East Multi-Regional Training
-Instructors' Library-
355 Smoke Tree Plaza

Crime Prevention at a Crossroads

Copyright © 1997 by Anderson Publishing Co. and the Academy of Criminal Justice Sciences

All rights reserved. No part of this book may be reproduced in any form or by any electronic or mechanical means including information storage and retrieval systems without permission in writing from the copyright holders.

ISBN 0-87084-511-X
Library of Congress Catalog Number 97-70841

Gail Eccleston *Editor*
Elizabeth A. Shipp *Assistant Editor*

Acknowledgments

Attempting to acknowledge all those who have contributed in some way to a book is fraught with danger since it is inevitable that someone will be inadvertently left out. This problem is magnified in an edited work when the many people who contributed to the individual works are unknown to the editor. Despite this fact, I am indebted to several people. First, this work emerged from several panels I coordinated at the 1995 ACJS Annual Meeting in Boston. The Program Chair, Bob Langworthy, asked me to undertake that task and suggested using those panels as a point of departure for this book. Second, I cannot thank the contributing authors enough for allowing me to include their papers. Having served as a journal editor in the past, I can attest to the quality of the papers I received and the fact that little copyediting was needed in these papers. When I had suggestions or questions, the authors responded immediately to my needs. Most of the delays in this project were my fault and I apologize to the authors, and thank them for sticking with me. Finally, I thank the Series Editor, Joy Pollock, the staff at Anderson, and the Academy for including this volume in their monograph series.

Preface

The ACJS/Anderson series has produced monographs that present important new information for criminal justice audiences. This addition to the series explores aspects of crime prevention—arguably, the central issue of the entire field. In this volume, Steve Lab has brought together a series of articles that explores every facet of crime prevention, from a historical description of early forms of prevention to current efforts, such as neighborhood policing. In the journey, authors also make contributions to our knowledge of criminology theories, especially rational choice theory and recent formulations of control theory. The effects of architecture on crime prevention are examined, as is crime prevention on college campuses and in our schools. Each of the articles contributes to a theme that historical and political influences shape our efforts at crime prevention.

Neighborhood policing might be described as the current "fad" in crime control and crime prevention. This volume offers several insights into the historical parallels between the current approach of neighborhood policing and older models of community involvement. Evaluations indicate that the association between neighborhood characteristics, police presence, and crime prevention are complicated and neighborhood policing efforts may have more effect on perception than reality in crime reduction.

The authors brought together in this volume contribute important insights to the field of crime prevention and the volume itself emphasizes the importance of prevention over punishment. Despite the inclination of some to dissect the problem of crime from other social realities, the influence of unemployment, disenfranchisement, broken families, a lack of political power, structural inequalities, and other social problems are clearly intertwined with crime prevention, and realistic efforts aimed at crime prevention cannot ignore their influence. This volume helps shed light on these important topics.

Joycelyn M. Pollock, Ph.D., J.D.
ACJS/Anderson Monograph Series Editor
Southwest Texas State University

Contents

1

Crime Prevention: Where Have We Been and Which Way Should We Go?

Steven P. Lab
Bowling Green State University

Crime prevention is not a new idea. Indeed, for as long as people have been victimized there have been attempts to protect one's self and one's family. The term "crime prevention," however, has only recently come to signify a set of ideas for combatting crime. Many recent activities classified as crime prevention can be seen throughout history. Indeed, "new" crime prevention ideas and techniques are often little more than reincarnations of past practices or extensions of basic approaches in the (distant) past. The form of prevention has varied greatly over the centuries—from retribution to surveillance to deterrence to social engineering to physical design, and beyond.

CRIME PREVENTION THROUGH THE AGES

In any discussion it is important to set forth the context from which our ideas and thoughts emerge. Perhaps the best place to start is with an understanding of what has happened in the past. The study of crime prevention is no exception. Indeed, many people suggest that what we are doing today is new and unique, particularly when we talk about citizen participation. In reality, it is only in the relatively recent past that the general citizenry has *not* been the primary line of defense against crime and victimization. The following discussion, therefore, represents a brief discussion of crime prevention throughout history. While necessarily general, it provides a framework from which to launch other discussions.

A Thumbnail Sketch of Early Crime Prevention

The earliest responses to crime were left to the individual and his or her family. There was no societal agency that would intervene on the behalf of an aggrieved individual. Instead, self-help was the primary response (Wormser, 1962). Retribution, revenge and vengeance were the driving forces throughout early history. While such actions would serve to make the victim whole again, they also would eliminate the benefit gained by the offender. An additional underlying assumption was that potential offenders would see little gain in an offense, thereby deterring the individual from taking action. Some of the earliest sets of laws, such as the Code of Hammurabi (dating roughly from 1750 B.C.), outlined retribution by the victim and/or his or her family as the accepted response to injurious behavior. *Lex talionis*, the principle of "an eye for an eye," was specifically set forth as a driving principle in the Hammurabic Law. The proscription of individual/familial retribution for crime appears in many other early laws, including the Justinian Code (534 A.D.) which appears almost 2500 years after Hammurabi laid out his code. These laws and practices provided legitimacy to individual citizen action.

For the most part, the existence of any formal system of social control is a relatively new idea. While it is possible to point to "policing" in some early civilizations (such as the Roman Empire and in France) (see, Holden, 1992; Langworthy & Travis, 1994), these efforts often displayed several features which mitigated their use by most citizens. First, they were highly concentrated in the cities. Second, most policing was done by the military. Third, and most importantly, the laws enforced by these "police" typically involved issues of the central state and the nobility (i.e., king), and not common concerns of the citizens (Holden, 1992). Due to the limited usefulness of these early forms of police, people were left with the need to continue self-help methods.

The Norman conquest of England in 1066 gave rise to an *obligatory* form of avocational citizen policing (Klockars, 1985). Following the conquest, male citizens were required to band together into groups for the purpose of policing each other. If one individual in the group caused harm (to a group or nongroup member), the other members were responsible for apprehending and sanctioning the offender. Failure to take action was itself an offense. While this practice served as a means of addressing harm against the individual, it was largely meant to eliminate threats to the Crown.

Beyond this obligatory action, a variety of cooperative practices emerged that relied on citizen participation to protect the community and one another. One practice, "watch and ward," rotated the responsibility for keeping watch over the town or area, particularly at night, among the male citizens. Should a threat be identified by this individual, he would raise the alarm and call for help ("hue and cry"). It was then up to the general citizenry to apprehend and (possibly) punish the offender. Those responding to the call for help were not employees of the state. Rather, they were other common citizens. This approach to policing was codified in 1285 in the Statutes of Winchester (Klockars, 1985). Besides the "watch and ward" and "hue and cry" ideas, the statutes also required men to have weapons available for use when called ("assize of arms"), and outlined the role of a "constable," which was an unpaid position responsible for coordinating the watch and ward system and overseeing other aspects of the law. Every able-bodied male in the community was supposed to take a turn at being constable. It is apparent throughout these actions that crime prevention was a major responsibility of the citizenry.

The individual, often voluntary, responsibility for crime prevention generally persisted until the 1800s. The exceptions to this trend can be seen in the development of paid, private security police for specialized industries or groups (Klockars, 1985; Langworthy & Travis, 1994). The Merchant Police of England, which was established in the sixteenth century to protect the wool industry, is a prime example of an early private police force. The "parochial" police, hired by the wealthy to protect their homes and businesses, is another example.

The passage of the Highwayman Act in 1692 in England set up a new entrepreneurial form of policing. This law outlined the practice of paying bounty to individuals for the capture of thieves and the recovery of property. While originally intended as a means of protecting shipments of goods from city to city, the idea had immediate implications for the general public. These voluntary bounty hunters came to be known as "thief takers" (Klockars, 1985; LaGrange, 1993). By the mid 1700s, the thief takers were organized under the leadership of English magistrates. These thief takers, who were often reformed criminals themselves, were "paid" to protect the public by being able to keep a portion of all recovered property.

The evolution of the thief takers from a wholly voluntary activity to a legitimized, organized group under government control was the beginning of a process which ended with the establishment of the Metropolitan Police in London in 1829. At this point, the main responsibility for law enforcement and public protection was shifted from volunteer citizens to paid, professional police. Key to this new police organization was the idea of crime prevention. Sir Robert Peel, who was the driving force behind the Metropolitan Police Act, and Charles Roman, the commissioner of the new organization, both saw crime prevention as the basic principle underlying police work (LaGrange, 1993). Even earlier attempts at formal policing, such as that in 17th century Paris, emphasized crime prevention through methods such as preventive patrol, increased lighting, and street cleaning (Stead, 1983).

The dominance of volunteer activity was not restricted to England and Europe. Similar citizen responsibility was common place in the new world colonies and the early United States. The vigilante movement, which mirrored early ideas of "hue and cry," was a major component of enforcing law and order in the growing frontier of the young country (Klockars, 1985). Posses of citizens were formed when an offender needed to be apprehended and (possibly) punished. Formal police forces, mirroring the movement in England, emerged in the mid-1800s and were restricted primarily to the largest U.S. cities in the northeast, leaving citizens to continue their efforts at self-protection.

While the foregoing discussion has emphasized the dominance of individual action and self-help that prevailed throughout most of history, it should not be construed as indicative that protective actions were solely a matter of retribution and revenge. There are numerous examples of alternative approaches to dealing with crime, many of which were preventative in nature. Two examples were the use of walls and moats around cities to protect the community from external invasion. Many of the approaches already discussed provided surveillance as a means of identifying problems before they got out of hand. Yet another prevention approach was the restriction of weapon ownership as a means of eliminating violent behavior (Holden, 1992). However, despite these examples, the dominant trend before the advent of formal policing in the 1800s was the reliance on individuals to protect themselves.

Twentieth Century Crime Prevention

The advent of the twentieth century witnessed a great deal of change in societal response to deviant behavior. Not only was a formal police force becoming the norm, other forces were emerging to address crime and deviance. Not the least of these changes was the growth of the scientific study of crime and criminal behavior. The emerging fields of psychology and sociology in the late 1800s and early 1900s were beginning to question the causes of deviant behavior. Rather than carry on the dominant tradition of attributing deviance to the battle between good and evil (God and the devil), researchers were starting to note patterns in where and when offenses occurred and who was involved in the offenses, and to relate these facts to changing social structure and personal relationships. The logical result of this growing study was a movement away from simple responses involving repression, vengeance, retribution, and the like to actions that would attack the assumed causes of deviant behavior. The emerging criminal and juvenile justice systems, therefore, responded by incorporating more prevention-oriented functions into their activity.

Save the Less Fortunate

One prime example of an early "crime prevention" approach was the development of the juvenile court and its efforts to combat the problems of poverty, lack of education, and poor parenting among the lower classes of society. While it can be argued whether this was a benevolent action or one driven by a desire to keep the status quo (see, for example, Platt, 1977; Krisberg & Austin, 1978), the reality is that an emphasis was placed on correcting a problem before it occurred. Children were separated from their problem households and neighborhoods in an attempt to provide the love, guidance, and education needed to lead a productive life (see Whitehead & Lab, 1996 for a more complete discussion).

The preventive nature of the juvenile system can be seen in its philosophy and operation. The *parens patriae* philosophy argued that youths needed help and that processing in adult courts was geared to punishment rather than prevention. Consequently, a new system was needed that emphasized molding proper behavior early in life, similar to the role of a parent. A natural companion to this philosophy was the expansion of the juvenile court's jurisdiction to cover *status offenses*. It was believed that curfew violation, smoking, playing in the street, incorrigibility, and other such actions (none of which were proscribed by the criminal code) were indicative of later criminal behavior. Thus, intervening in these status offenses was a means of preventing later crime. The juvenile system, therefore, was clearly an attempt at crime prevention.

Altering the Social Fabric

A more recognized form of early preventive action is the work of the Chicago Area Project. This project was based on the research of Shaw and McKay (1931, 1942) in which they found crime and delinquency concentrating in the central areas of Chicago, and persisting in those areas despite demographic changes over time. Identifying a high level of transiency and an apparent lack of social ties in these areas as the root cause of the problems, Shaw and McKay (1942) labeled the problem as *social disorganization*. What this meant was that the constant turnover of residents resulted in an inability for the people to exert any informal social control over the individuals in the area. People were more interested in improving themselves and moving out of these neighborhoods than in improving the area and staying there. Consequently, offenders could act with some degree of impunity in these neighborhoods.

Shaw's proposed solution to the problem of social disorganization was to work with the residents to build a sense of pride and community, thereby prompting people to stay and exert control over the actions of people in the area. The Chicago Area Project (CAP) was founded in 1931 as a vehicle for building a self-help atmosphere. The key to the CAP was the generation of community support through the use of community volunteers and existing neighborhood institutions. Recreation for youths, vigilance and community self-renewal, and mediation were the major components to building that support (Schlossman & Sedlak, 1983). In essence, the project sought to build ongoing, thriving communities that could control the behavior of both its residents and those who visited the area.

The Physical Environment

Crime prevention experienced perhaps its biggest boost with the emergence of physical design as a topic of debate. Led by the work of Jane Jacobs (1961) and Oscar Newman (1972), flaws in the physical environment were identified as causes of, or at least facilitators for, criminal behavior. Newman (1972), an architect, argued that the physical characteristics of an area have the potential to suggest to residents and potential offenders that the area is either well cared for and protected, or it is open for criminal activity. Design features conducive to criminal behavior would include common entrances for a large number of people, poorly placed windows inhibiting casual surveillance of grounds and common areas, hidden entrances, easy access for illegitimate users, isolated buildings, and other features which make it easier for an offender to commit a crime and escape with minimal risk of detection and apprehension.

Where Newman focused primarily on housing projects, Wilson and Kelling's (1982) discussion of *broken windows* extended this reasoning to entire neighborhoods. "Broken windows" refers to physical signs that an area is uncared for. Abandoned buildings and automobiles, the presence of trash and litter, broken windows and lights, and graffiti may all invite further social problems by indicating to potential offenders that there is no one around who will stop them (Lewis & Salem, 1986). Besides the physical indicators, social manifestations of the same problems may be loitering youths, public drunkenness, prostitution, and vagrancy (Taylor & Gottfredson, 1986). Both the physical and social indicators are typically referred to as signs of *incivility* that attract offenders to the area. Removal of such signs should make the area appear more protected and a less promising site for crime.

The interest in environmental causes, both physical and social, prompted a great deal of research and intervention in the 1970s and 1980s. Programs aimed at altering the construction of public housing, altering traffic and road patterns, installing better lights and locks, marking property with identification numbers, cleaning up buildings and neighborhoods, and promoting citizen interaction were instituted under the rubric of crime prevention. The aim of all these efforts was twofold—encourage citizens to take control of their area, and present an image to potential offenders that there is increased risk in offending in the area.

Organize the Public

Early evaluations of the physical design movement demonstrated that such changes, by themselves, are not sufficient for altering the level of crime (see Lab, 1997). In essence, physical design changes cannot stop a truly motivated offender and cannot capture the offender for further processing. Further, altering the physical environment does not guarantee that residents will become involved and take action. It became clear that direct efforts to enhance active citizen involvement was a necessary companion to physical design changes.

The 1970s saw the rise of community-based crime prevention programs, typically referred to as Neighborhood or Block Watch. These programs used the same premise as physical design approaches—that potential offenders will not commit a crime if they perceive citizen activity, awareness, and concern in an area. In essence, the focus is on citizen surveillance and action. Signs of resident activity, social cohesion, and social support should work to protect the neighborhood. A second component to the growth of citizen involvement was the recognition by law enforcement that they could not stop crime or solve the problems on their own. Instead, there was a growing acceptance among the police that they needed the active help of the citizenry.

A wide array of activities and ideas have been subsumed under the general heading of neighborhood watch. Surveillance is one of the cornerstone ideas, with variations ranging from conducting block parties to get to know the neighbors; to cutting back bushes, installing lighting, and removing obstacles in order to enhance sight lines; to organizing citizen patrols (both walking and vehicular) of the neighborhood. Security surveys are another important service provided by many neighborhood watch groups (Garofalo & McLeod, 1988). The information gathered in these surveys often form the basis for property marking, installing locks and unbreakable glass, notifying neighbors when the house is to be vacant, leaving lights on when away, and removing signs that indicate the house is unoccupied (such as overgrown grass and piling up mail). Yet another common element of neighborhood watch is the distribution of crime and crime prevention news. This can be accomplished through meetings or through the publication of newsletters that contain crime data and/or crime prevention suggestions (Lavrakas, 1986).

Evidence for the effectiveness of community organizing for crime prevention purposes is mixed, although there are examples of programs that reduced crime or the fear of crime (Lab, 1997). Evaluation results show that direct attempts to engender citizen participation and action is more effective than assuming such participation will follow physical design changes. The greatest point of failure for neighborhood watch is in organizing those neighborhoods and areas most in need of help. Rosenbaum (1987, 1988) notes that even concerted efforts to organize high crime communities often fail. Despite this fact, the move to organize citizens and enlist their support in crime prevention activities is a major effort of many police departments and communities.

Situational Approaches

The most recent move in crime prevention has been to focus efforts and interventions on attacking specific problems, places, and times. Clarke (1983) proposed *situational prevention* as "measures directed at highly specific forms of crime that involve" environmental changes that "reduce the opportunities for crime and increase its risks" (p. 225). In essence, situational prevention uses many of the existing crime prevention ideas and techniques to target specific problems in more localized environments. Examples of situational prevention include the installation of surveillance equipment in a parking lot experiencing vandalism, erecting security screens in banks to stop robberies, altering traffic patterns in a drug market neighborhood, use of electronic tags in library materials, and establishing "Caller ID" in response to obscene phone calls (see Clarke, 1992 for additional examples).

The situational approach borrows heavily from a variety of different ideas, theories, and research. One close companion to situational prevention is problem-oriented policing. In both approaches the idea is to define the problem, identify the contributing causes, seek out the proper people or agencies to assist in identifying potential solutions, and work as a group to implement the solution. The police and criminal justice system become both initiators and participants in this process, rather than the sole responsible parties. Other participants may include public health officials, fire marshals, the clerk of courts, the tax department, private businesses, schools, and utility companies.

The fact that the problem drives the solution in situational prevention means that a wide array of theories could be brought to bear on different problems. Among the theoretical approaches most identified with situational prevention are *rational choice*, *routine activities*, and *lifestyles*. Each of these perspectives deals with choice and behavior of both offenders and victims. Understanding the range of options available to the different actors and their decision-making processes would provide insight to the type of preventive action most likely to impact on the identified problem (see, Clarke, 1995 for a more complete explanation of these ideas). Since the problem drives the solution, virtually any theory could be used under the rubric of situational prevention. Clarke (1992) offers a classification of situational techniques (that is further developed later in this book), each of which rely on varying theoretical premises. As such, different solutions would be needed for the problems.

Summary

This short presentation demonstrates that crime prevention is an idea that has been around as long as there has been crime. While the form has changed and the term "crime prevention" is relatively new, the concern over safety is age-old. Perhaps the most interesting point to note is the circular movement back to a reliance on the general citizenry for preventive action. Throughout most of history it was the individual's responsibility, either voluntarily or through obligation, to deal with crime and offenders. It has only been in the recent past that society has moved to a system of police, courts, and corrections that has assumed the primary responsibility. Since the late 1960s, however, there has been a growing movement toward bringing the citizenry back as active participants in crime prevention. While many see this type of community action as "new," in reality it is more a movement back to age-old traditions of individual responsibility than a revolutionary step forward in crime control.

This presentation also illustrates that crime prevention need not be, and is not, restricted to the publicly recognized ideas of neighborhood watch and property marking. Indeed, prevention includes a wide range of ideas not usually considered as prevention. Social inequality, developmental theories, deterrence, community-oriented policing, juvenile court processing, economic development, and other ideas are integrally related to crime prevention.

CONTINUING CHALLENGES FOR CRIME PREVENTION

While crime prevention is not new, there are numerous issues and challenges yet to be addressed. Among these are concerns over competing theoretical bases for interventions, the implementation of programs, the political reality within which any program must develop and exist, reliance on poor or inadequate evaluation, and concerns over displacement and diffusion of benefits. The following discussion highlights some of the more important issues facing the future of crime prevention efforts.

Theoretical Competition

Underlying all crime prevention efforts (hopefully) is some theoretical argument. At the same time, any criminologist can attest to the fact that there is a great deal of debate over the proper explanation for deviant behavior. The social-disorganization, rational-choice, and routine-activities perspectives already discussed are common theoretical bases for crime prevention programs. Many other theories, however, also provide valuable insight to interventions. Learning theory, developmental approaches, strain theory, control theory, deterrence, and critical theories are only a few of the potentially useful frameworks that have been, and should be, considered in designing crime prevention. The unfortunate reality of many prevention programs, especially community-based, is the lack of attention paid to theory. This is particularly noticeable in programs that arise from indigenous community leaders and groups, and that tend to avoid entanglements with outside agencies or experts. The end result may be a jumble of bits and pieces from different, competing theories working at cross purposes to one another. More emphasis needs to be placed on the theoretical development of crime prevention programs.

Program Implementation

A key issue for any program, whether it be related to crime or anything else, is the degree to which the program is adequately implemented. Interventions that are poorly or only partly implemented have a good chance of failure, no matter how well-intentioned or thought-out. For example, a neighborhood watch scheme in a crime-ridden, ethnically divided area that is only able to gain participation from 20 percent of the residents, and that 20 percent exclusively from one of three ethnic groups, should not be expected to have much of an impact on the entire neighborhood or community. Key elements of a successful neighborhood watch, such as enhanced social cohesion, higher recognition of residents, and group action against crime, will not be realized if you cannot gain the participation of the citizens.

The problems of implementation can come from a variety of sources. Poor conceptualization of the problem can lead to a "grab bag" approach in which a little of everything is tried instead of focusing on a few key items. Even if the problem is properly identified, many crime prevention programs operate with a small group of highly committed but poorly trained and supported individuals. Good intentions can only go so far. A program may need specific expertise, outside help, and/or significant funding in order to have an impact. The lack of resources (both personnel and monetary) may mean that only parts of the solution can be implemented. Unfortunately, no matter how well a program addresses one of the causes of the problem, the inability to address other key components will undermine the efforts.

Another potential problem with implementation is the possibility that key agencies, actors, or community members will only half-heartedly participate. Many law enforcement and criminal justice system personnel have questioned the motivations and approaches of individuals and groups who have become involved in crime prevention. Some of this may be due to the "we-versus-them" attitude between the police and the public that has developed over time, particularly in large, heterogeneous cities. It may also be attributable to feelings that the police have the training and the public does not, or to fear of a return to vigilante justice. Breaking through these attitudes and fears has not been easy, as indicated by police opposition to community-oriented policing. The cooperation and participation of criminal justice professionals is often a key to successful implementation, continuation, and effectiveness of crime prevention programs.

The Political Reality

Crime prevention exists and must compete in the political arena, just as any other program or agency. In the United States, citizen crime prevention programs and methods remain secondary to more punitive responses to crime. This is evidenced in the fact that, while there is an established Sentencing Commission, a Drug Czar, and a Department of Corrections (to name a few), there is no similar focal point or agency for crime prevention. In recent years, the political debate in the United States has been whether to increase funding for prisons or enhance crime prevention initiatives.

At a more basic level, many people would argue that politics plays a deciding role in whether crime prevention addresses the immediate problem (crime and victimization) or the root problems (such as poverty, economic inequality, and lack of power). Some would argue that true crime prevention will require an alteration of the economic system under which most western, industrial nations operate. The majority of both offenders and victims come from the disenfranchised groups in society. These groups have little or no political or economic power with which to improve themselves, their neighborhoods, or, for that matter, society. A conflict theorist would suggest that there is a need to make major changes in the social system in order to truly impact crime.

A less extreme view of the political reality can be seen in Hope's (1995a) distinction between *horizontal* and *vertical* dimensions of power. The horizontal dimension refers to the sharing of experiences and the ability to engender action at the local level between residents and citizens in the area. The degree to which the indigenous populace can relate to one another and work together will greatly influence the effectiveness of any prevention program. Of perhaps greater importance, however, is the vertical power of the local constituents. Vertical power refers to the ability of the local groups to marshal support and action by other elements of the community or society. What Hope (1995a) argues is that, no matter how much horizontal effort is expended, if needed funds and assistance are not provided by the vertical dimension, the program will fail. The fact is that some neighborhoods and groups simply do not have the political power to mobilize the vertical interaction and response. Both the horizontal and the vertical dimensions must be at work for crime prevention to be effective (Hope, 1995a).

Poor Evaluation

Crime prevention suffers from the same malady from which many interventions suffer—poor or nonexistent evaluation. Most evaluation efforts are secondary to the implementation of the program and may actually be a last minute addition to a project. As such, the evaluation component of most programs is poorly conceived, marginally funded, after-the-fact, and short-lived. Program evaluation should be an integral part of the planning of any intervention.

Two types of evaluation can be identified in the crime prevention literature. The most prevalent form is simple *process evaluation*. Process evaluations focus on what was done, who did it, how often it occurred, how many people were involved, and other similar measures. This type of evaluation dominated most early examinations of citizen crime prevention programs, and can be found throughout the government-sponsored research in this area. Process evaluations typically proclaim success when some level of participation, implementation, or coverage is attained. What is missing from this approach is an assessment of impact on crime and victimization. The closest these evaluations come to such assessment is to relate people's impressions of success. Unfortunately, this type of evaluation still appears all too often today.

The more useful form of evaluation is an *outcome* or *impact evaluation*. These evaluations, which typically include process information, focus on whether the intervention achieved the expected outcome—typically reduced crime and victimization. Assessments of this type require more planning and effort. Typical consideration must be given to the selection of comparison groups, follow-up time frame, measures of the outcome variables, potential confounding factors, and analytic techniques. Many program participants, both citizen and criminal justice system based, do not have the training to undertake such an evaluation and fail to search out those who can do this for the project. Even when evaluation is planned, the funds and time are often so limited that the evaluation provides only minimal insight. As a consequence, many promising programs never know whether they really work. This leads to one of two negative outcomes—perpetuation of an ineffective program or the demise of a program that works.

A great deal of additional attention needs to be paid to the evaluation of crime prevention initiatives. While there has been increased support for this evaluation in the United States, England, Canada, and other countries, there are still a large number of programs, particularly local, that are not adequately evaluated.

Displacement and Diffusion

Two related issues that emerge in almost any discussion of crime prevention are crime displacement and the diffusion of benefits. *Crime displacement* refers to the idea that, rather than eliminate crime or victimization, interventions simply result in the movement of crime across a variety of dimensions. Examples of displacement include moving crime from one area to another, shifting offenders to new targets within the same area, altering the methods used to accomplish a crime, and prompting offenders to change the type of crime they commit (Lab, 1997). The *diffusion of benefits* argument proposes that not only does the preventive action benefit the specific target area or group, it also reduces crime and victimization experienced by others not targeted. For example, if the installation of anti-theft devices in some merchandise also reduces theft of unprotected items, this would be considered a diffusion of benefits.

What makes these two possibilities a concern is the fact that they are often ignored in discussions and evaluations of crime prevention. Each has implications for whether an intervention should be continued, expanded, or modified. One prime reason for the lack of attention paid to displacement and diffusion is the difficulty in assessing them. Identifying the occurrence of either one may require an evaluation targeting people and places *not* part of the prevention program. Additionally, Clarke (1995) points out that increased knowledge about the decision-making processes of (potential) offenders is necessary to adequately assess the degree and possibility of displacement and diffusion. The issues of displacement and diffusion are a special concern for program evaluation that should be explicitly included in the design of a program and its evaluation.

CRIME PREVENTION AT A CROSSROADS

So where do we go from here? Suggesting that crime prevention is at a crossroads may bring to mind images that the area is at a crucial stage of development and that a misstep will cause irreparable harm. That is not the case. My choice of a crossroads analogy is meant to suggest that there are a variety of directions from which to choose—each with its share of challenges (some seen and some unseen) and each holding out promise of success. Some of the roads appear straighter than others due to the knowledge we have accumulated, the theoretical basis of the ideas, its potential political acceptability, and our ability to marshal the resources needed to travel that path. A look down the other roads may indicate sudden turns or many speed bumps and stop signs that will make the journey a longer, more difficult one, although not necessarily impossible. Choosing this direction may reflect philosophical beliefs, despite political roadblocks or a lack of past scientific research.

No choice of direction is inherently wrong or right. Instead, whatever choice is made should be based on the best knowledge and planning possible. History, past successes and failures, theory, logic, and research should inform and guide the choice of direction. The only wrong choice is the uninformed choice.

The papers in this book offer a number of different roads to take. Some of the ideas are more closely related to one another. This is to be expected when there is a wealth of research and literature underlying an area such as crime prevention. Other papers offer different insights and suggestions that may challenge common wisdom or the more popular approaches. Again, they are based on insight, theory, and research and deserve to be examined. In every case, these papers, by some of the leading writers on crime prevention, offer ideas that may lead down different roads. At the same time, moving forward in any direction is better than standing still, and (I expect) each one will bring us closer to "crime prevention."

INTRODUCTION TO CHAPTER 2

The failure of many broad-based community crime prevention efforts of the 1960s and 1970s to bring about significant changes in crime and fear of crime prompted a number of different responses. Perhaps the most notable was Ronald Clarke's offering of *situational prevention* as an alternative orientation to understanding crime prevention. Under the situational approach, instead of attempting to make sweeping changes in an entire community or neighborhood, prevention efforts are targeted at specific problems, places, and times in an attempt to alter the opportunities for crime. From a situational perspective, target hardening, passive and active surveillance, physical design changes, increased lighting, removal of targets, property marking, alteration of street layouts, and other familiar crime prevention efforts are brought to bear on problems in a more micro-environment than an entire community. Further, situational prevention follows a problem-oriented approach that avoids the blind imposition of an existing crime prevention program. Rather, situational prevention argues that the most fruitful approach is to identify the problem, identify possible solutions, marshal support and cooperation from a variety of sources and actors, implement the proposed solution, evaluate the impact, and make changes in the intervention as necessary.

In his 1992 book, Clarke proposed 12 techniques of situational prevention that reflected three general payoffs—increased effort to commit crime, increased risks of being observed and apprehended, and reduced rewards of crime. Besides offering a list of prevention ideas, Clarke based his suggestions on a variety of theoretical perspectives. Foremost among those perspectives were rational choice, routine activities, and defensible space.

In the following paper, Clarke and Homel revise and expand the original list of 12 situational techniques to reflect what has been learned in recent years about the adequacy of the original classification and about new techniques. Beyond simply expanding the list of situational categories, the discussion incorporates a wider array of theoretical orientations in explaining how or why an intervention will prevent crime or criminal behavior. The revised categorization incorporates the ideas of guilt, shame, and embarrassment into the discussion of situational prevention. The merging of new ideas, knowledge, and experiences is basic to any discussion of "situational" prevention. The cornerstone of their discussion, however, remains the rational choice perspective.

Clarke and Homel present this revision as one step forward in a dynamic, evolving process. Indeed, they suggest that their classification may already need revision, and they recognize the need to constantly "re-classify techniques to reflect recent experience." This recognition of the need and desire to utilize a wide range of approaches and ideas in prevention offers an excellent point from which to launch later chapters.

2

A Revised Classification of Situational Crime Prevention Techniques[1]

Ronald V. Clarke
Rutgers, The State University of New Jersey

Ross Homel
Griffith University

INTRODUCTION

A broad distinction can be made between crime prevention measures designed to reduce criminal motivation and those designed simply to reduce opportunities for crime. The latter measures include crime prevention through environmental design (Jeffery, 1971), "defensible space" architecture (Newman, 1972), problem-oriented policing (Goldstein, 1979, 1990), and situational crime prevention (Clarke, 1980). The most criminologically developed of these is situational crime prevention, that is supported by a variety of "opportunity" theories including routine activity theory and the rational choice perspective. Essentially, it involves introducing discrete environmental or situational changes to reduce the opportunities for highly specific categories of crime.

Due largely to government-sponsored research programs in Britain and Europe, a considerable body of experience now exists about the effectiveness of a range of situational techniques (Clarke, 1995). Various classifications of these techniques have been made in the interests of systematizing current knowledge, orienting research, and communicating (and learning) fundamental concepts. By showing that opportunity reduction involves more than simple target hardening, these classifications have also served to engage the creative or critical interest of a broad spectrum of theoretical criminologists.

The present paper reports a new classification that builds upon earlier work by one of the present authors (Clarke, 1992), in which a rational choice framework was used to sort 12 situational techniques into three groups: those designed to increase the effort involved in crime, to increase the risks, or to reduce the rewards (see Table 2.1). Our modified classification encompasses a wider range of techniques within a broader interpretation of rational choice theory that places more emphasis upon the social and psychological contexts of offending. Specifically, it incorporates the threat of feeling guilty when contemplating a morally wrong act and the fear of shame and embarrassment arising from the disapproval expressed by significant others when offending is revealed. An important result of our modification is that it moves situational prevention techniques beyond the largely physical manipulation of costs and benefits depicted in Table 2.1.

Table 2.1
Clarke's (1992) 12 Techniques of Situational Prevention

Increasing the Effort	Increasing the Risks	Reducing the Rewards
1. Target Hardening	5. Entry/Exit Screening	9. Target Removal
2. Access Control	6. Formal Surveillance	10. Identifying Property
3. Deflecting Offenders	7. Surveillance by Employees	11. Removing Inducements
4. Controlling Facilitators	8. Natural Surveillance	12. Rule Setting

Our modification is also congruent with a large literature suggesting that one of the main reasons why people refrain from offending is moral commitment to the law (e.g., Hirschi, 1969; Norstrom, 1981; Grasmick & Bursik, 1990). It is also congruent with an important body of theory dealing with ways that offenders neutralize feelings of guilt when committing a criminal act (Sykes & Matza, 1957). Finally, it is consistent with a long tradition of criminological research into the critical role of peer influences in offending (Sutherland & Cressey, 1966), and a more recent resurgence of interest in public (but non-stigmatizing) shaming as a crime control measure (Braithwaite, 1989). While these literatures have mostly been concerned with long-standing criminal dispositions, there are implications of specific concern to us here for influencing the situational calculus at the point of committing an offense.

Clarke's classification was developed from one produced by Hough et al. (1980), that had become out-of-date, principally because it could no longer accommodate the range of situational techniques developed through experimentation. The pace of development has accelerated in recent years, and Clarke's classification is itself no longer sufficiently comprehensive. In addition, experience has shown that some of his techniques were defined imprecisely or too broadly. The present attempt to re-classify situational techniques has thus been prompted by concerns for greater precision and comprehensiveness as well as the need for a strengthened theoretical foundation.

THE NEED FOR GREATER PRECISION

Four of the 12 techniques in Table 2.1—deflecting offenders, controlling facilitators, removing inducements, and rule setting—each contain two distinct ways of reducing opportunities that we felt should be separated in our revised classification.

"Deflecting offenders" is a situational technique derived from routine activity theory (Cohen & Felson, 1979) that holds that the occurrence of crime requires the convergence in space and time of a likely offender, a suitable target, and the absence of a capable guardian. "Deflecting offenders" reduces the scope for such unfortunate convergences, for example, by street closures in residential neighborhoods or by coordinating public transport schedules with the late-night closing of pubs and other entertainment facilities. Clarke's description of the category also includes the distinct, though related, idea that offenders might be "deflected" from a range of incivilities by the provision of graffiti boards, litter bins, public lavatories, supervised venues for cruising automobiles, and so forth. We suggest below that this form of deflection, which we call "facilitating compliance," has more general applicability and should be considered a situational technique in its own right.

Weapons, vehicles, telephones, credit cards, and a variety of other objects can facilitate criminal action. "Controlling facilitators," by such means as vehicle licensing and gun controls, was identified by Clarke as a distinct situational technique. His definition also included controls on alcohol and drugs, that in certain circumstances (e.g., rapes where the offender has plied the victim with alcohol), can be "tools" to make crime easier. However, these substances may not only make crime easier for the offender by making victims more vulnerable, they might also make it more psychologically comfortable; for example, because of impairment of perceptual or cognitive processes, offenders are sometimes unaware that they are breaking the law, or their usual social or moral inhibitions are undermined (White & Humeniuk, 1994).

The distinction between physical facilitation and psychological disinhibition is important and we propose that "controlling disinhibitors" should be considered a situational technique in its own right; encompassing such measures as promotion of responsible drinking practices, server intervention training for bar staff, and ignition interlock systems that require someone starting a car to pass a breath test. We should note that apart from drugs and alcohol there is a range of possible disinhibitors that might be controlled situationally. These could include propaganda, that can be directed at the dehumanization of target groups (such as Jews—see Bauer, 1990) and can provide the moral certainties and justifications that ordinary people need to commit atrocities and war crimes (Ellul, 1965). Also included could be television violence, which like propaganda, might "reduce or break down those inhibitions against being violent that parents and other socializing agencies have been building up in boys" (Belson, 1978:17). These are fertile areas for further research from a situational perspective.

"Removing inducements" in Clarke's schema has two meanings. The first is "reducing temptation," for example, by gender-neutral phone lists that reduce the temptation for obscene phone calling. The second is "denying benefits," examples of which include ink-tags that spoil merchandise unless they are removed by the retailer and the rapid removal of graffiti so that the tag artist cannot enjoy the rewards of "getting up" (Sloan-Howitt & Kelling, 1990). This distinction is reflected in our new classification by the inclusion of both "reducing temptation" and "denying benefits."

The main purpose of "rule setting," as described by Clarke, is to remove any uncertainty about impermissible behavior in particular settings, since this uncertainty may be interpreted by the offender to his or her own advantage. Schools, libraries, shops, offices, factories, and a host of other private and public organizations find it necessary to make such rules or regulations. Sometimes new rules have to be made to deal with developing problems; in other cases, existing rules need to be clarified or made more widely known. However, Clarke's description of "rule setting" also included some actions such as improved library checkout procedures or improved design of income tax forms, that make it easier to conform to existing rules. These actions would more properly be described as "facilitating compliance," that we have already suggested above should be identified as a distinct situational technique.

BROADER EXPERIENCE OF SITUATIONAL MEASURES

Some situational techniques such as "target hardening" and "identifying property" are specially applicable to certain broad categories of crime (in these cases, varieties of theft), and early classifications of situational prevention reflect their origins in government-sponsored programs of research into "street crimes" of autotheft, burglary, and vandalism. As situational prevention began to be applied in a wider range of contexts, the range of identifiable techniques also expanded. Clarke's classification reflects subsequent experience of using situational measures in the commercial sphere (for example, against shoplifting, employee theft, and convenience store robbery) and of employing them to deal with drunkenness and disorder at sporting events, in town centers, and other public places. The implicit model of the offender underlying all these applications, both early and later, has been the predatory, hard-core young criminal or, in the case of disorder and drunkenness, the ill-disciplined and loutish youth.

More recently, situational measures have been increasingly applied against income tax evasion, traffic offenses (including drunk driving), sexual harassment, and theft of official property, which are as much the province of "ordinary citizens" as of "hardened offenders" (see Gabor, 1994, for a review of these crimes, and the earlier seminal paper by Ross, 1960, on traffic offenses as "folk crimes"). Opportunities for these offenses arise in the course of everyday life for most people and do not have to be sought in the same way as opportunities for autotheft or burglary. The very frequency of these opportunities, together with the generally higher social status of offenders, may contribute to the relative lack of moral opprobrium attached to taking advantage of them. This lack of condemnation and the relative ease of commission suggest that, rather than by increasing the risks of detection, these offenses might more effectively be prevented by increasing the incentives or pressures to comply with the law (Sparrow, 1994).

This may be a subtle distinction, but its importance is borne out by examination of the techniques employed to-date in dealing with these everyday crimes. The techniques are somewhat different from those used against predatory street crime and include three that we have discussed above: (1) "facilitating compliance" by such measures as subsidized taxi rides home for those who have been drinking, (2) "rule setting" by such means as codes of practice designed to reduce sexual harassment in the workplace, and (3) "controlling disinhibitors" through, for example, low alcohol beer, server intervention and ignition interlock systems.

In addition to use of these three techniques, attempts have also been made in highly discrete settings to manipulate the guilt or shame attached to offending.   For example, license plates of cars observed cruising in red light districts have sometimes been published in local newspapers both as a specific and a general deterrent. Signs announce that "Shoplifting is stealing," and in the Port Authority Bus Terminal in Manhattan signs proclaim that "Smoking here is illegal, selfish, and rude." Mobile roadside speed monitors have been used to give immediate feedback (without issuing fines) to individual cars traveling above the speed limit (Casey & Lund, 1993).

An example of a more intensive and coordinated attempt to increase such informal sanctions is provided by recent advertising campaigns mounted in Australia to reinforce the deterrent impact of random breath testing (Cavallo & Drummond, 1994). The campaigns sought to create a climate in which it would be more acceptable for males to abstain from drinking when driving. To help them resist peer pressure, as well as to increase the stigma associated with drinking and driving, one of the campaigns portrayed anyone ignoring the newly omnipresent risk of being breathalyzed as being "a bloody idiot." Another campaign played upon guilt by the slogan: "Good mates don't let mates drink and drive." A further example is the attempt being made by the Australian tax authorities to change attitudes about tax paying so that cheating the government is no longer regarded as acceptable behavior and even something to be proud of, but as dishonest and selfish (Sparrow, 1994). Finally, in Britain, government television campaigns, used to supplement crackdowns on television license evaders, portray those caught as being treated by the police and courts as "common criminals."

The British government has been repeating its advertising campaigns for more than a decade and claims (though without producing evidence) that applications for television licenses sharply increase whenever the campaigns are mounted. The introduction of random breath testing in Australia, accompanied by the kinds of advertising campaigns described above, has led to a marked drop in alcohol-related traffic deaths (Homel, 1988; Cameron & Newstead, 1994), and significant increases in revenue have resulted from the Australian tax authority's compliance-increasing measures, including the deliberate attempt made to change attitudes (Sparrow, 1994). Altogether, there seems sufficient evidence of the usefulness of this approach to identify "strengthening moral condemnation" as a distinct situational technique. We will discuss below the dangers of confusing the highly specific and situational use of this technique with society's more general approach to social control.

A BROADER CONCEPTION OF RATIONAL CHOICE

None of the situational techniques used in securing the conformity of the general population—rule setting, facilitating compliance, controlling disinhibitors, and strengthening moral condemnation—fit well under the familiar rational choice categories of increasing the effort or risks and reducing the rewards. "Rule setting" had been placed by Clarke under reducing the rewards because the existence of explicit prohibitions means that offenders can no longer excuse their behavior by rationalizations such as, "Everybody else does it." They must therefore be prepared to incur higher costs in terms of guilt or shame. Raising the costs of crime, however, is not the same as reducing its rewards and, indeed, confusing the two reduces the value of the classification.

Rather than attempting to fit "rule setting" under the other rational choice categories that concern the *physical* effort of crime and the risks of apprehension, we propose adding a fourth rational choice category, "inducing guilt or shame." This category would include, not just rule setting, but also the other situational techniques employed in regard to everyday crimes, all of which seek to raise the costs of specific crimes in terms of painful feelings of guilt or shame. Thus, facilitating compliance makes it harder to find excuses for ignoring the law. Controlling disinhibitors, such as alcohol, removes the means of neutralizing guilt and inhibiting the higher order mental processes involved in conscience. Finally, strengthening moral condemnation is specifically intended to raise the costs of crime in terms of shame.

As mentioned above, utilizing this broader conception of the rational choice perspective enables explicit links to be made with the literature on the role of moral commitment (Hirschi, 1969; Grasmick & Bursik, 1990) and peer approval (Sutherland & Cressey, 1996) in committing or refraining from crime. Specifically, the addition of this fourth rational choice category represents more explicit recognition of the fact that offenders make judgments about the morality of their own behavior and that they frequently rationalize their conduct to neutralize what would otherwise be debilitating feelings of guilt or shame by employing such excuses as, "He deserved it," "I was just borrowing

it," and "I only slapped her." These rationalizations may be especially important for ordinary people responding to everyday temptations to break the law.
Though overlooked in Clarke's classification of situational techniques, the role
of rationalizations was clearly identified in the original formulation of the rational choice perspective on which he drew (Clarke & Cornish, 1985; Cornish &
Clarke, 1986). Rationalizations are also given a central role by two other criminological theories, Sykes & Matza's (1957) social deviance theory of "techniques of neutralization" and Bandura's (1976) social learning theory of
violence, that makes use of the concept of "self-exoneration" (Wortley, 1986).
The parallels between these concepts are remarkable (though Bandura appears
to have been unaware of Sykes and Matza's earlier work) and this degree of
congruence gives further reason to think that promoting feelings of guilt or
shame may be an important preventive strategy.

One result of developing the conceptual underpinnings of the rational
choice perspective is that the subjective perceptual and evaluative processes
involved in criminal decisionmaking are further emphasized. In keeping with
this direction, we propose to re-label Clarke's three rational choice categories
to reflect the *perception* of risks, effort, and rewards in the classification of situational techniques we present below (for example, "increasing the effort" is
replaced by "increasing perceived effort").

THE 16 TECHNIQUES OF SITUATIONAL PREVENTION

As explained above, a lack of conceptual clarity in Clarke's classification
and an expanded repertoire of situational techniques resulting from developments in practice and theory have made necessary the revision of his classification presented here. A particularly important trend has been the increasing
use of situational measures in preventing everyday crimes committed by the
public, that has led to the identification of several new techniques.

Eight of the 12 situational techniques identified by Clarke were left
untouched in the course of the revision. Two other techniques ("deflecting
offenders" and "controlling facilitators") also survived, but with more restricted
definitions. Of the remaining techniques, one ("removing inducements") was
divided into two ("reducing temptation" and "denying benefits") and the other
("rule setting") was moved from the category of measures to reduce the rewards
of crime into the new category of inducing guilt or shame. Also falling under
this category, are three new situational techniques: "facilitating compliance,"
"controlling disinhibitors," and "strengthening moral condemnation."

The resulting classification is shown in Table 2.2, together with examples of
each of the 16 techniques. Some of the examples in Table 2.2 could easily fall
under more than one situational technique (for example, the alcohol countermeasures could be included under "controlling facilitators" as well as "controlling disinhibitors"), but to simplify presentation we have not shown this in the table.

Table 2.2
16 Techniques of Situational Prevention

Increasing Perceived Effort	Increasing Perceived Risks	Reducing Anticipated Rewards	Inducing Guilt or Shame
1. *Target Hardening:* Slug rejector device Steering locks Bandit screens	5. *Entry/Exit Screening:* Automatic ticket gates Baggage screening Merchandise tags	9. *Target Removal:* Removable car radio Women's refuges Phonecard	13. *Rule Setting:* Harrassment codes Customs declaration Hotel registrations
2. *Access Control:* Parking lot barriers Fenced yards Entry phones	6. *Formal Surveillance:* Burglar alarms Speed cameras Security guards	10. *Identifying Property:* Property marking Vehicle licensing Cattle branding	14. *Strengthening Moral Condemnation:* "Shoplifting is stealing" Roadside speedometers "Bloody idiots drink and drive"
3. *Deflecting Offenders:* Bus stop placement Tavern location Street closures	7. *Surveillance by Employees:* Pay phone location Parking attendants CCTV systems	11. *Reducing Temptation:* Gender-neutral phone lists Off-street parking	15. *Controlling Disinhibitors:* Drinking age laws Ignition interlock Server intervention
4. *Controlling Facilitators:* Credit card photo Caller-ID Gun controls	8. *Natural Surveillance:* Defensible space Street lighting Cab driver ID	12. *Denying Benefits:* Ink merchandise tags PIN for car radios Graffiti cleaning	16. *Facilitating Compliance:* Improved library checkout Public lavatories Trash bins

Emphasizing perceptions in the three original rational choice categories and adding the dimension of "inducing guilt or shame" brings about an important change in the way that situational prevention is conceived. In Clarke's classification, the individual techniques of situational prevention are presented as influencing the objective probability of incurring costs and receiving benefits. In our new classification, situational measures are conceived as affecting not just objective costs and benefits, but also the offender's assessments of these realities. This is wholly consistent with the rational choice perspective and it means that manipulating perceptions may sometimes be as important as changing the objective realities. In turn, this calls attention to the role of publicity in reinforcing the effect of changes in the cost/benefit ratio resulting from the implementation of situational prevention. This role has previously been discussed by Sherman (1990) in relation to enhancing the deterrent effect of police crackdowns and by Clarke and Weisburd (1994) in relation to enhancing the "diffusion of benefits" of focused, situational action. More needs to be learned about how to devise effective publicity of this kind.

While an emphasis on offender perceptions should increase the scope for situational crime prevention, there is a danger of blurring the lines between its highly specific, immediate opportunity-reducing focus and the more general, longer-term preventive approach involved in modifying criminal dispositions. When proposing "rule setting" as a distinct situational technique, Clarke (1992) noted the fine line that exists between the opportunity-reducing and character-forming purposes of rules and that some "rules" may serve both purposes. For example, discussions of corporate ethics (e.g., Nalla & Newman, 1990) often emphasize the repeated presentation and clarification of rules, not just as a constant reminder, but also to foster a corporate climate in which it becomes more difficult for employees to behave unethically without incurring the disapproval of colleagues. Some of the measures that we would include under "strengthening moral condemnation," such as the Australian advertising campaigns to reinforce random breath testing, may also have the dual purpose of affecting both immediate decisions and longer-term dispositions. We feel justified in including them as situational techniques because they are focused on particular forms of offending in particular contexts. Thus, the objective of the "bloody idiot" drinking and driving campaigns is to reduce the chances of a specific kind of act being committed. It is not intended to produce more generally law-abiding and responsible people, which is the objective of developmental and community crime prevention. We would feel especially comfortable in regarding moral condemnation as a situational technique when it is employed directly in the situations in which decisions to offend are made. Thus, the message "Shoplifting is stealing" is much more likely to affect the situational calculus, and thus qualify as a situational measure, when displayed in high risk stores than when displayed on school notice boards.

CONCLUSIONS

We believe that our new classification of situational techniques more fully reflects the richness and complexity of the rational choice perspective on crime. In particular, the incorporation of a set of techniques intended to induce feelings of anticipatory shame and guilt has shifted the focus of situational prevention from the largely physical and material determinants of crime to the equally important dimension of internalized controls.

We have discussed the danger (inherent in dealing with non-material sanctions) of entangling situational prevention in attempts to bring about long-term changes in dispositions to offend, which is a fundamentally different approach to crime prevention. It seems, however, that a choice must be made between maintaining the clarity of the situational approach but limiting its application, or extending its reach and complicating its definition. We have chosen the latter route and believe that, so long as the measures to induce guilt or shame are focused on highly specific categories of offending and are delivered at the point when criminal decisions are being made, the danger can be avoided of confusing the nature of situational prevention.

Expanding the classification of techniques in the way we have suggested potentially enhances the relevance of the research on situational prevention to such fields as tax compliance (Thurman et al., 1984; Smith & Kinsey, 1987; Weigel et al., 1987; Bardach, 1989), the control of corporate and white-collar crime (Jamieson, 1994), and the regulation of business (Ayres & Braithwaite, 1992). In all these areas control efforts are increasingly focused on moral suasion, negotiation, and compliance, with a corresponding reduction in emphasis on punitive measures such as license revocation, fines, or imprisonment, except in extreme situations in which negotiation and self-regulation break down.

We suspect that as these efforts develop our new classification may as quickly become outdated as the one it replaced, if for no other reason than our category of "inducing guilt or shame" reflects two fundamentally distinct processes—one socially mediated through approval or disapproval and the other internally mediated through conscience.

This can be illustrated by reference to the advertising campaigns used to reinforce the introduction of random breath testing in Australia discussed previously. The ways that these seem to have affected the decision whether to drink and drive are quite complex. We referred to the guilt-inducing message of "Good mates don't let mates drink and drive." Homel (1988) has also shown that peer pressures that made it embarrassing for young drinkers to comply with drinking and driving laws were mitigated by the well-publicized threat of random breath testing, because the need to avoid being tested provided an acceptable excuse to limit alcohol consumption when drinking with friends. Moreover, there is some evidence that, as a result of the sustained publicity backed with enforcement, the social stigma adhering to this offense has increased in Australia and that this cultural change has importantly contributed to the decline in alcohol-related accidents (Homel, Caseldine & Kearns, 1988).

These different means of affecting decisions about drinking and driving might eventually be reflected in a more refined classification of situational measures. Indeed, as examples multiply of ways to induce guilt or shame, we expect to distinguish more clearly between internally mediated and socially mediated processes, perhaps through the addition of a "fifth column" that explicitly represents the social dimension of embarrassment. This column would take account of the extensive literature on group processes in identifying situational means to increase anticipated shame and embarrassment.

Hughlings Jackson (1874) observed that, "Classifications in all sciences make distinctions more exact and abrupt than any that exist in nature." We have had to make some difficult compromises in our own classification between accuracy and clarity. These difficulties, together with the knowledge that, even if useful now, our classification might not survive for long, have led us to consider delaying our modifications. However, situational prevention has many years of development ahead. The constant re-classifying of techniques to reflect recent experience plays an important role in this development by assisting analysis of possible ways to reduce new, or previously unaddressed, forms of crime.

NOTE

[1]   We should like to thank Griffith University for making our collaboration possible through the award of a visiting fellowship to Ronald Clarke for July and August 1994. We are also grateful to Marcus Felson and Richard Wortley for their helpful comments on a draft of this paper.

INTRODUCTION TO CHAPTER 3

The broad theoretical scope that is relevant to crime prevention initiatives is evident in the situational techniques presented in the previous paper. This breadth is further demonstrated in Felson's discussion of Hirschi's control theory and Gottfredson and Hirschi's general theory of crime. In his paper, Felson sets out to do a number of things. First, he tries to reconcile the bases of these two related theories. Second, he examines the implications of self-control theory for everyday life. In doing so, Felson takes the more abstract concepts and attempts to demonstrate how people with different levels of self-control require varying degrees of outside control on their behavior. Third, he shows how the idea of self-control is intimately related to crime prevention.

Throughout Felson's presentation, it is easy to see parallels to routine activities and the rational choice perspectives—key ideas in crime prevention. The discussion reflects crime prevention ideas, even before he explicitly introduces the routine activities approach. The degree to which guardians of various forms are necessary for controlling behavior differs based on the individual's level of self-control. Felson outlines how the proximity of others (guardians) can provide behavioral input ranging from subtle "reminders" to overt "coercion." As Felson notes, "self control is implicit in any discussion of offender decisions and choices or responses to crime opportunities."

Perhaps the greatest contribution of this paper is the demonstration of how theory can inform and direct crime prevention efforts. It also shows how different theories and perspectives can inform and extend the utility of one another. This discussion of self-control has clear implications for situational crime prevention and provides further explication of the various situational techniques proposed by Clarke and Homel in Chapter 2.

3

Reconciling Hirschi's 1969 Control Theory with the General Theory of Crime

Marcus Felson
Rutgers, The State University of New Jersey

Control theory is one of the most important theories of criminal action. Yet its two most famous versions differ, sometimes confusing student and teacher alike. Perhaps the most important exposition of control theory for its era was Travis Hirschi's (1969) *Causes of Delinquency*. Hirschi emphasized that crime needs no special motivation: there is no problem explaining why people commit crime but rather explaining why people do not. The answer to the latter question lies in social control. Through social bonds the larger society gets individuals to forego their selfish motivations and to follow rules. Without social bonds, people would revert to their selfish interests and hence fall into crime and delinquency.

Many crime theorists emphasize rules and how well people learn them or fail to learn them. Hirschi avowedly avoided that theoretical emphasis. Instead, he made clear that virtually everyone knows the rules and has them internalized. Hirschi recognized that it is very human to internalize the rules and still break them (see also Felson, 1994), following basic human weaknesses. Social bonds help people to overcome these weaknesses and to follow the conventions of society. Such bonds include attachments to other people, commitments to future achievements, and involvements in conventional activities. Those lacking such controls tend to get involved in a wide variety of actions classified as crime and delinquency.

ANOTHER CONTROL THEORY?

Twenty-one years after that work appeared, Michael Gottfredson and Travis Hirschi (1990) presented *A General Theory of Crime*. This volume once more emphasized the notion that crime needs no special motivation. The general theory of crime went beyond crime alone, explaining social controls that help people; for example, to do a good job, perform well in school, drive a car safely, function as good parents, and consume moderately. Conversely, the absence of controls leads not only to crime and delinquency, but also to poor work performance, school failure, reckless driving, poor parenting, substance abuse, and more (see Hirschi & Gottfredson, 1994).

Many social and behavioral scientists have noted correlations among such human tendencies, and refer to some people as belonging to a general category of "deviants" or "antisocials." However, Gottfredson and Hirschi decidedly avoided such terms. Those committing crimes or having other problems in society are not necessarily "defective." Since they have no special motivations, it is misleading to call them antisocials or deviants simply because they get into a variety of troubles. It is also a mistake to treat offenders as a distinct population (see Rowe, Osgood & Nicewander, 1990; Fattah, 1991).

Gottfredson and Hirschi argued that people varied not in motivation but rather in *self*-control.[1] Those very low in self-control tend to get into more trouble more often, but are not the only ones who get into any trouble. Nor can one tell from low self-control alone into which kind of trouble they will get. They tend to get involved in crime if opportunities are present (see Hindelang, Gottfredson & Garafolo, 1978; Cohen & Felson, 1979); or they may follow general human temptations into other mischievous or harmful directions when opportunities entice and make it possible (see Hirschi & Gottfredson, 1994). One can also find in social psychology a general construct defined on the basis of self-regulation, taking into account such behaviors as losing attention, failing to set goals, procrastinating, mismanaging money, falling into unwanted thought processes, and giving in to impulses, appetites, and moods (Baumeister, Heatherton & Tice, 1994).

Gottfredson and Hirschi were not dustbowl empiricists, relying on *in*duction, rather they acted as theorists employing *de*duction. They picked self-control above its correlates because it could sum up the most information and could make the theory hold together. Self-control was consistent with their prior assumption that everyone has forbidden desires, while some people have more trouble resisting these desires. Whereas the 1969 work emphasized social bonds producing social control, the 1990 work considered how self-control could accomplish the same thing.

RECONCILING TWO CONTROL THEORIES

In his evaluation of social control theories, Akers (1997:91) notes not only the lack of self-control in Hirschi's 1969 theory, but also that

> Gottfredson and Hirschi (1990) do not clarify how their self-control theory relates to Hirschi's (1969) social bonding theory . . .

Is Hirschi (1969) compatible with Gottfredson and Hirschi (1990)? This is more than a question for the history of criminology; it raises a theoretical issue going beyond what the authors mentioned: How does control of one's self relate to control through ties to other people?

Theoretical nicety is not the only reason to reconcile the two control theories. Control implies prevention. If we can sharpen our thinking about control, that might help us to formulate better means for preventing crime.

To reconcile the two control theories, I shall work backwards from Gottfredson and Hirschi (1990).[2] They conceived a single continuous variable, the degree of self-control, ranging very widely among individuals. They summed up a great deal of information with this continuum, offering us a good theory. Although it is possible to treat self-control as multidimensional (Tedeschi & Felson, 1994; Longshore, Turner & Stein, 1996), Gottfredson and Hirschi sacrificed such specificity in offering us a more general model of criminal inclinations. Hirschi's 1969 control theory also had something concise to offer. The challenge here is to draw the best of Hirschi (1969) and fuse it with the best of Gottfredson and Hirschi (1990). In the process, something slightly new may emerge.

SEGMENTING THE SELF-CONTROL CONTINUUM

A continuum is difficult for nonstatisticians to visualize. On the other hand, dichotomizing this very wide scale does it an injustice, also giving the false impression that the population can be divided clearly into offenders and nonoffenders. I propose a communications compromise, using an ordinal variable with five segments to summarize individuals by level of self-control:

Self-Control Level	Usual Response To Control From Others
STRONGEST	
1	scarcely needing to be reminded
2	responsive to anyone nearby
3	responsive to special people nearby
4	responsive to imminent coercion
5	ignoring imminent coercion
WEAKEST	

This ordinal scale makes self-control theory a little simpler and easier to apply to everyday life. Each segment can be described in terms of types of people and their proximity to other people. This simplified model links two analytically distinct concepts, self-control and responsiveness, to others. This makes sense mainly because those who have more self-control can better respond to the influence of others, whose proximity thus becomes more relevant.

Segment 1 includes those with the greatest self-control. This includes those who usually obey the rules of society with little or no reminder from others. Although many people may think they fit this segment, their self assessments should probably be dismissed by the independent analyst. Most people need frequent reminders from others, however subtle or inadvertant.

Segment 2 includes people who usually respond to informal social control delivered by almost anyone nearby. Even silent strangers may succeed in reminding them to follow society's rules. Jane Jacobs (1961), Oscar Newman (1972), C. Ray Jeffery (1971), Barry Poyner (1983), and Brantingham and Brantingham (1991, 1995) have studied and explained how places can be designed for natural interactions, even among strangers. Some good examples of these ideas were found in the redesign of the Port Authority Bus Terminal in New York City. This public facility was plagued on a daily basis by hundreds of male hustlers, female prostitutes, luggage thieves, and squatting transients. The sprawling building had many corners and crannies for which no one took specific responsibility. This explained why illegal activities tended to take over. Participants included a good number of customers for illegal goods and services who were otherwise law-abiding citizens, presumably with moderate levels of self-control. The Port Authority applied several inexpensive design methods (Felson et al., 1996). A good part of this was putting in push-carts and small shops to enhance the flow of ordinary legal activities. These legal activities inadvertently replaced illegal activities. Normally law-abiding citizens were now embarrassed to purchase illegal goods and services.

We now turn to Segment 3—people not high enough in self-control to be readily influenced by simple proximity of strangers (see Felson, 1995). However, they usually respond well to proximate social influences from those whom they know personally. *Hirschi's 1969 concept of social control fits best with members of Segment 3.* Physical proximity between people is essential to put such social control into action (Felson, 1986). It is delivered informally by "handlers," that is, parents, neighbors, teachers, or others whose physical and social proximity combine to supervise individuals and hence discourage their participation in crime. In the example mentioned above (Felson et al., 1996), the Port Authority social workers got to know street people by name. Some of the more innocuous street people may have thus become more responsive to instructions and suggestions and less likely to flagrantly break the rules.[3]

Some people seldom respond to gentle social control from anyone. Segment 4 includes those who usually have only enough self-control to respond to imminent coercion. Some youths follow the law only so long as the officers of coercion are looking.

Segment 5 is lacking even that bit of self-control. These people attack those stronger than themselves, strike policemen, break into the wrong places, and can barely function in society, even as criminals. Segment 5 members probably end up institutionalized in one way or another for much of their lives.

CAVEATS FOR THE SELF-CONTROL SCALE

Self-control segments are merely for heuristic purposes. Self-control remains a very wide continuum. Each segment contains significant variations within it. For example, some people classified in Segment 1 may need a slight reminder about the rules from time to time. Some people within Segment 3 need several explicit reminders, while others respond to the mere presence of one relative. Someone just over the line into Segment 5, who cannot resist the urge to strike a single policeman, may control the urge to attack two.

So far I have treated each individual as having one and only one point on a self-control scale. However, in reality, each individual probably varies significantly in self-control hour-by-hour and day-by-day. Alcohol and other disinhibiting chemicals may temporarily move someone down the scale. For example, someone normally in Segment 1 may, after a drink or two, come to require reminders by others to follow the rules. Someone usually in Segment 4 might, under the influence of alcohol, move into Segment 5, becoming quite a bit more dangerous.

However wide the overall scale, I do not believe that a large percent of the population belongs either to Segment 1 or Segment 5. Most of the population can be categorized into Segments 2, 3, and 4. I have rotated and redrawn the line segments thusly:

| 1 | 2 | 3 | 4 | 5 |

This depicts most of the population having self-control levels requiring reminders from others, then responding to these reminders. This links self-control intimately to social interaction. Through Segment 3, this five-point scale incorporates Hirschi's 1969 control theory within the 1990 general theory of crime. The latter is the larger theory, and the two are quite consistent with one another. However, this consistence depends upon making control theory tangible. As in Felson (1986), the proximity of various agents of social control is essential for reconciling the theories.

VARIATIONS IN TEMPTATION AND CUMULATIVE SELF-CONTROL

The previous section noted the heuristic purposes of this scale. That point is further illustrated by considering variations in temptation and their interplay with self-control. Not all temptations are equal. Some are only slightly alluring; others take strong effort to resist. The self-control scale can best be understood in juxtaposition to a temptation scale. Even people relatively high in self-control may find it difficult to resist a powerful temptation. This in turn means that members of self-control Segment 1 are not immune to committing a crime, even a major one, when temptations are great. Sexual release is the best example of a strong temptation that can reach almost anyone, even those generally known to be high in self-control. In addition, such people are probably subject to temptation by large illegal gains, but not readily tempted by small ones. At the same time, those with little self-control (e.g., in Segment 4) are subject to temptations of many types, not only sexual temptation and large illegal gains, but also petty crime and errors leading to poor performance in school, job, and family.

MULTIPLE CONTROLS ON ONE PERSON

The importance of temptation leads us to use the word "usual" or "usually" in describing self-control. Those who are usually self-regulating may not always be so dependable. This makes multiple forms of control relevant. The five types of control mentioned above have cumulative effects, forming a Guttman Scale:

Usually Responsive to...	SEGMENT				
	5	4	3	2	1
a. unassisted self-control					X
b. anyone nearby				X	X
c. special people nearby			X	X	X
d. imminent coercion		X	X	X	X
e. overwhelming force	X	X	X	X	X

This scale illustrates the very wide range of social control. Segment 1 responds to all five types of control: unassisted self-control, influence of anyone nearby, influence by special people nearby, imminent coercion, and overwhelming force. Segment 5 responds only to overwhelming force. Segment 2 responds to all but unassisted self-control. Segment 4 responds only to imminent coercion of overwhelming force. Segment 3 responds to three of the five types of control, including the impact of special people nearby. The 1969 control theory especially addresses this segment, as stated earlier. Note that overwhelming force applies to all five segments, but is hardly necessary with the other tools of social control present.

TANGIBLE REQUIREMENTS OF SOCIAL CONTROL

Only in Segment 1 can social control be accomplished generally in the physical absence of others. In the other four segments (hence for the vast majority of the population), social control depends upon the tangible structure of activities assembling people and delivering on-the-spot influence. For all five segments, the proximity in time and space of various temptations to break society's conventions is very important. Indeed, the fundamental postulate of this analysis is that most control is activated by the proximity of others. Control is a tangible process, varying by level of self-control but also responsive to other conditions influencing the convergence of likely participants in crime or its prevention.

CONTROL SEGMENTS AND
THE ROUTINE-ACTIVITY APPROACH

The emphasis on tangibility helps bring control even closer to the routine-activity approach. That approach was originally applied to direct-contact predatory offenses (Cohen & Felson, 1979; Felson, 1994). An offense is predatory when at least one person takes or damages the person or property of another. Most predatory offenses involve direct and close physical contact, but threatening letters or phone calls and computer crimes transcend space and are exceptions. A direct-contact predatory crime requires a likely offender, a suitable target, and the absence of a capable guardian to protect a target, however inadvertently. The target may be animate or inanimate, and the guardian is usually not a police officer or security guard but rather a citizen, friend or family member, or property owner. The offender needs to find a target with no guardians near.

The routine-activity approach has been broadened to include other types of crimes, such as sales of illegal goods and services (Felson, 1983; Eck, 1995), as well as suicide (Felson, 1983; Clarke & Lester, 1989), and fights lacking an innocent victim (R. Felson, 1993; Felson, 1994; Tedeschi & Felson, 1995).

The routine-activity approach was further extended by Felson (1986), then Eck (1995) to produce Eck's Triplets, taking into account three types of supervision: (1) guardians/targets, (2) handlers/likely offenders, and (3) managers/places. In general, in order to commit a crime, a likely offender must escape handlers, then find a target in the absence of guardians, in a location without a manager.

All three types of supervision illustrate the tangible requirements of social control, depending on the routine activities of everyday life.

The effectiveness of guardians, handlers, and place managers will not be constant across self-control segments. For example, Segment 2 may respond well to strangers acting in these three roles, while Segment 4 is responsive to more obtrusive supervision. Segment 3 may commit little crime close to home, yet respond to temptations elsewhere. Segment 4 may even get into trouble close to home. Segment 5 could get into trouble any place, any time. Even so, changes in community life may alter the crime opportunities available to this segment. The basic routine-activity principle is that crime risks respond to changes in community structure, shifting the quantities and varieties of people and things assembling in space and time. This principle may play out differently for different self-control segments, since they are not equally responsive to temptation or supervision.

SOCIETY'S LINES OF DEFENSE

Paralleling the self-control segments, society has five lines of defense against crime, at least so far as potential offenders are concerned. The first line of defense is to get people to regulate themselves. This first line has few spatio-temporal requirements, since it does not depend upon the presence of other people.

Society's second line of defense is to get people to remind each other, even without intimacy, to follow the rules. This second line depends upon a physical organization of microenvironments so that those who are tempted to commit a crime will, at that time and place, note the likely presence of others. These others must implicitly or explicitly discourage responding to a temptation with an illegal act.

The third line of defense puts intimacy to work to get people to obey laws. At the moment of temptation, potential offenders must feel they will be seen and recognized by intimates or by others who can report to intimates (see Felson, 1986). This third line of defense depends upon social bonds having been formed, self-controls being strong enough to respond to such bonds, and proximity of those who can deliver on such bonds.

Pure self regulation and natural controls from strangers or intimates can all fail. The fourth line of defense is a threat of imminent force. The fifth and final line of defense is to use full force to obtain compliance with society's rules.

I regard the combination of the second and third lines of defense as "natural social control," imitating long-standing human experience to enhance self regulation without widespread coercion (see Felson, 1994).

This moderate course is not followed in every society. Some nations have relied on heavy-handed use of force as their only means of control. More sophisticated dictatorships also employ informal social control to assist the police. American society offers a befuddling combination of the first and fifth lines of defense, with the self regulation failures leading to extreme dependance on force. That dependance largely results from a public policy that neglects the second and third lines of defense.

APPLICATIONS TO SITUATIONAL CRIME PREVENTION

It seems that an emphasis upon prisons is wasteful when large segments of the population can be systematically kept away from crime with simpler, less costly and less draconian methods. The most direct of these is situational crime prevention (Clarke, 1995). It acts directly to remove crime opportunities, for example, by increasing risks or reducing rewards to potential offenders. This usually is done simply and directly, and relies on some measure of self-control on the part of people. Indeed, some self-control is implicit in any discussion of offender decisions and choices or responses to crime opportunities (see Clarke & Felson, 1993).

However, crime prevention does not influence everyone in the same way, since people vary in self-control. This is why self-control segmentation helps us to think about crime prevention. Clarke and Harris (1992) review evidence that car crime prevention methods work differently for young offenders and older ones, for parts strippers and for joyriders. Although it is tempting to make a distinction between "amateur" and "professional" offenders, repeat offenders are perhaps too clumsy in their behavior over time to deserve the term "professional." Perhaps self-control segmentation offers us a useful alternative way to think about different offenders and how to prevent their illegal actions. Those who are high in self-control may be discouraged from an illegal act with a very small disinhibitor, such as a sign that says, "Keep Off the Grass," or "Shoplifting is Stealing." Others can be discouraged from shoplifting by very good lighting or clear aisles, with potential scrutiny by strangers sufficing, even with low risk of punishment. The Japanese use of school uniforms, with schools kept small, reduces shoplifting by increasing personal visibility (Tanioka, 1989). And yet it may be necessary to organize shopping to increase the shopkeepers' own chances to monitor goods and discourage thefts. Each method is effective with a different self-control segment.

Situational prevention and environmental criminology tell us that many people need to be reminded over and over again what they are supposed to do and not to do. These reminders need not be verbal; any number of environmental cues can get the message across (Brantingham & Brantingham, 1991, 1995; Clarke, 1995). How responsive people are to reminders varies greatly, and some will not pay much attention. However, enough people do pay attention, especially those in Segments 2 and 3. For those in Segment 2, the message is that people are watching, even inadvertently. For Segment 3 members, the message is that parents (or other specific people important to the decision-maker) may find out, however indirectly. If criminal activity can be largely limited to those in Segments 4 and 5, then crime rates will decline greatly. Even these offenders may be guided toward more legal behavior by microenvironments designed to make illegal actions stand out boldly and clearly.

NOTES

[1]   I have chosen to treat "self-control" as two unhyphenated words. Akers (1997) prefers to hyphenate the term.

[2]   My approach diverges from Akers's intuitive remark that ". . . other social bonds affect crime only indirectly through their effects on self-control" (1997:92). I suggest that social bonds apply mainly at middle levels of self-control.

[3]   Social control applies not only to offenders themselves, but also to those who might put pressure on offenders. Dividing the bus terminal more effectively left specific shopkeepers and their employees clearly responsible for particular parts of the terminal. Not only would each business suffer financially from proximate lawbreaking, but managers and employees would now feel personal responsibility for a specific area. See also Felson (1995).

INTRODUCTION TO CHAPTER 4

Our discussion of crime prevention thus far has concentrated primarily on actual crime, the individuals who commit the crime, and the methods that may be used to address the problem. What has not been addressed is a second major concern—the fear of crime. Much past research has demonstrated that fear of crime and actual victimization do not correspond to one another. Many people fear crime even though they have never been victimized and have little risk of being victimized in the future. Indeed, young males are at the greatest risk of being victimized, but typically express the lowest levels of fear.

This discrepancy between actual crime and the fear of crime raises some interesting problems for crime prevention planning and programming. The next paper by the Brantinghams tackles this double-edged problem of crime and fear. One important lesson to be learned from the presentation is that crime and fear may require different interventions. For example, increased lighting may reduce fear but have little impact on crime, especially if the area was not prone to victimization in the first place. Another consideration in trying to deal with both crime and fear is that efforts to improve one may be counterproductive for the other. An example of this is where the reduction of fear may lead to an individual taking fewer precautions (or greater risks) and, ultimately, becoming a victim. Similarly, successful efforts to reduce the actual level of crime may be meaningless if residents retain a high level of fear and stay locked within their homes. What is needed are prevention programs that address both crime and fear in a positive fashion for both problems.

The Brantingham's paper also discusses the geographic distribution of crime and fear, and its implication for crime prevention programming. Many familiar ideas emerge in the discussion—routine activities, rational choice, and situational approaches. These factors help to explain why crime occurs in certain areas (and not others), as well as to provide a framework in which to consider the appropriate responses to the problems. They conclude their investigation by calling for what amounts to a problem-oriented approach toward crime and fear. They note, "We need to know more about what people are afraid of at particular times and places. When we do, we will be able to design prevention intervention tactics that will balance fear management with crime prevention."

4

Understanding and Controlling Crime and Fear of Crime: Conflicts and Trade-Offs in Crime Prevention Planning

Paul J. Brantingham
Patricia L. Brantingham
Simon Fraser University

INTRODUCTION

The term *crime prevention* has a range of meanings (Lab, 1992). For the police and for private security firms, it frequently focuses on finding ways to decrease the actual number of crimes. For social service practitioners it is frequently oriented towards reducing the incidence of a range of incivilities—littering, vandalism, rudeness, and mean-spirited selfishness—that only tangentially overlap with the criminal law. For citizens at large, crime prevention often really means the management of fears that may not have anything to do with the underlying patterns of crime incidence or risk, or even the visible patterns of social incivilities.

All three of these meanings of crime prevention—reduction in the incidence of crimes, reduction in the incidence of incivilities, and management of fears about crime and incivilities—are important in the practice of crime prevention. They are important because accomplishment of each of them is central to the production of a civil society that is comfortable with itself. But they are also important because they are often at variance with each other. People's fears of crime do not always correspond with their objective risks of crime. This has been demonstrated frequently in the victimization literature with respect to age and sex (see Fattah, 1991 for a complete review). It is also true of people's fear of crime in time and space (see e.g., Bartnicki, 1989; Brantingham & Brantingham, 1984; Brantingham, Brantingham & Butcher, 1986; Brantingham, Brantingham & Molumby, 1977).

This separation of crime and fear poses a set of major problems for crime prevention planners and practitioners. Programs that reduce the incidence of crime may not necessarily reduce the fear of crime in society at large, and may not produce the levels of political civility that real reductions in crime ought to bring. This appears to describe the American experience of the past two decades, when real overall crime levels, as measured by the National Crime Survey, have declined, but public fears of crime have increased.[1] At the same time, programs that reduce fear levels may well produce routine-activity changes (Felson, 1994) that increase both exposure to, and the incidence of, crime.

Crime prevention involves simultaneous adoption of programs to reduce crime and programs to manage fear. These programs may often argue for the application of *different* situational[2] interventions at particular times and places, and actual implementation by crime prevention planners and practitioners may require trade-offs between conflicting intervention choices. An understanding of the processes that contribute to criminal events and to perceptions of crime is critical to making these choices.

IMPACT OF MULTIPLE MEANINGS OF CRIME PREVENTION

Since crime prevention as a general approach may have as its goal the reduction of actual crimes, the reduction of incivilities, or the reduction of fear of crime, it becomes essential to explore how these goals relate to the actual behavior and perceptions of people and then use the results of this exploration to develop crime prevention programs that are more likely to work.

This is another way of saying that sites, situations, or general socioeconomic, demographic, and media conditions that create fear may not necessarily relate to actual risks of victimization or patterns of crime. For example, it is well-known that the elderly express high levels of fear of crime, but run low risks of actual victimization; teenagers and young adults generally express low levels of fear of crime, but run the highest risks of criminal victimization (Fattah, 1991). Note that places marked by darkness and isolation are generally feared as likely crime sites, but (with a few exceptions) tend to be relatively low frequency crime locations (Brantingham, Brantingham & Seagrave, 1995). Introduction of higher levels of street lighting into high fear locations appears, in general to have little beneficial impact on crime levels (Atkins, Hussain & Storey, 1991; Lab, 1992; Ramsay & Newton, 1991) Vandalism, litter, and graffiti are known to make people feel uneasy, to raise their fears of crime in an area, but do not often constitute territorial markers of actual crime hot spots (Ley & Cybriwsky, 1974; Skogan, 1988a). The public view of "crime" often turns out to be tied to the presence of noise, traffic, panhandlers, alcoholics, and contact between groups of "different" people as much as to criminal code events.

Crime may often be high in situations and at sites where people feel safe and express little fear. This is predicted by Angel's (1968) target density model and by what is known about the environmental psychology of crime (Brantingham & Brantingham, 1993). So, robberies are known to be concentrated along busy shopping streets (Wilcox, 1973) where people generally express little fear. University crimes in general are concentrated in high activity areas such as the library, the student union, or dormitory laundromats where students say they feel safe (Brantingham, Brantingham & Molumby, 1977; Brantingham, Brantingham & Seagrave, 1995). Auto thefts and thefts from autos are concentrated in and around parking lots where people feel their cars are safe (Brantingham & Brantingham, 1994a; Eck & Spelman, 1992; Poyner, 1992), or in exposed locations such as the street close to home where people feel their cars are safe (Clarke & Mayhew, 1994).

Crime and fear may both be problems at particular locations in space and time, of course. Such dual hot spots of crime and fear often occur along the edges of "entertainment" districts—42nd Street in New York, or Granville Street in Vancouver, for instance. They occur in danger zones 100 to 300 meters away from major transit stops (Block & Davis, 1995; Brantingham, Brantingham & Wong, 1991). They occur on the edges or borders between neighborhoods of distinctly different character and social status (Brantingham & Brantingham, 1975; Brantingham & Brantingham, 1993; Brantingham, Brantingham & Molumby, 1977). They occur on major pathways and at major nodes where large numbers of potential offenders are brought together, through routine activities, with large numbers of potential victims and targets.

This array of possibilities means that it is important to understand the process behind the choice of targets and target areas by offenders; and the development of fear on the part of individuals. It is very important to understand what happens when areas that create fear are also high risk areas for crimes and nuisances. Interventions that reduce crime may not reduce fear if fear is not grounded on the frequency of the crimes. Interventions that reduce fear will have no impact on crime if there is no real crime problem at the intervention location. In fact, interventions that reduce fear in some high crime areas might actually increase the frequency of crime by inducing potential victims to expose themselves (or their target possessions) more than they previously did (thus increasing the number of criminal opportunities). This can be compounded because some interventions have a generic impact: they reduce potential victims' fears but also reduce potential offenders' fears, making the offenders more likely to sense and act upon the expanded number of opportunities for crime generated by the reduced fears of the potential victims.

To explore how this may work, we will present two basic process models that are consistent with the line of work in rational choice theory (Brantingham & Brantingham, 1978; Cornish, 1994; Cornish & Clarke, 1986). One model deals with crimes and other uncivil acts; the other model deals with fear of crime and incivility.

CRIME CHOICE MODEL

It is important to remember that what we know about crime is typically filtered through a funnel of decreasing information. This point is made over and over by criminologists, but it is sufficiently fundamental that we illustrate it here again, using data from Nova Scotia, Canada, for 1991. Figure 4.1 shows a *crime funnel* that ranges from about 180,000 estimated criminal code victimizations, to about 90,000 *actual*[3] offenses known to the police, to about 20,000 offenses cleared by charge, to about 11,000 adult convictions, to about 2,400 prison or jail sentences.

Figure 4.1
Nova Scotia Criminal Code Funnel—1991

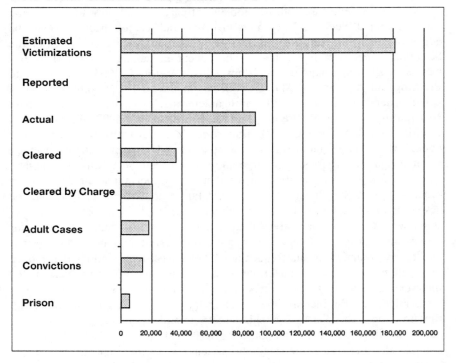

This, of course, is an overall funnel for serious crimes. The funnels of information and case processing can look quite different for different types of crime. The crime funnel for murder, for instance, is not steeply graded: most murders are in fact reported to or discovered by the police, most murders are cleared by charge, most murder charges result in convictions from some kind of criminal homicide (often manslaughter), and most convictions result in some sort of prison term. The crime funnel for solicitation for the purposes of prostitution, a nuisance crime, is very steeply graded: few instances of criminal solicitation are ever brought to the attention of police, though most that are result in charges and convictions, though few convictions result in prison or jail sentences. When looking at the aggregate crime pattern, it is also important to remember that most calls for police service involve relatively minor crimes, incivilities, and noise.

Crime choice behavior is also a funnel. There are many potential offenders, but only a few actually commit offenses. Only a few of the actual offenders commit serious offenses. Criminal choices are funneled by motivation levels and by situations. The motivation levels and search processes of potential offenders provide a good basis for beginning to think through the possibilities for situational interventions into crime-prone times and places.

Motivations[4] vary across individuals, but they also vary over time and in different situations for almost every individual. Almost anyone is motivated strongly enough to be tempted into doing some minor kinds of crime when the opportunity arises: pilfering a few office supplies from work, driving faster than the posted speed limit, etc. Some crimes require very high levels of motivation so that very few people are ever tempted into committing them: serial murder, payroll robbery, etc. In between lie a wide range of offenses that some people, but not most, are tempted into from time to time: residential burglary, theft from an auto, common assault in a bar, experimenting with illegal drugs.[5]

Search processes are a function of location, situation, and motivation. Some searches for criminal targets are very short, perhaps instantaneous, because motivation flares in a situation of proximity to a potential victim or target. Some searches for victims or targets are extended, the product of strong continuing motivation and premeditation.

Figure 4.2 presents a basic model of the criminal choice process and links it to the criminal justice process. When discussing crime prevention, focus should fall on the first part of the model. An expansion of the first part of the model is presented in Figure 4.3.

For crime prevention purposes a distinction must to be made between opportunistic crimes and premeditated crimes. In *opportunistic* crimes, the search is a by-product of routine daily activities. Target selection can be virtually instantaneous when a criminal opportunity appears during the course of daily routines: bar assaults, joy riding, theft from auto, and shoplifting can all serve as examples of this (although some proportion of all of these offenses are planned and strongly motivated). Sometimes criminal opportunities are noticed during the course of routine activities and exploited at a later time, when the situation for criminal action is less risky or requires less effort (Cromwell et al., 1991; Letkemann, 1973; Maguire, 1982). In *premeditated* crimes, the offender *begins* with the intention of committing a crime and conducts a conscious search until a suitable target is found, then awaits the right situation for the criminal act. A large proportion of burglaries are premeditated, as are high "take" robberies. Even for premeditated crimes, however, it is important to remember that search patterns are typically constrained by routine

Figure 4.2
Crime Process Model

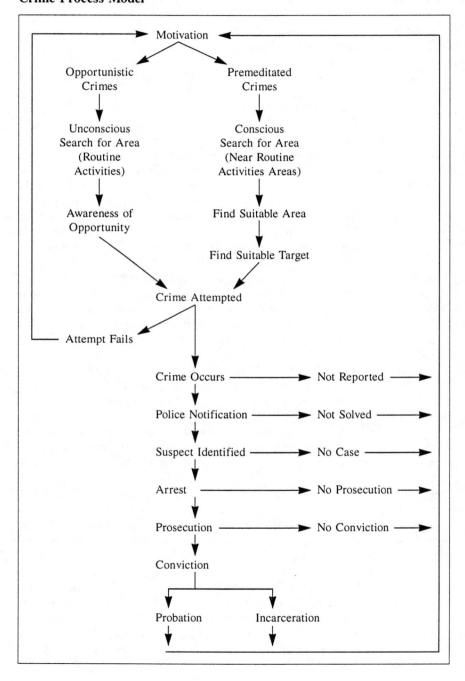

Figure 4.3
Crime Process Model: Target Selection

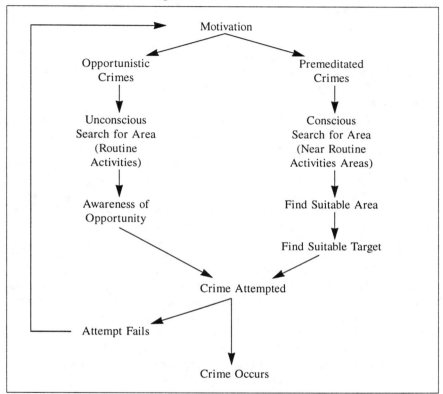

activities and awareness spaces. The places an intending burglar will search to find a burglary target are likely to be constrained by an awareness space shaped by routine activities (see e.g., Cromwell et al., 1991; Maguire, 1982; Rengert & Wasilchick, 1985; Reppetto, 1974).

For most offenders, criminal action is nested within a daily, weekly, and monthly routine of non-criminal activities. Crime follows some triggering event that draws the offender's attention to an opportunity in a situation in which it can be exploited at risk, effort, and emotional levels that seem acceptable to the offender at the time. Nearly all such triggering events occur in normal behavior spaces. Assaults, auto thefts, house break-ins, acts of vandalism, shoplifting, and noisy behavior all typically happen in the offender's normal behavior spaces. Even very unusual and serious crimes—serial murders and serial rapes—have been shown to occur within the offender's normal behavior spaces most of the time (see e.g., Alston, 1994; Rossmo, 1994).

CRIME PREVENTION FOR HOT SPOTS

Efficient crime prevention, then, should use intelligence information about routine-activity patterns and the opportunity spaces they create. Crime prevention can be oriented to: (1) reduce opportunistic crimes by reducing easy opportunities in routine activity spaces; and (2) reduce premeditated crimes by introducing preventive obstacles into those routine situations that specifically attract intending offenders. This, of course, follows the situational model developed by Clarke (1992).

Reducing opportunistic crimes by reducing the volume of easy opportunities clustered at particular times and places involves analysis of the characteristics of hot spots. Opportunistic crimes cluster at places we call crime generators.

Crime generators are particular areas to which large numbers of people are attracted for reasons unrelated to any particular level of criminal motivation they might have or the particular crime they might end up committing. Typical examples might include shopping precincts, entertainment districts, office concentrations, or sports stadiums. In New York City, these might include Fifth Avenue around Rockefeller Center or the Grand Concourse, the Theater District and 42nd Street off Times Square, and the areas around Madison Square Garden and Yankee Stadium. Major subway interchanges such as Grand Central or Columbus Circle would also probably qualify. In metro Vancouver these might include the downtown core, the Granville Island shopping and theater district, the stadium complexes on False Creek, and the Metrotown complex in suburban Burnaby. In Montreal one might think of the St. Catherine shopping strip, the St. Denis bar and theater strip, or the Olympic stadium or the Forum.

Crime generators produce crime by creating particular times and places that provide appropriate concentrations of people and other targets (Angel, 1968) in settings that are conducive to particular types of criminal acts. Mixed into the people gathered at generator locations are at least some potential offenders who have sufficient general levels of criminal motivation who, although did not come to the area with the explicit intent of doing a crime, notice and exploit criminal opportunities as presented (either immediately or on a subsequent occasion). Both local insiders and outsiders may be tempted into committing crimes at crime generator locations.

Application of situational prevention strategies to crime generators is likely to produce substantial reductions in high volume, low seriousness crimes— property offenses, minor assaults, and nuisance offenses—without inducing much displacement into other times, places, or crime types. Instead, removal of easy opportunities will deflect many potential offenders into non-criminal activities—the crime generator becomes merely a social activity node, and ceases to be a hot spot (Brantingham & Brantingham, 1984; Kohfeld & Sprague, 1990; Pease, 1994). Moreover, despite the individual seriousness of violent crime, and despite media-induced concerns with lethal violence, this is the kind of crime that most concerns and most directly affects most North

Americans (see e.g., Canadian Centre for Justice Statistics, 1995; Kennedy & Forde, 1990; Maguire & Pastore, 1994).

Reduction of premeditated crimes requires the use of similar but much tougher situational interventions. Premeditated crime hot spots often concentrate at places we call crime attractors.

Crime attractors are particular places, areas, neighborhoods, or districts that create well-known criminal opportunities to which strongly motivated, intending criminal offenders are attracted because of the known opportunities for particular types of crime. Examples might include bar districts, prostitution strolls, drug markets, large shopping malls (particularly those near major public transit exchanges), and large, insecure parking lots in business or commercial areas. The intending offender goes to rough biker bars looking for fights or other kinds of "action." The intending offender goes to hooker strolls looking to solicit an act of prostitution; or, in the case of serial offenders, looking for a victim (Alston, 1994; Rossmo, 1994). The intending offender is drawn to a drug market area to deal in drugs. The intending offender is drawn to malls or stores with poor security arrangements looking to shoplift or rob. The intending offender is drawn to large, insecure parking lots looking for cars or car parts to steal.

Crimes in such locations are often committed by area outsiders. Strongly motivated offenders will travel relatively long distances in search of a target (Capone & Nichols, 1976). (When insiders commit crimes in such areas, they may have previously moved to those areas because of their crime attracting qualities or, as in many cities, because poor areas are located near commercial areas thus creating many accessible targets near home.)

The attraction is created by an ecological label (Brantingham & Brantingham, 1991, 1993), often supplemented by the intending offender's personal past history, establishing that particular location as a known place to go for that kind of crime. As studies by Rengert (1995) and Langworthy and LeBeau (1992a, 1992b) have shown, such crime attracting areas can also *generate* other types of crime that are auxiliary or serendipitous by-products of the intending offender having been attracted to the area by the prospect of committing the primary crime.

The application of situational crime prevention techniques to premeditated crimes occurring at crime attractor locations is much more likely to produce displacement to other places, other times, and, to a lesser extent, to other crimes. This suggests that crime prevention planners must consider the likely alternatives open to premeditating offenders and also intervene at those times and locations in order to make effective preventive interventions.

It is worth noting that there are also *crime neutral* areas in most cities. Crime neutral areas neither attract intending offenders because they expect to do a particular crime in the area, nor do they produce crimes by creating criminal opportunities that are too tempting to resist. Instead, they experience occasional crimes by local insiders. Simple distance decay and pathway models can describe the geography of crime in such locations. The offense mix is different from the offense mix at either crime attractor or crime generator locations (Brantingham & Brantingham, 1994a).

It is important to note that most areas are unlikely to be pure attractors, pure generators, or purely neutral. Most areas will be mixed, in the sense that they may be crime attractors for some types of crimes, crime generators for other types of crime, and neutral with respect to still other types of crime.

Reducing opportunistic crimes at crime generator locations may only require minor changes to the site or situation: new walkways through a store; access limited through the placement of a door; introduction of minor levels of semi-official surveillance—"viewers" from an observational distance. Reducing premeditated crimes at crime attractor locations may require stronger specific changes: tightly controlled access; constant unofficial observation; obvious official surveillance.

Depending on the mix of criminal opportunities and criminal offenders at particular sites and situations, mid-range interventions may increase some criminal opportunities and crimes while reducing targeted crimes. Consider for instance, a patio fence. The fence can reduce casual thefts of bikes or barbecue grills by kids who pass by and do not see the targets. A burglar, in contrast, can use the fence as a screen behind which to commit a break-in, free from observation by neighbors and passersby. Consider, as another example, a private security guard at a shopping mall who follows a predictable patrol route. The visible presence of this official guardian may discourage casual shoplifters (there may be other guards as well), but the predictability of the guard's route enhances the ability of drug dealers to traffic in the mall's food fair. Longer periods of observation allow the drug dealer to establish the rhythm of when guardians will be present and when they will not, and set up lookouts to notify them when security guards are approaching.

Mid-range preventive intervention attempts are also important as they relate to fear reduction efforts. Fear reduction may sometimes increase actual risk. The importance of distinguishing between fear and crime reduction is covered in the next section.

FEAR GENERATOR MODEL

Fear of crime is complex. There are many types of fear, but they seem to fall into five broad categories:

- Direct fear of another person.
- Fear of being alone.
- Fear at night (in the dark).
- Fear in unknown areas.
- Fear of encounters with "scary" people.

Fear of crime is a general fear of being attacked, of suffering some physical harm, of suffering an intrusion that destroys privacy and dignity. It is not generally tied to a concern for property loss. Fear is increased by:

- *Personal physical vulnerability.* People who, because of age or lack of strength feel much more susceptible to harm if attacked, feel much more fearful than people who do not feel vulnerable.

- *Lack of control over the situation.* People who feel they have no control over a situation are much more fearful than people who believe they have the ability to control that same situation. This is why subway trains are so "scary": a passenger cannot be sure who might get on at the next station and, if someone "scary" gets on, there is no help and no escape until the next station.

When crime prevention practitioners seek to reduce fear of crime, the model used must focus on people's perceptions and feelings, and how different people react to different situations. Figure 4.4 presents a general model of fear generation.

Figure 4.4
Fear Model

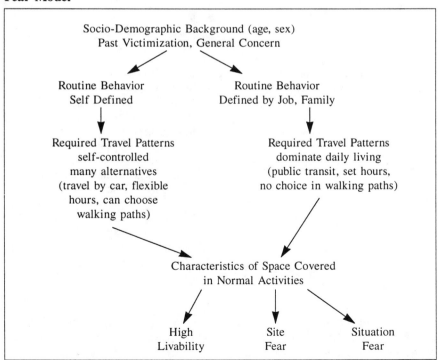

Fear increases with increases in perceived vulnerability, with increased isolation from "known" others, or with perceived reduction in the ability to control what might happen. Fear is higher for a potentially vulnerable person when alone in public space with no sure knowledge of what is around, when essential pathways cross those of other people seen as "potential attackers," and when there are signs of problems such as Wilson and Kelling's (1982) "broken windows" or indicators of incivility such as litter and graffiti (Skogan, 1988a) in the area. Table 4.1 lists some characteristic fear generators.

Table 4.1
Fear Generators

Limited knowledge of what is around:	• Lack of lighting • Blind corners • Lack of prospect • Hiding places
Presence of "scary" people, that is, people who are seen as different and potentially aggressive:	• Teenagers • Panhandlers • People of different ethnic groups
Trouble markers:	• Litter, trash • Graffiti • Bars on windows • Alarms
Absence of choice in routes that must be traversed on foot:	• One entry, one exit • Single pathways • Requirements to work at specific locations • Requirements to travel a specific way (bus stops, tunnels to transit) • Requirements to enter unknown space behind a solid door
Isolation:	• No one near whom you know or believe you could call on for help

Crime prevention may reduce fear in public places by increasing lighting, increasing view angles, eliminating hiding places, or providing alternative walkways that allow someone to keep a separation from areas or people they do not want to approach. For example, there might be a walkway through a park that a person would like to follow between his or her home and bus stop during the day, but at night that same person would prefer to stay on a street with stores and with well-lighted display windows while walking between the same destinations. A person might feel less fear if elevator waiting areas were surrounded by glass walls and doors, not solid walls and doors. A senior citizen might feel less fear if he or she were to walk past a group of teenagers across the street, but feel more fear if he or she must walk *through* the group or wait with them at a bus stop in order to reach his or her destination.

In most instances fear generation is not necessarily related to actual risk. Crime is concentrated in time and space. Figure 4.5 shows the spatial distribution of criminal code calls for service in Burnaby during 1991. Note that Burnaby has multiple hot spots.[6] Figure 4.6 shows the spatial concentration of burglaries in Vancouver in 1993. Vancouver has a single major crime hot spot of great intensity.[7] Yet people who live far from the crime hot spots, who rarely venture into high risk areas, and who therefore run little objective risk of victimization often express the highest levels of fear and are most willing to participate in crime prevention exercises such as neighborhood watch programs.[8]

Figure 4.5
Spatial Concentration of Criminal Code Calls
Burnaby, British Columbia, 1991

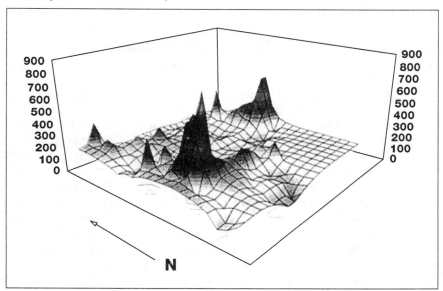

Figure 4.6
Spatial Concentration of Burglaries
Vancouver, Canada, 1993

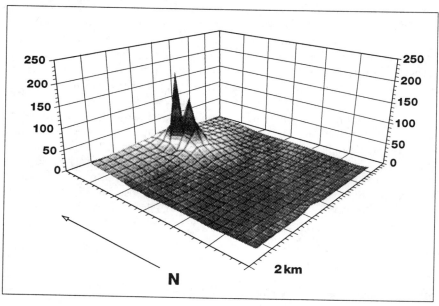

FEAR AND CRIME MODEL:
TRADE-OFFS TO CONSIDER

There are some sites and situations that both generate fear and experience much crime. In these times and places crime prevention practitioners may face a potential conflict between fear reduction and crime reduction. This potential conflict comes from several sources. First, fear may cause potential victims to be more cautious and to take more care of their property, reducing exposure, thus reducing the volume of criminal opportunities and thereby reducing crime at the site and in the situation. In such circumstances, a fear reduction program could have the effect of increasing crime by lulling potential victims. Second, potential offenders are people, too. They often experience the same fears in the same places where potential victims feel fearful. This may reduce the use of the particular site by the potential offenders as well, thereby reducing the actual risk of victimization accruing to others. A fear reduction program might make such a place feel comfortable to potential offenders and thus generate additional crimes. A number of strategies for reducing fear of crime may have counterproductive results. This may be illustrated through several examples.

Lighting

Ask citizens at large what should be done to improve street safety and the first response is almost universal: more street lighting. In the Simon Fraser University (SFU) victim survey in British Columbia, for instance, students indicated that the reason that they felt fearful at particular locations was a sense of isolation, of being alone in case they needed help. When asked what should be done to improve the situation, more than 70 percent responded that more lighting was needed. This response did not address the stated reasons for feeling afraid, and it was directed at the most brightly lighted area on campus, a remote parking lot. Moreover, because SFU is a commuter campus, a large proportion of the students who called for more lighting in the parking lot also said that they almost never remained on campus late enough in the day that lighting would matter (Brantingham & Brantingham, 1994b; Brantingham, Brantingham & Seagrave, 1995).

In many settings, but particularly at crime and fear hot spots, attempts to reduce fear by improving lighting, increasing view angles, and increasing the number of alternative of escape routes (Nasar & Fisher, 1992, 1993) may actually increase the incidence of crime by increasing public use of the area by both potential victims and potential offenders, thereby increasing the volume of opportunities at the site and triggering more criminal events. Examples of fear-reducing attempts that increase criminal activity include:

- Street drug dealers probably want well-lighted places so they can see when police or others are approaching. They need a broad view angle to make the lighting work most effectively. Users also need light to use needles.[9] Dealers would probably like escape routes to use should they see something—police, a rival dealer—they do not like.

- Female prostitutes want well-lighted corners for visibility. They want other people around as customers, but also probably for personal safety.

- Auto thieves interviewed for the British Columbia Association of Chiefs of Police auto theft study (Fleming, Brantingham & Brantingham, 1994) stated that they want good lighting so that they can see what they are doing when they steal a car. They also want broad view angles so that thugs cannot sneak up on them and rob them while they are busy trying to steal a car.

- Better lighting and good view angles with good escape routes make it easier for highly motivated robbers or burglars to know whether there is reasonable time to actually commit the crime (complete the robbery or break into the building) before someone can intervene.

These examples are not characteristic of every part of every city. Although the bulk of evidence demonstrates that the introduction of higher levels of street lighting does little to reduce crime and may be counterproductive (Atkins, Hussain & Storey, 1991; Lab, 1992; Ramsay & Newton, 1991), it is also the case that the introduction of lighting into dark spots where predatory crimes are occurring can sometimes prevent crimes at such locations (Painter, 1994). There is a policy trade-off between fear and crime that needs to be explored situationally at each specific site.

Traffic Flows

Traffic flows are a matter of substantial concern to the residents and users of neighborhoods. The little research that has been done suggests that fear of crime follows a U-shaped trajectory—fear is high when traffic (pedestrian or vehicular) is so low that people feel isolated and alone, and fear is also high when traffic volumes are very high and people feel crowded by pedestrians and vehicles (Appleyard, 1981). This suggests that modification of traffic flows to produce intermediate levels of traffic at particular sites will reduce fear of crime at those sites.

Unfortunately, the little research that has been done seems to show that crime volumes follow the reverse trajectory—crime is low at sites with very low traffic volumes, high at sites with intermediate traffic volumes, and low again at sites with very high traffic volumes. This theoretical model was developed by an urban planner (Angel, 1968) and has been confirmed in the few studies that have addressed it (e.g., Duffala, 1976; Wilcox, 1973).

This means that efforts to reduce fear through manipulation of traffic flow density are likely to produce increased volumes of crime. Moreover, although crime prevention efforts based on traffic flow modifications sometimes prove to be successful (Matthews, 1990), they do not invariably prove successful (Cromwell & Zahm, 1991). This means that this approach to fear reduction and crime control may be a poor trade-off, although it is often politically tempting at the local level.

Our Ignorance About Fear of Crime

One of the problems in trying to take things further in this analysis is that we actually have very little information about what "fear of crime" really means. The fear of crime industry that criminologists have constructed out of a question put in victimization surveys—"Is there any place in your neighborhood (within a mile or so) where you would be afraid to walk alone at night?"—provides almost no useful information to crime prevention practitioners. If people respond "yes" we have no idea:

- Of what they are afraid.
  It could be they fear physical attack by strangers, robbery, or assault. But in questions put to various groups in New Westminster, a suburban city node within greater Vancouver over more than a decade (e.g., Brantingham & Brantingham, 1981; Brantingham & Brantingham, 1984; Brantingham, Brantingham & Fister, 1979), we found that, when asked, people state that they are concerned about being hassled by teenagers, or that they are afraid of traffic moving too fast, or that they expect to be accosted by panhandlers or drunks. We need to know much more about what people have in mind when they indicate they fear "crime" at particular locations. On the basis of the skimpy evidence presently available, most people are thinking of incivilities rather than crime, most of the time.

- Where, exactly, they have in mind.
  Different people can have sharply different ideas about where the crime hot spots are and where they feel afraid. Residents, businessmen, and the police, as groups, in the suburban city of New Westminster identified quite different places when asked to circle the high crime places on a map of the city.[10]

- How maps of fear relate to maps of crime.
  Until recently we could relate a map of fear of crime with a map of known criminal events in any North American city. Recently, George Rengert (1995) has demonstrated that people's cognitive maps of crime and the objective crime patterns in central Philadelphia are quite different. Until we have done this for a great many cities, we are likely, without realizing it, to undertake crime prevention efforts that are counterproductive along one or the other dimension—fear and crime—of the thing we are trying to manipulate.

What we must do now is work with sites and situations using some of the underlying principles previously described. With current general levels of concern and fear we should begin looking at the *public's* understanding of what constitutes the crime problem; and in our analyses of the crime problem, we should ensure that we do not commingle fear-reducing strategies with crime-reducing strategies in counterproductive ways. We need to know more about what people are afraid of at particular times and places. When we do, we will be able to design preventive intervention tactics that will balance fear management with crime prevention.

North East Multi-Regional Training
-Instructors' Library-
355 Smoke Tree Plaza
North Aurora, IL 60542

CONCLUSION

Crime prevention—from both a theoretical perspective and in actual practice—is making great progress. Future improvements in crime prevention should be linked to better understandings of time and place, particularly how a site or situation can be a crime generator or a crime attractor, and how fear, incivilities, and crime are different and require different crime prevention approaches.

NOTES

[1]   Canada has experienced a similar phenomenon, although the longer five year spacing between national victimization surveys renders the pattern less clearly (Canadian Centre for Justice Statistics, 1995).

[2]   For a clear understanding of situational crime prevention in practice, see Clarke, 1992.

[3]   In the Canadian Uniform Crime Reporting System the term *actual offenses* is used to describe a count of offenses reported to police minus those reports in which preliminary investigation establishes that no criminal event in fact occurred.

[4]   By *motivation* we refer both to the reasons people have for committing crimes and to the strength of their commitment to the idea that the crime must be committed.

[5]   For instance, while 88 percent of the American high school class of 1993 admitted having had a fight or argument with their parents during the previous 12 months, less than three percent admitted having committed an armed robbery. In between these extremes, more than one-quarter of the class of 1993 admitted having committed a burglary during the preceding 12 months, and about one-third admitted a minor theft (Maguire & Pastore, 1994:308-309).

[6]   Burnaby data are from the RCMP PIRS information system and were collected during the course of the auto theft study sponsored by the British Columbia Association of Chiefs of Police (Fleming, Brantingham & Brantingham, 1994).

[7]   Vancouver data are from the Vancouver Police Department's CAD system and represent calls for service.

[8]   University students tend to fear areas of campus where little real crime occurs, and to feel safe in the very areas in which crimes most frequently occur (Brantingham, Brantingham & Seagrave, 1995). Little is known about the spatial and temporal distribution of fear in cities. We think that much could be learned from a concerted effort to develop fear maps for a number of cities utilizing a variety of mental mapping techniques. A starting point would be Pyle's *Spatial Dynamics of Crime* (1974).

[9]   It is hard to find a vein sometimes.

[10]   See Brantingham, Brantingham and Fister (1979) for cognitive maps of crime in New Westminster.

355 Smoke Tree Plaza
North Aurora, IL. 60542

INTRODUCTION TO CHAPTER 5

The influence of signs of incivility on crime and fear of crime has been a focal point of discussion in crime prevention. Incivility can be reflected in both physical signs (such as litter, graffiti, abandoned buildings, and broken windows) and social signs (such as vagrants, prostitutes, and drug markets/sales). The assumption has been that signs of incivility indicate that the area is poorly taken care of and controlled and, therefore, that offenders can act with a reasonable degree of impunity. The logical implication for crime prevention is that efforts to reduce incivility will lower the levels of crime and fear in the area.

These assumptions about the impact of incivility have been accepted at face value and have gone largely unchallenged. Taylor, however, challenges these assumptions and suggests that signs of incivility, particularly physical signs, are not as important as we are led to believe. Based on an evaluation of data from Minneapolis-St. Paul, Taylor finds that signs of incivility are only minimally related to fear of crime, perceived risk of victimization, and attachment to the area. The most significant predictors of the outcomes are differences in actual victimization between residents in the same areas. Perceptions of incivilities, not actual differences between neighborhoods, also predict fear and perceived risk.

Taylor suggests that the heavy focus of many crime prevention initiatives should shift away from allocating significant amounts of time, money, and energy to reducing signs of incivility. Based on his results, these efforts will have only a minimal impact on fear and perceived risk. Other forms of crime prevention would have a greater impact than combatting incivility, particularly efforts to improve resident interaction with one another and the police, reducing perceptions of incivility, and building community stability. Does this mean that reducing physical problems and other signs of incivility in a neighborhood should be abandoned? Taylor says no. Changes in incivility should be a secondary part of a larger program, rather than the focal point of a community's efforts.

5

Crime, Grime, and Responses to Crime: Relative Impacts of Neighborhood Structure, Crime, and Physical Deterioration on Residents and Business Personnel in the Twin Cities[1]

Ralph B. Taylor
Temple University

ISSUES ADDRESSED

In this project, I sought to gain a better understanding of the factors influencing people's cognitive and emotional responses to crime in a community context. How afraid people are to walk the streets of their neighborhood at night, or how likely people gauge their chances of being a crime victim, or how much people worry about their property while away, or how serious residents gauge order-related problems to be in their neighborhood, all reflect how people are dealing with and responding to crime and related problems in their neighborhood. Each of these responses has been extensively researched (see DuBow et al., 1979; Ferraro, 1994; Miethe, 1995; Skogan & Maxfield, 1981). In addition, work has shown that these responses relate to a range of psychological, social psychological, and ecological outcomes. These include behavioral withdrawal, anxiety and depression, weakened resident-based control on the street, and less commitment to the community. Why conduct another study?

The answer has three parts. First, researchers have made a strong case that physical deterioration and disorderly behavior on the street deepens the reactions to disorder mentioned above. These signs of incivility include: vacant, trash-filled lots; abandoned and badly deteriorated housing and stores; extensive graffiti; public drinking, drunkenness, or drug dealing; "hey honey" hassles; large groups of rowdy youths or adults; and street crazies or homeless persons. Examinations of this question, however, have been limited in some important ways.

The researchers have suggested the following scenario. Over time, signs of neighborhood incivility may not only deepen residents' concerns for their personal safety, they also may speed processes of increasing crime in the neighborhood and neighborhood decline.[2] Deterioration and disorderly street conduct, independent of other neighborhood conditions, might be partially responsible for making crime increase faster in a neighborhood, or for weakening residents involvement in formal and informal neighborhood affairs. To properly gauge the merit of such an argument requires information on how neighborhoods change over time.[3]

But if the incivilities thesis has merit, I also should probably see, in data from several neighborhoods collected at one point in time, impacts of physical deterioration and disorderly social behavior on responses to crime like fear and perceived risk. Studies looking for such impacts observe them when they use resident perceptions of deterioration and disorderly behavior, as reported in surveys (see e.g., Skogan, 1990). But when measures use on-site assessments made by independent raters, different patterns emerge depending in part on the level of analysis. At the neighborhood level, the impacts are nonexistent, or conditional, or much weaker than observed with perceived measures (Covington & Taylor, 1991; Taylor et al., 1985). At the block level the impacts may be weaker than observed with survey-based measures, but sometimes they are stronger (Perkins and Taylor, in press; Perkins et al., 1990; Perkins et al., 1993).

In short, despite the earlier work on responses to disorder, some outstanding issues deserve attention.

- We are not yet certain if, and under what conditions, signs of incivility make independent contributions to responses like fear of crime and perceived risk;

- If signs of incivility do contribute independently to cognitive and emotional responses to crime and related problems, what are the relative impacts of assessed versus perceived signs, and how do these impacts depend on whether the focus is individuals or larger units like neighborhoods?

Understandably, extensive use has been made of perceived measures of incivilities, based on surveys of residents, because they are easy to collect and generally available in many different studies. Far fewer studies have included on-site assessments of the relevant features, made by trained raters.[4] But from a policy perspective, what is of interest are the features as they exist in the residential environment. It is these extant conditions that have been the focus of some elements of community policing and community improvement efforts (see e.g., Spelman & Eck, 1987).

Community policing has many different elements, only one of which is helping communities remove or manage signs of incivility (Bayley, 1994). Nevertheless, when community or problem-oriented police are focusing on signs of incivility, the clearest way of learning how successful they have been may be to assess the changes taking place in the targeted settings, rather than by asking residents about perceptions of problems.

Perceived incivilities, I suggest, may reflect more than the extant conditions surrounding a resident. They also may reflect something about the resident, or something about the resident's sensitivity to local conditions. The typical perceived incivility question asks "How much of a problem is condition x? Is it a big problem, somewhat of a problem, or not a problem at all? in your neighborhood [on your block]." Some people may see bigger problems in their neighborhood simply because they are the kind of person to complain more. Another explanation for differences in perceived incivilities, beyond extant conditions, is varying awareness of those conditions. If cognitive processes of adaptation to disorder are ongoing in an urban environment, some residents are going to tune out their surroundings more than others (Riger, 1985; Taylor & Shumaker, 1990). Those who are less adapted to the local disorder are going to report more problems.[5] Evidence that these perceived problems encompass more than the assessed signs of incivility receives support from work finding independent impacts of both on outcomes like fear of crime (Covington & Taylor, 1991).

In short, the work to date suggests perceived signs of incivility reflect psychological and social psychological factors, as well as ecological conditions. On-site assessments of signs of incivility, although not perfectly reliable and not completely free of rater bias, do largely reflect setting conditions. Therefore, it may be appropriate to include perceived incivilities when predicting responses to disorder, provided one does so at the individual level, and recognizes that these perceptions reflect varying responses to the same surrounding conditions. These variations reflect internal psychological attributes, or differences in how people interact with the locale. It is appropriate to use on-site assessments of signs of incivility, when these are available, to gauge setting conditions and differences between settings. When on-site ratings are available they are preferred as the indicators of setting conditions because they most directly represent a possible focus of community policing initiatives.

Thus, the first purpose of this study was to examine independent impacts of assessed and perceived signs of incivility on responses to crime. The assessed measures come from on-site ratings made by trained raters. The perceived measures come from residents' survey responses. I will allow assessed incivilities to predict differences between locations, and perceived incivilities to predict differences between people in the same location.

While examining differences between places, I want to control for overall neighborhood structure. Three independent elements of community structure emerging from extensive ecological work are: status, race/ethnicity, and stability (Berry & Kasarda, 1977). I will take out their effects in our analyses. At the individual level, similarly, when we are examining effects of perceived incivilities, we will control for other characteristics that might influence responses to crime.

The second purpose of the current investigation was to carry out the above assessment using analytical techniques separating between-place from between-person differences. Techniques used in prior studies, such as contextual regression, have some limitations (see e.g., Hauser, 1974). Recently developed hierarchical linear models, emerging from educational sociology, address some of these limitations (Bryk & Raudenbush, 1992; Taylor, 1995c). Most notably, they allow clear separation of impacts due to differences between places, and impacts due to differences between people in the same place.

The third purpose of the investigation was to examine responses to disorder reported by local merchants. Most work to date has focused on residents' reactions to disorder. But the responses of local merchants, those in charge of small neighborhood businesses, also merit attention. Merchants who perceive significant risk of harm, or who become extremely concerned about protecting their establishment, may change their operations in one of several ways. They may become less trusting of local customers, carrying out security procedures making even harmless customers feel less welcome; they might limit their hours and services in ways that inconvenience local residents; or they may decide to locate their businesses elsewhere. The present study examines if the disorderly neighborhood conditions influence merchants' responses to disorder in the same way they do residents' responses.

DATA SOURCES AND PROCESSING

I carried out a secondary analysis of a dataset originally collected by researchers at the Minnesota Crime Prevention Center in the early 1980s.[6] The original researchers focused on small commercial centers (SCCs) in Minneapolis and St. Paul (MN). In 1981, on-site assessments were completed of 93 such centers, with raters noting land use, physical conditions, and business types. Micro-neighborhoods, about one-third of a mile in diameter around each center, were defined, and crime information was collected for the centers and the surrounding neighborhoods.

In 1982, researchers selected a stratified sample of 24 SCCs. Assessors visited each center a second time, again noting land use, physical conditions, and types of businesses. During the summer, systematic behavioral observations were completed in each center. In the late summer, telephone interviewers completed about 35 interviews in each neighborhood surrounding each center. In-person interviews were completed with approximately 200 business personnel working in businesses in the centers in the early fall. Most of the merchants interviewed were owners or managers.

In the resident interviews, interviewers confirmed that the respondent was familiar with the commercial center in question. The interview covered a wide range of topics including perceived problems in the center, views about the neighborhood, fear, perceived risk, worry about crime, informal social control, attachment to the neighborhood, views about the neighborhood future, recent victimization experience, and background demographic questions. Particularly useful for the present purposes, the protocol asked about fear and worry while in the center itself, as well as fear and worry while abroad in the larger neighborhood. The focus on fear and worry while in the center allows consideration of reactions in a specific location.

The merchant interviews, where possible and appropriate, asked questions paralleling those in the resident interviews. Merchants were asked about fear and worry while in the center, perceived risk of victimization, perceived problems in the center, and steps taken to protect their businesses. Background questions included how many hours a week were spent at work, and how long they had been located there.

To better appreciate the ecological contexts within which the data were collected, I visited the Twin Cities in June of 1995. With a key informant who was a life long resident of St. Paul, I toured all 24 commercial centers and the adjoining neighborhoods. In several locations we talked to both merchants and/or some local residents. From those visits I collected no "new" data. But I will use the impressions gained to provide more extensive context for some findings.

From the resident interviews I constructed indexes to reflect the outcomes of interest. Three outcomes assessed perceived vulnerability: fear and worry while in the center; fear and worry while abroad in the neighborhood; and perceived risk of being victimized by street crime. I also developed an index for informal social control on the resident's block, an index of the respondent's attachment to his/her neighborhood, and an index for perceived incivilities.

With the merchant surveys I concentrated on four outcomes, each captured in reliable indexes: fear and worry while in the center; perceived risk of victimization; steps taken to protect the business from crimes; and perceived incivilities in the center.

RESULTS AND IMPLICATIONS

Resident Outcomes

I examined how much the outcomes from the resident interviews varied across persons, and how much they varied across places.

- On average, about 11 percent of the variation in the outcomes was due to differences between places.

The bulk of the variation in the outcomes was due to differences between people in the same location. The amount of the outcome due to differences between places varied from three percent for fear and worry while in the neighborhood to 33 percent for perceived incivilities. In all cases, the amount of variation due to differences between places was statistically significant. For the three indicators of vulnerability, less than 10 percent of the variation was due to differences between places.[7]

This pattern suggests theoretical and practical implications. In the theoretical realm, several researchers have proposed that fear of crime may be as high as it is in urban locations because it is capturing an urban malaise or urban unease residents feel in response to disintegrating and disorderly conditions (see e.g., Garofalo & Laub, 1978). If we concentrate on feelings *that can be linked directly to the specific external condition*, then the results I see here suggest such a conceptualization is responsible for about one-tenth of the fear differences across settings in one city. Nine-tenths of the variation in fear is capturing individual differences, including measurement error, in how people respond to similar conditions.[8] The ecological sources of fear are, at most, responsible for about one-tenth of the variations in fear.

By ecological sources, I mean sources that can be attributed to locational differences, that is, living in a different neighborhood. I am not including as an ecological source variations in perceived conditions arising from individuals living in the same location.[9]

Practically speaking, and assuming the partitioning observed here applies equally well to other samples, places, and times, the pattern suggests that efforts to improve local disorderly and dilapidated conditions, even under the most optimistic scenarios, can never directly shrink fear by more than about 10 to 20 percent.

Imagine that we could isolate a single neighborhood condition, such as the amount of graffiti, that completely explained the between-location differences in fear. Imagine further that subsequently we could eradicate the graffiti.[10] If graffiti was a direct cause of fear, and all residents were aware of its removal, its removal would result in shrinking fear by no more than 10 percent.

Of course I am ignoring for the moment the means by which the graffiti is removed. The cleanup campaign may evolve from local community development efforts. Here there might be "side effects" of the effort itself, such as increased citizen empowerment and more residents getting to know one another through the cooperative effort. These social-psychological outcomes might result in shrinking fear beyond the 10 percent due to graffiti removal itself. By contrast, the removal may occur because community policing officers, after talking with local leaders, enlist city agency personnel to remove the graffiti.[11] In this case the side effects noted above would not accrue.

But the theorists working on this problem maintain that it is the conditions themselves that cause concern. They either do not address how the problem is fixed; or argue in favor of a public agency response; or argue for initiatives from a public-private partnership. Given such a perspective, we should not presume that additional side effects will necessarily occur. We should not count on shrinking fear beyond the 10 percent that arises from the conditions themselves.

In short, if public agencies are concerned about reducing residents' fear of crime, and seek to do so by eradicating local social and physical ecological conditions that might inspire fear, they are limited to reducing fear only by a small amount. The bulk of the causes of fear arises from differences between residents responding to the same exact ecological conditions. These would be largely untouched by a community policing effort built around the "broken windows" thesis or a problem-oriented policing framework oriented solely toward grime reduction.

If the above data and supporting reasoning are correct, and broadly applicable, policymakers have two questions to address. First, is it worth dedicating problem-solving police officers to these tasks? Are fear reductions on the order specified above worthwhile, from an agency perspective? This answer can only be answered in a specific jurisdiction, with detailed knowledge about the settings in question, and specific agency and program goals. Second, those formulating community policing policies for their jurisdiction may want to consider relative priorities assigned to these officers considering the above scenario. What efforts should be devoted to eradicating these conditions, in comparison to efforts focused on different elements of community policing? For example, these findings might suggest police managers increase community policing resources devoted to police mini-stations, or bicycle patrol, or attending community meetings, and decrease resources allocated to coordinating environmental improvements such as cleaning out vacant lots, boarding up vacant houses, or cleaning graffiti.

- Neither assessed incivilities, nor local crime rates, make independent contributions to between-neighborhood differences in outcomes after controlling for neighborhood structure.

Assessed incivilities and the local personal crime rates failed to significantly predict between-neighborhood differences in the outcomes after I had controlled for neighborhood race, status, and stability. Their failure to contribute arose from one of two causes. In some cases, assessed incivilities and/or crime were so strongly related to neighborhood structure that it was simply not possible for them to make an independent contribution.[12] In other cases, once the three dimensions of neighborhood structure had been entered as predictors, no significant between-location differences on the outcome remained in need of explaining.

Prior studies also have observed strong correlations between neighborhood structure and assessed incivilities (Taylor et al., 1985). The correlations were stronger at the neighborhood level than at the streetblock level (for some block level correlations, see Perkins et al., 1990). Researchers need to systematically examine the size of these correlations and decide if physical deterioration and other assessed indicators of incivilities can be reliably distinguished from the broader status, ethnic composition, and stability of neighborhoods. Are these signs of incivility so strongly driven by community conditions that they are best viewed as symptoms of those conditions?[13]

The implication of the current pattern of findings is that between-location differences in responses to crime are caused more by community characteristics than by anything else.[14] The community feature linked most closely to the responses was neighborhood stability. Results suggested it was far more important than status or neighborhood racial composition. This finding is fully in keeping with human ecological theory underscoring the central importance of neighborhood stability (McKenzie, 1921).

For policymakers advocating neighborhood stabilization programs, these results provide further impetus to their projects. Neighborhood stability will, beyond enhancing overall neighborhood life, contribute significantly to lower levels of fear and personal safety concerns. Greater perceived safety may represent an important latent function arising from these programs.

- Victimization experience, and perceived incivilities, both consistently predicted responses to crime.

Controlling for other individual level factors, recent victimization experience emerged as a significant predictor for each outcome save attachment to the neighborhood. Recent victims, as compared to non-victims, were more afraid in the neighborhood and in the commercial center, perceived more incivilities in the center, and reported less informal social control on their own block. The impacts, although statistically significant and consistent, were moderate in size.[15]

Perceived incivilities in the commercial center contributed significantly to every outcome except informal social control. The impacts were sizable and significant.[16] Perceived incivilities in the commercial center contributed most significantly when the outcome was fear and worry while in the center itself. This is plausible since in this situation the arenas for the predictor and outcome matched perfectly. But even when asking about different locations, perceived incivilities in the center still display sizable impacts. Apparently residents were making cross-location inferences to the greater neighborhood, based on the problems they discerned in the commercial center itself. This pattern supports, but also extends, the counter-dependency thesis (McPherson & Silloway, 1986). McPherson and Silloway argued for such a thesis when they originally examined the data we are working with here.

The dependency thesis suggests that the commercial activity in a small commercial center is almost wholly dependent on the characteristics of the surrounding clientele and neighborhood. In their counter-dependency thesis McPherson and Silloway (1986) argued that the center itself could have independent effects on residents' involvements in their neighborhoods. The effects observed here strongly support that thesis. At the same time they further articulate that thesis by grounding it firmly in the *psychological* realm. In the same location, and confronted with the same commercial center, residents are making strong connections between what they think is taking place in their center, and how safe they feel not only in the center, but elsewhere in their neighborhood. The counter-dependency dynamics are operating intrapersonally.

To sum up on this last point, then, the effects of crime and disorder on responses to disorder are operating largely at the psychological rather than ecological level. Once we control for neighborhood structure, we do not see independent impacts of crime and assessed disorder on between-neighborhood differences in responses to crime. But when we control for individual characteristics such as age, education, and sex, we still see independent contributions of victimization and perceived incivilities to differences between individuals.

For policymakers, this last finding suggests a potential program focus for community policing efforts—how to reduce residents' perceptions of physical and social problems. Perceptions of signs of incivility are important to outcomes like fear, and are independent of extant conditions. They reflect psychological and social psychological dynamics. Police-citizen door-to-door contacts on this topic, or community police addressing this matter at organization meetings, may prove useful venues for addressing these concerns.

At this point, it is not clear how to address these concerns, what the best vehicle for doing so is, or the appropriate roles of community police officers, but perceived signs of incivility certainly appear to be appropriate targets for community policing efforts.

Merchant Outcomes

I observed significant variation in merchant responses to disorder for all outcomes, save protection. Again, as with the resident-based outcomes, the between-neighborhood differences, although statistically significant, were not extremely large. There were no significant between-neighborhood differences in the number of steps merchants took to protect their businesses from crime.

In several ways the merchant results paralleled the resident results. For example, perceived incivilities contributed significantly, in the expected direction, to fear and worry in the center, perceived risk, and steps taken to protect businesses. As with the residents, this was analyzed as a predictor telling us about differences between merchants in the same location, so again it reflects social psychological and psychological dynamics, rather than ecological processes.

Another interesting difference between merchants in the same location emerged from differences in exposure. In businesses open more hours per week than nearby businesses, merchants took more steps to protect themselves, and perceived themselves to be at more risk of crime. This could reflect mere exposure, or different types of clientele served by businesses such as bars and convenience stores that are open more hours per week.

When I examined the contributions made by crime and assessed incivilities to between-neighborhoods outcome differences, I saw some expected and some unanticipated results. As expected, centers with one or more bars, and a higher crime rate, had merchants experiencing more serious problems. Centers with one or more bars had merchants taking more steps to protect their businesses.

Quite unexpected impacts appeared when the outcomes focused on merchants' feelings of vulnerability. For fear and worry in the center, merchants felt safer in centers in which there was a greater volume of vehicles on the street. This is the opposite of the resident-based research on safe neighborhoods, which finds crime is lower in neighborhoods with smaller, lower volume streets (Greenberg et al., 1982). With perceived risk, merchants felt less vulnerable in centers in which teenagers made up a higher portion of pedestrian traffic in the center. Again, this is the opposite of the resident-based theory. The latter argues that the presence of unsupervised teens contributes substantially to and reflects weak informal control in the locale (Sampson & Groves, 1989). These last two findings suggest that the contributions of ecological characteristics to responses to disorder made by those filling non-resident roles in the neighborhood may be markedly different from what we are given to expect based on a resident-centered theory.

SUMMARY

The current project has clarified how much responses to disorder, such as fear and informal control, differ across neighborhoods. I find these between-neighborhood differences to be significant but relatively small. This descriptive information puts an upper limit on the effectiveness of community policing programs designed to clean up social and physical signs of incivility.

In addition, the between-neighborhood differences, for residents, reflect the kind of neighborhood in which they live, rather than the amount of assessed disorder and crime taking place there. Assessed incivilities, in part because they are so closely related to neighborhood structure, make no independent contributions to resident differences across neighborhoods.

For merchants, assessed incivilities make some independent contributions to the outcomes, but some contributions are opposite what we would expect given the resident-based theory that has developed in this area.

At the individual level, perceptions of incivility contribute strongly to both resident-based and merchant-based outcomes. Victimization among residents contributes significantly to several outcomes. In short, the kinds of contributions made by disorder, as measured by reported crime and/or victimization, and incivilities, as measured by assessed features or perceptions, depend on the level of analysis. The main contributions appear to be at the individual-level, reflecting psychological and social psychological rather than ecological differences.

The policy implications are threefold. Those directing community policing efforts may want to reconsider the relative effort expended on reducing physical problems in neighborhoods, compared to other initiatives, such as mini-stations, getting to know residents, or communicating crime information to local organizations. Such considerations will of course be influenced by the relative priority assigned to responses to disorder like fear, and other setting, departmental, and jurisdictional factors. Second, such directors may also wish to explore ways community policing efforts, perhaps working collaboratively with local resident-based organizations, can reduce *perceptions* of incivility. These perceptions contribute substantially to the outcomes examined here.

Finally, results here have underscored the sizable impacts of neighborhood stability on responses to disorder like fear. It should be recognized that those responsible for maintaining stable neighborhoods, and those seeking to stabilize changing locales are, as an indirect result of their efforts, probably making residents feel safer.

NOTES

[1]   The work reported here was supported by grant 94-IJ-CX-0018 from the National Institute of Justice. Points of view or opinions in this document are solely the author's, and represent neither the opinions nor the official policies of the Department of Justice or the National Institute of Justice. I also received support from grant 93-IJ-CX-0022 during the course of this project. Data analyzed here were originally collected by Marlys McPherson and Glenn Silloway under grant 80-IJ-CX-0073 from the National Institute of Justice while they were affiliated with the Minnesota Crime Prevention Center, and were provided by the ICPSR at the University of Michigan. I thank Pamela Lattimore, without whose support this project would not have been possible. Grant Snyder provided invaluable field assistance. Joachim Savelsberg also encouraged and supported this project in various ways. David Linne, Ruth Eichmiller, and Mary Poulin assisted in data processing. Jack Greene, Doug Perkins, and Ron Davis provided helpful feedback on an earlier draft. Address correspondence to RBT, Department of Criminal Justice, Temple University, Philadelphia, PA 19122 (Internet:V5024E@VM.TEMPLE.EDU).

[2]   The incivilities thesis comes in several varieties. See, for example, Lewis and Salem (1986), Skogan (1990), Wilson (1975), and Wilson and Kelling (1982). For comments on the thesis see Greene and Taylor (1988) and Taylor (1987).

[3]   Such a project is currently underway in Baltimore. See, for example, Taylor (1995a).

[4]   I will use "assessed" and "on-site" to refer to measures of signs of incivility collected by trained raters using standardized assessment forms. The raters may be residents in the locale, or they may be outsiders. They also include standardized ratings made of photographs of the settings. I will use "perceived" and "survey-based" to refer to measures gathered from closed-ended surveys of residents, where

they are asked to gauge how much of a problem various signs of incivility are for their block or their neighborhood. For more background on the advantages and disadvantages of these different approaches to measurement see Taylor (1995b).

5   Crenson (1983) makes a similar argument.

6   The principal investigators were Marlys McPherson and Glenn Silloway. Some results from the study were reported in McPherson and Silloway (1984).

7   These between-within breakdowns on fear agree with what we have seen in multi-neighborhood datasets from other cities like Atlanta and Baltimore. This partitioning of the variance takes place *after* the hierarchical linear model carries out precision weighting. This process takes several features of the data into account. However, for our purposes here, the most important point is that it considers variations in group size and data quality. The ecological variations might be slightly more substantial if we focused on raw rather than precision weighted group means. Work with datasets in other locations, however, that has not used precision weighting, finds variance partitions comparable to those observed here.

8   Of course, different residents live in different parts of their neighborhood. Thus, at a micro level, each resident is confronted with a different neighborhood, but one outcome asked about fear and worry while in the center. These centers are quite small, and thus represent the same setting for all residents in the neighborhood. Although we do see more between-neighborhood differences when residents are asked about the center than when they are asked about their neighborhood, the amount of between variation is still quite small (7.5%). Because we do have this focused setting for the fear variable, I feel comfortable asserting that residents are responding to the same conditions. The between-within breakdowns we observe here may vary across samples of neighborhoods, and across cities. In samples with a broader range of neighborhoods than used here, the proportion of between variance may be somewhat higher. In cities in which the differences between neighborhoods are more extreme than was observed for these cities, the between portion also may be somewhat higher.

9   For example, residents living on the same block may have varying perceptions of the amount of graffiti on the block. Since these variations arise in response to one setting, with one level of graffiti, I view them as not having an ecological source. Ecological variation can arise if setting conditions have varying impacts on residents in different locations. In the current models these variations are folded into the overall between-neighborhood partition cited. Analyses exploring place x person interactions suggested they were generally quite small.

10   Of course, it is extremely unlikely that we would be able to identify one condition responsible for explaining all of the between-location differences. But even in situations in which we might be able to do so, I could do no better than the percentage noted. I am trying to present a best-case scenario here.

11   This assumes, unrealistically of course, that such public funds are available for the effort.

[12]   Some would argue that the choice of which to enter first as a predictor—neighborhood structure or assessed signs of incivility—is an arbitrary one. I would counter that we can have a neighborhood population without having signs of incivility, but we cannot have signs of incivility, in a residential context, without having a surrounding neighborhood population. The neighborhood population is the context within which the signs of incivility emerge.

[13]   Buerger (1994) has made a somewhat similar argument.

[14]   This statement presumes a direct rather than a mediating model for impacts of community structure and signs of incivility impacts on between-neighborhood outcomes. With a mediating model, community structure may have its impacts via the signs of incivility.

In the direct model we anticipate:

Community structure ───────▶
Signs of Incivility   ───────▶   Responses to disorder

But a mediating model, depicted below, also may be warranted:

Community structure ──▶ Signs of incivility ──▶ Responses to disorder

In the latter model, we would say that the between-neighborhood impacts of community structure are transmitted via signs of incivility. The latter are the proximal cause, the former the distal cause. With a direct model, by contrast, we model the correlation between structure and signs of incivility as correlations between two predictors. HLM, however, cannot test mediating models. But if I did test a mediating model, I would still be viewing community structure as the "ultimate" source of the impacts.

[15]   Generally, for every one standard deviation change in the predictor, the outcome changed about one-tenth to one-twelfth of a standard deviation.

[16]   Generally, for every standard deviation change in the predictor, the outcome changed about one-third to one-sixth of a standard deviation. These size effects are comparable to what has been observed elsewhere. See, for example, Covington and Taylor (1991).

INTRODUCTION TO CHAPTER 6

How do you build successful community organizations? What are the key ingredients to effective, long-term efforts to fight crime and fear at the neighborhood level? These are questions that have not been clearly answered. Research on community crime prevention has shown that groups have better success when they have strong indigenous leadership, focus on more than one issue, arise in areas of residential stability, and have a unified vision of the problem and solution. Unfortunately, it is just these factors that are lacking in most high-crime, high-fear areas. The challenge then becomes one of trying to build community involvement in those areas that are the hardest to organize and need it the most.

Despite evidence that even concerted efforts to organize high-crime areas are rarely successful, community leaders and activists continue to work at building effective coalitions. The next paper by Dennis Palumbo and his associates examines the problems and issues involved in building community-based organizations in high crime, poor neighborhoods of major cities. The two projects they examine, Project Intervention and The Community Partnership of Phoenix, rely on a range of approaches illustrative of those found in other programs. A number of problems and issues emerge from their study to which others should pay heed in future endeavors.

One major concern is the issue of defining "community." While this may seem to be an easy task, it is actually one of the large stumbling blocks in organizing communities. A community or neighborhood is more than just a name or boundaries on a map, and too often those types of definitions are used (particularly by outsiders) in trying to establish a community group. More appropriate means of defining the community's parameters are needed.

A second major issue emerging from the paper is the recognition that changing attitude, building local leadership, effectively empowering the citizens, and making other important changes are not short-term processes. Indeed, it may take an extended period of time to bring about such changes. At the same time, however, residents facing crime, fear, neighborhood deterioration, and other problems may not have the patience needed to wait for success. The slow pace of change may bring more discouragement than encouragement.

The results set forth in the paper provide a good illustration of the problems faced by any program trying to build community crime prevention programs in the areas that need them the most. Most of the time, success will take time and a great deal of effort. Perhaps the most important feature of successful endeavors must be the ability of the program and implementors to adapt to the unique needs, problems, and situations faced in different communities. What may work in one location may not work in another. In essence, the suggestion is that, not only should individual interventions consider a problem-oriented approach, community-based groups must be built with problem-oriented methods in mind.

6

The Conditions Needed for Successful Community Crime Prevention

Dennis Palumbo
Jennifer L. Ferguson
Judy Stein
Arizona State University

INTRODUCTION

Although community-based crime prevention programs have been receiving support in recent years from both ends of the political spectrum, the question of whether they can succeed in reducing crime is unclear. The research that does exist comes to mixed conclusions. For example, on the one hand, Lewis, Grant and Rosenbaum (1988) conclude that programs that are aimed only at crime prevention cannot succeed in low-income communities and may actually direct the attention of neighborhood organizations away from their real interests, which are to fight inequality, police brutality, and social injustice. Bursik and Grasmick (1993:176) tend to agree when they conclude that "no program has been designed that has any degree of success in those neighborhoods with the highest rates of crime." On the other hand, Curtis (1987) and Greenberg, Rohe and Williams (1985:133) conclude that such programs can be successful in reducing crime and the fear of crime. However, regardless of the disagreements, both the negative and positive findings, as well as the evaluations we will describe in this chapter, provide a basic outline of what conditions can produce successful community-based crime prevention programs.

In this chapter, we first review the literature and then describe research we have conducted in community crime prevention in Arizona. This research includes evaluations of Project Intervention, conducted out of the Governor's Office of Community Relations, and the Community Partnership of Phoenix, that is supported by a grant from the Center for Substance Abuse Prevention.[1] In our conclusions we evaluate the prospects for success in community crime prevention in each of these two programs and for community crime prevention in general.

REVIEW OF THE LITERATURE

Community Crime Prevention (CCP) is an umbrella term that covers a host of different strategies that include changing the social, economic, and physical conditions that influence offending in residential communities, preventing the occurrence of crime in specific situations by environmental modification, community surveillance through block watches, preserving order, and protecting the vulnerable (Hope, 1995a). We are interested only in the first strategy; that is, attempts to organize and empower communities so as to make them the key to preventing crime.

There are two major dimensions to empowering communities and both are needed for success to occur (Hope, 1995a). One is the horizontal dimension of promoting social relations and connecting individuals and groups within a community (sometimes called "communitarianism" [Braithwaite, 1989]), and the other is the vertical dimension that connects local institutions to outside sources of power. The two dimensions are equally important and interrelated in their effect on crime prevention efforts (Hope, 1995a:24).

The first dimension of promoting social relations among individuals and groups is difficult to accomplish, especially in low-income communities. Getting people in poor, disorganized communities to participate in organized efforts to reduce crime is very, very difficult. The paradox is that research shows that disorganized communities cause crime, but it is these very same disorganized structures, plus a lack of resources and commitment, that prevent poor communities from organizing (Hope, 1995a). People in such communities are overwhelmed with daily needs, have little belief in their ability to change things, and have few leadership and other skills.

Mobilizing a community is more successful in stable, middle-class communities in which there are more married people, people who have lived in the community for a long time, and who own their own homes. It is people who have roots in the community who will participate in organized efforts (Wandersman et al., 1987; Skogan, 1988b), but this is the very thing that is lacking in communities that have high levels of crime (Hope, 1995a:45).

Getting people to participate in community organizations is a function of inclination and opportunity. Skogan (1988b:46) notes: "Few people will be inclined to participate if there are no available opportunities or if they judge the prospects of successful community organization in the community to be poor." In block watch programs in Minneapolis, despite substantial block level organizing efforts, participation was still low; and even though efforts were greatest in poorer, African-American and higher-crime areas, attendance at meetings was highest in white and middle-to-upper-income areas where crime problems were not substantial (Rosenbaum, 1988). It is the feeling of hopelessness, of not being able to make a difference, that is prevalent in low-income communities.

Poor communities also are lacking in the vertical dimension of political power; they do not have the outside ties that are essential to effective community action. Knoke and Wood (1981:290) found that the most successful organizations were able to form strong ties to politically and financially powerful organizations. However, top down strategies wherein the government provides resources to poor communities generally are not successful because the resources that have been provided are so meager and uncertain that little might be expected of them (Rosenbaum, 1988). Because governmental agencies that provide some programs pull out after a few years, most residents in poor communities do not trust the government. Thus, unless mobilization efforts arise from within the community, they are not likely to be sustained (Lewis et al., 1988). Moreover, multi-purpose organizations that focus on more than crime are more likely to succeed than those that focus on crime alone (Skogan, 1988b).

Middle- and upper middle-class areas have relatively little turnover in residents, a high percentage of home ownership, relatives and friends living close by, businesses that provide jobs for residents and their youth, houses that are well taken care of, and a sufficient tax-base to support good schools, parks, and recreation. These things do not exist in high crime areas of central cities. Building community in such areas is much more difficult. Hope (1995a:75) believes that community defense strategies will work in these areas provided there is less emphasis on communitarianism and more on establishing effective communications between individual households and the police "who would then—with a commensurate allocation of resources—be able to provide more efficient guardianship of the residential space." The residents can be the "eyes and ears" of the police. High crime areas are ones in which there is a linkage between economic conditions and community social structure.

A high rate of male joblessness influences the crime-rate through its effect on the disruption of families and on family formation among residents (Hope, 1995a:75). Given a lack of access to job markets and networks, and given the social isolation of their communities, youth turn to street robbery and drug dealing in their own neighborhoods as the only source of supplemental income in their middle to late teen years (Sullivan, 1989:76). Hope (1995a:77) notes that the residential concentration of youth poverty seems to be creating communities with concentrations of high-risk offenders; young, jobless men and multiple victims, most of whom are single mothers "linked together in a powerless, victimizing—and victimized—culture of primary relationships." Thus, Hope (1995a:77) concludes that the horizontal dimension of creating a social structure is not likely to work in poor communities.

Communitarian approaches to community crime prevention (CCP) programs are built on the theory that "cultural commitments to shaming are the key to controlling all types of crime" (Braithwaite, 1989:55). In particular, reintegrative shaming, wherein the offender is accepted back into the community, is most likely to succeed. "The best place to see reintegrative shaming at work," Braithwaite (1989:56) says, "is in loving families." In addition, the role of a stable community, as exists in Japan, is also important. The main ingredients of neighborhood stability are relatively little turnover in residents, relatives and acquaintances living close by, businesses that provide jobs for residents and their youth, houses that are well taken care of, and a sufficient tax base to support good schools, parks, and recreation.

The process by which neighborhood stability breaks down is fairly clear. In neighborhoods where there is limited and poor education, lack of an adult labor market, and an overall lack of jobs, youth turn to income-oriented crime. They join gangs because this increases their ability to obtain scarce resources (Jankowski, 1991). The resulting increase in crime drives out law-abiding citizens and legitimate economic activity (McGahey, 1986). This is followed by a concentration of the poor, a high percent of single parent families, political ineffectiveness, and a loss of a local tax base. In addition, intimate primary ties deteriorate and, as a result, ostracism fails as a means of social control. Gang behavior is taken for granted and gang members are *not* marginal members of the community (Reed, 1982). Instead, they have a symbiotic relationship with the local residents (Jankowski, 1991); gangs need the approval of their community and the community allows the gangs to exist because they provide some useful services such as keeping out extreme criminal elements.

CCP programs attempt to reverse this process of economic and social deterioration by recreating a sense of community. Curtis (1987:13) describes several "models of success." The underlying principles of success, he writes, are "the creation of an extended-family setting with strict rules and nurturing, through which self-respect is instilled, education is pursued, training is undertaken, and employment is found by high-risk youth." What seems to be crucial in creating these conditions is that "the community always takes the lead vis-à-vis police among these model initiatives" (Curtis, 1987:13). He goes on to say that although the police began to cooperate, even in the communities where they opposed the programs initially, internal development by community members themselves was a crucial factor in their success.

Whether communities can be organized to fight crime by external agents, such as government programs, is doubtful. Lewis et al. (1988) believe that community organizations must solve the problem of their own maintenance by recruiting people and finding the resources to keep the group growing. Receiving funds from outside can undermine their effectiveness in pursuing their necessary mission, which is to challenge the status quo. The Lewis et al. study of the Urban Crime Prevention Program in Chicago, which received a major grant from the Ford Foundation to develop block watches, concluded that "the problems facing Northeast Austin may be beyond the reach of block watch alone to affect" (Lewis et al., 1988:108). Outside interventions are doomed to fail, they believe, because lower-income people have no incentive to change their culture. Communitarian reforms feed on a desire for attachment to community, but offer a faulty program to bring this about because these programs fail to change the culture of individualism that exists in these communities.

Bursik and Grasmick (1993) agree that programs initiated from the outside face resentment from local residents who feel that the outsiders have a limited degree of understanding of the community's problems. They believe a combination of block watches, promoting a sense of community, and social action designed to mobilize disadvantaged groups have a greater chance of success when they are integrated into the activities of more general, multi-issue neighborhood organizations. Organizations cannot survive on the basis of a single issue such as crime. Our research in Project Intervention and the Community Partnership of Phoenix help point to what is necessary for successful community-based organizations.

PROJECT INTERVENTION

Project Intervention (PI) began in July, 1993 in six different sites in Arizona: two in Phoenix, two in Tucson, one in Tempe, and one in Flagstaff. All of the sites were in very poor, high crime, drug and gang activity areas, in which houses were dilapidated and yards and alleys were strewn with trash and junk. Each of the sites was awarded grants by the Governor's Office of Community Relations. The grants were given to established community organizations such as the Tucson Urban League, which in turn, worked with neighborhood associations that, in most cases, were created prior to the grant program. Thus, PI is a case of community crime prevention that first began by internal organizing, and then was helped by external funding.

The funds provided through Project Intervention allow the opportunity for neighborhoods to create a better quality of life. There were three primary areas that were emphasized across all sites. These were housing assistance or rehabilitation, job training, and substance abuse education. What differed across sites were the approaches taken to address these areas, as well as which area received the most emphasis.

Other differences also existed across the six sites. Some were doing very well, while others were floundering. Some had active neighborhood associations that played important roles in policymaking; in others, the neighborhood association played much less of a role. Some were in very old neighborhoods in which residents had lived all their lives; other neighborhoods had a large number of transients, or were in the process of adjusting to new ethnic groups (primarily Latino) moving in.

The six Project Intervention sites are identified in Table 6.1 along with characteristics of the neighborhoods in which they are located. Table 6.2 identifies the activities engaged in at the various sites. Taken together, the six sites offer important clues to what conditions lead to successful crime prevention efforts. It is these conditions on which we will focus.

Table 6.1
Project Intervention Sites

Site	Year Assoc. Formed	Neighborhood Characteristics
A. Community Excellence Project, South Phoenix Village Assoc.	1989	• 53% African American, 39% Hispanic, 8% other • Increased number of Hispanics • Oldest African-American community • Large numbers of rental properties • Long-term residents are elderly
B. Tucson Urban League	1985	• Shift in ethnic composition from 56% African American, 35% Hispanic to the reverse • High percent of homeowners • Many elderly but average age is 25
C. Escalante Neighborhood Assoc., Tempe	1990	• 70% Anglo, 25% Hispanic, 5% other • Ethnic community is geographically divided
D. Citizens Against Substance Abuse, Sunnyside Block Watch, Flagstaff	1990	• 33% American Indian, 33% Hispanic, 33% other • Highly transient area
E. Chicanos por la Causa, Wedgewood Community Council, Phoenix	1988	• Predominantly Hispanic with small percentage of other • Not highly transient
F. City of South Tucson	No Assoc.	• One of the older Hispanic communities in Tucson • Influx of African Americans is changing the composition somewhat

Specifically, we address several questions:

1. Does a high level of turnover of residents in a community inhibit crime prevention?

2. Is a strong indigenous neighborhood association essential to successful crime prevention?

3. Can "outside" experts alone succeed in developing a strong crime prevention program?

4. Can a program succeed if it focuses only on crime prevention?

5. Is a feeling of community and a sense of "neighborliness" essential to successful community crime prevention?

Table 6.2
Project Intervention Activities and Characteristics by Site

A. Community Excellence Project
  - Community police officer located in the project building
  - Demolish burned out houses
  - Neighborhood clean ups
  - Rehabilitate houses (average $3,500 per house)
  - Solicit people to serve as youth mentors
  - Refer youths to substance abuse treatment
  - Job training classes and job placement
  - GED courses
  - Local businesses hire community residents

B. Tucson Urban League
  - Repair houses (average $4,200 per house)
  - Neighborhood clean ups
  - Train community members for painting and carpentry jobs
  - Recreational opportunities for neighborhood youth
  - Presentations for youth on gangs and drugs
  - Skill-building in areas of problem solving and conflict resolution
  - GED classes
  - "English-as-a-second-language" classes
  - Job placement

C. Escalante Neighborhood Association
  - Community police officer located in community center
  - Neighborhood improvements
  - House repairs ($12,500 per house)
  - Classroom education for substance abuse
  - Gang Resistance Education and Training (GREAT) program
  - Outreach program—regular counseling sessions
  - $50 stipend for attending job training classes
  - Career shadowing

D. Sunnyside Block Watch
  - Patrol of neighborhoods on bikes by police and National Guard
  - Community improvements
  - Repair houses (average $1,500 per house)
  - Recreational activities for youth
  - Films and speakers about drugs
  - Career education classes
  - Monthly job training workshops

E. Wedgewood Community Council
  - National Night Out
  - Roof replacement and house painting
  - Teen program to target youth at risk for substance abuse
  - Job training center—GED classes and vocational training
  - Summer job training program for at-risk youth

F. City of South Tucson
  - Substance abuse presentations at elementary schools
  - Adult education classes
  - English as a second language
  - GED preparation
  - Job training and job referrals

Methods

This research used non-structured, open-ended interviews. We began with some structured, Likert-type questions but soon found that the people we interviewed were not inclined to respond to these types of questions. Most of the residents and neighborhood association members had limited educational backgrounds and we soon found that it was better to use open-ended questions. The same questions were asked, however, in each of the sites. Thus, this research can be classified as a qualitative, ethnographic study. It should be stressed that we have not tried to determine if our findings are valid and reliable in the traditional, positivist sense. We tried to obtain data on police-reported crime but found that the data for the specific areas were hard to obtain. In some cases the police were not cooperative. However, since we have observed the six programs over a period of two years we conclude that our findings are believable and trustworthy (Guba & Lincoln, 1989). Also, we do not say that the conditions we will describe cause community crime prevention to be successful, only that they were present in the more successful of the six sites.

A total of 72 interviews were conducted in the six sites. Those interviewed included project directors, program coordinators, neighborhood association members, program clients, community board members, and police officers. This was the second time that we evaluated the program. The first time was at the end of the first year of operation. The data being reported here are for the second year of the program.

Responses to Questions

Does a High Level of Turnover of Residents in the Community Inhibit Crime Prevention?

While several sites were experiencing changes in the ethnic composition of their residents, only one (Flagstaff) had a large transient population. It is clear that a large number of transients does inhibit successful crime prevention. The Sunnyside Block Watch area in Flagstaff had about 5,000 people, of whom one-third were American Indian, one-third were Hispanic, and one-third mixed Anglo, Hispanic, and Indian. The school in the area served twice as many children during the school year as its total enrollment, which was a good indication that there was a large transient population. Due to limited job opportunities, many of the residents lived in rundown motels for short periods of time. The director of the neighborhood organization reported that there was a gang and a crime problem due to the large number of transients in the community. One indicator of this was the presence of beer cans, alcohol bottles, and syringes on the school grounds on Monday morning when the clean-up crews began work. Fencing of the school grounds eliminated this problem.

In another site the ethnic composition of the neighborhood was changing (Community Excellence Project in South Phoenix). This was the oldest African-American community in Phoenix and more than one-half of the residents had lived there all their lives. In recent years, a number of Mexican immigrants had moved into the area. As a result, according to one informant, they were having trouble getting a block watch program started because the newer residents lived in rental units and it was difficult to get the people who lived there involved. In addition, the long-term residents were elderly and could not contribute much to clean-up campaigns or block watch.

One of the Tucson sites was having similar problems. Originally, the racial make up was approximately 56 percent African American and 35 percent Hispanic, but by 1990 the ethnic proportions were reversed. It also had a high crime and gang problem—one that had gotten worse in the recent months. According to most respondents, some parts of the neighborhood were no longer safe. In addition, the problem had worsened since community policing ended in 1993. When discussing the loss of community policing, the head of the neighborhood association, Pat Garcia told us "It's too bad because the community policing effort was very effective."

In a fourth site in Tempe, there had not been a large turnover in residents. According to most respondents, the crime and gang problem had improved. Part of this may be due to the fact that a community policing station, as well as relative population stability exists in this site. Overall, it seems to be the case that higher levels of population turnover and ethnic change make community crime prevention more difficult.

Is a Strong Indigenous Neighborhood Association Essential to Successful Crime Prevention?

The answer to this is clearly yes, but it also is true that support from an external source can help rather than undermine the viability of the neighborhood association. Four of the six sites had strong neighborhood organizations that began prior to the grant program. All four were doing well, including one whose neighborhood association was not very active (this was due to a recent change in directors). The two sites that did not have strong neighborhood associations—one of the two did not have one at all—were not doing very well. The City of South Tucson program, for example, was run by the city and it had just about collapsed because the city was facing a budget crisis. The other site, the Wedgewood Community Council located in Phoenix, was dominated by an agency that received the grant money but rarely met. This program was not doing well and it was difficult to determine how much of the grant money was being used for community crime prevention because the agency mingled the grant money with its regular budget.

Can "Outside Experts" Alone Succeed in Developing a Strong Crime Prevention Program?

The answer here is clearly no, although they can help support a strong indigenous neighborhood association. In most of the sites, it took six months to a year before the neighborhood association trusted the grant recipient agencies. It was only in the second year that the suspicions of the local groups were allayed. In the case of the Tucson Urban League, as in a few other sites, the distrust stemmed from government failure to follow through with past promises. In Tucson, the government promised to build a small lake as mitigation for loss of property when it built a parkway through the middle of the neighborhood. The parkway was built but the lake never materialized. This, of course, greatly alienated the residents.

At the same time, outside experts can help in situations where there is a strong indigenous association. This was the case in the Community Excellence Project in South Phoenix. The neighborhood served by the Community Excellence Project was comprised of about 2,250 people who were 53 percent African American, 39 percent Hispanic, and eight percent "other." The South Phoenix Village Association was established in 1989, prior to the formation of the Community Excellence Project, when a number of concerned citizens got together to form a "plan of action" to rehabilitate and revitalize the neighborhood. It had a strong board of directors consisting of 70 percent local residents and 30 percent representatives of local businesses. Strong support was provided by business firms within and from outside the community. It also had a community police station located in the facility that housed the Community Excellence Project. The community police officer, as well as almost all of the other interviewees, agreed that crime, drug and gang activity, and prostitution had gone down as a result of the activities of the neighborhood association and Project Intervention.

The success in this case was due in large part because of the strong neighborhood organization, the community policing operation, and the dedicated efforts of the "outside expert," as well as the local residents. It also was due to the fact that it did not focus only on crime prevention, which leads to the next question.

Can a Program Succeed if it Focuses Only on Crime Prevention?

The answer here seems to be clearly no. All six sites were involved in three activities: housing rehabilitation, job training, and substance abuse education. In addition, several of the sites were involved in block watches, neighborhood cleanups, and neighborhood nights out—planned, usually national efforts, in which residents come out at night to show community activity. These activities brought community members together, and in almost all cases led to safer neighborhoods in which people said they felt safe to walk outside at night and sit on their front porches or in their front living rooms. In the past, they could not do the latter because of drive-by shootings and fear of crime.

As a result of the housing programs a number of the run-down, dilapidated houses were fixed (new roofs, improved plumbing and electrical work, exteriors painted) and abandoned houses were demolished so they could no longer serve as havens for drug users and prostitutes.

Is a Feeling of Community and a Sense of "Neighborliness" Essential to Successful Community Crime Prevention?

We asked interviewees in each site if some of their relatives lived in the neighborhood, if they had friends there, and if people tended to talk to and greet each other on the street. In the two most successful sites (Community Excellence Project in South Phoenix and Tucson Urban League in Tucson) the answer was yes. Most of the residents in these two communities had lived there all their lives, although as we noted above, the neighborhoods were changing. In these two areas people knew each other, relatives lived close by, and there was a sense of community. In some of the other sites, such as Sunnyside Block Watch in Flagstaff and the City of South Tucson, this was not the case. These areas were not as successful in their housing and job training efforts. However, although Flagstaff had a large transient population, the established community—the longer-term residents—knew each other and were active in the block watch program and with the police and the schools.

THE COMMUNITY PARTNERSHIP OF PHOENIX

It was stated earlier that the strategy of the community crime prevention programs discussed in this chapter is to change the social, economic, and physical conditions that influence offending in residential neighborhoods. As discussed above, Project Intervention aims to achieve this by providing programs and services such as housing rehabilitation, job training, substance abuse education, block watches, and community policing. The Community Partnership of Phoenix (CPOP), however, aims to achieve this in a different way. This project is specifically focused on community empowerment. It is different than Project Intervention in that only a small portion of its budget (about one-third) is for delivery of services. The rest is for organizing and empowering the community. The actual changes that CPOP hopes will be made are not specified a priori but are identified by community residents.

Empowerment is not a value neutral term. Whether it should be individuals or communities that should be empowered, and whether it is the poor alone who should be empowered depends on the advocate's values and ideology. Conservatives stress empowering individuals to take responsibility for their condition. In this view it is bad individuals who are responsible for community crime (Wilson & Herrnstein, 1985). Liberals, on the other hand, focus on empowering communities, particularly the poor. Breton (1994), for example, argues that there would be no need for empowerment if we lived in a just society—one in which power and resources are distributed equitably. Thus, she defines empowerment as "gaining control over factors that are critical in accounting for one's state of oppression or disempowerment" (1994:24). The difference between conservatives and liberals is significant because policy responses vary depending on explanations of crime causes. Reiss (1986:22) notes: "Policies based on variation in individual behavior typically opt for direct intervention in the lives of persons . . .," whereas those that explain crime rates of collectivities lead to interventions that alter the cultural or social structure of collectivities.

Individual empowerment is not the same as community empowerment. Individuals in a community can become empowered without the community becoming empowered, but a community cannot become empowered if the individuals who comprise it have a personal sense of powerlessness (Staples, 1990:35). Staples believes that "individual empowerment is not now, and never will be the salvation of powerless groups." Thus, there is more to successful community empowerment than empowering individuals. It involves collective action as well. This is what CPOP hopes to accomplish.

CPOP is funded through a grant from the Center for Substance Abuse Prevention (CSAP) through the Community Partnership Study Program. While CSAP focuses on preventing alcohol, tobacco, and other drug problems, there is also a recognition that substance abuse problems are linked to other community problems. Therefore, the funds provided by CSAP are used to create "comprehensive, long-term, prevention demonstration programs tailored to local needs through effective public/private sector partnerships." The local communities that receive funds from CSAP identify the needs of their community and prioritize how those needs will be met. All of this is to be done in a way that promotes community involvement and the formation of partnerships across all sectors of the community.

The Office of Substance Abuse Prevention (OSAP) promotes a community empowerment model that is distinct from a typical service delivery model. Community empowerment involves "doing with" and not "doing for." This model shifts responsibility for planning and decisionmaking from agencies and professionals to the community. It also advocates the inclusion of all community groups, both formal and informal, in all prevention efforts. This model represents a "new paradigm" that OSAP says:

> no longer considers agencies and professionals solely responsible for solving the community's AOD (alcohol and other drug) problems, instead, that responsibility lies with the community itself. In this context, agencies and organizations work to facilitate the community's acquisition and

effective use of the knowledge, skills, and resources necessary to respond to the needs and problems as expressed and
defined by the community (OSAP, 1991:1).

In Phoenix, an attempt was made to implement a process that incorporated many components of the community empowerment model. The process that was adopted allowed community members to become active participants in identifying the needs of the community. At the initial workshops, participants were asked to list three things that would make their community more livable. From that list, five issues of importance were identified. A forum was created for each of the five issues. The purpose of the forums was for citizens to meet to identify the problems in Phoenix related to each issue, as well as to identify strategies to help address those problems. The five issues these forums addressed were: crime, neighborhood empowerment, prevention services, public education and awareness, and youth involvement. The youth involvement forum was for adults to discuss issues pertaining to youth, but a youth leadership forum was also created so that youth could become directly involved in the process of voicing concerns about their community. In August of 1995 a faith forum was also created to encourage involvement from the faith community.

The forums met for the first time in May of 1995. The purpose of the forums was to get the participants to identify the tasks that each forum should take on and identify the key resources (organizations, individuals) that could be called upon to help accomplish the tasks. The importance of community input was emphasized at the forum meetings. Although a steering committee was created as a formal decision-making body, CPOP policy was that the steering committee could not effectively make decisions without input from the community. The decisions that emerged should be community driven and the steering committee should not make judgments on their own. Thus, the steering committee had representatives from each of the forums as well as members who were specifically steering committee members.

Methods

After the initial meeting of the individual forums, we conducted interviews with forum participants and staff members in June of 1995 to collect data on how the Community Partnership of Phoenix was being implemented. The interviews consisted of both open- and closed-ended questions. About one-half of them were conducted face-to-face while the other one-half were conducted over the phone. We also attended forum and steering committee meetings. Thus our methods included participant observation as well as interviews.

The people who were interviewed were taken from lists of those who attended the initial forums. There were a total of 70 people on these lists. Interviews were conducted with 40 individuals, including 33 who attended the various forums and seven staff workers. This resulted in a response rate of 47 percent. There are three reasons why not all individuals were interviewed. One was that it was difficult to contact many of the individuals, a number of them did not return several phone calls. A second reason was the short time frame allotted in which the interviews were to be completed. Finally, a few individuals decided not to continue to participate in CPOP.

Support of CPOP

One component of successful community empowerment is that the community members need to believe in what they are doing and they must believe that they can make a difference. The Community Partnership of Phoenix adopted the motto "People will support what they create." Our initial interviews suggest that the respondents embraced this motto and that they had great expectations for what CPOP should accomplish. For example, 90 percent disagreed with the statement "I don't expect any concrete results to happen from CPOP." Only one person agreed with the statement. The median response to the item was 1.0 on a 1 to 10 scale where 1 is completely disagree and 10 is completely agree.

Agreement about the goals of a program and support of them are crucial to a program's success. If there is a lot of disagreement about what CPOP should accomplish then it will not be able to move forward. Table 6.3 gives the median response (on the same 1 to 10 scale) and the percentage of people who agreed, disagreed, and were neutral for each statement pertaining to the goals of CPOP.

It is apparent that respondents were in agreement about what CPOP should do and what it could do. Reducing drug and alcohol abuse were the two most important things respondents believed CPOP should accomplish. While the agreement is not as strong, there also was a belief that CPOP could have an impact on reducing crime. There also was agreement about the way city agencies should respond to community problems. It was expected that they would respond better and more effectively. Communities themselves were also expected to be more effective in using resources. Finally, community residents were optimistic that CPOP would build self-trust and there was a belief that change could occur, as well as a belief that they could overcome the apathy of community residents so they would be willing to participate. As the literature review noted, these are especially important conditions for community empowerment.

In addition to expressing optimism and support for what CPOP should accomplish, respondents also exhibited support for the way CPOP was being implemented. The city received reasonably good marks from respondents for the job it was doing. Table 6.4 illustrates that 81 percent agreed that the city had done a good job in getting CPOP implemented. Eighty-three percent believed that the right individuals had been involved and 70 percent believed the right decisions had been made about how to get CPOP going.

Table 6.3
Agreement with Goals of CPOP[1]

Statement	Median	% Agree	% Neutral	% Disagree
Reducing drug abuse in this community is very important for successful community development.	10	100	0	0
Reducing alcohol abuse in this community is very important for successful community development.	10	97	0	3
The principal task of CPOP is to rebuild self-trust and belief that change can occur.	9	87	3	10
CPOP is a grass roots program with communities having the major say in what it will do.	9	87	5	8
Communities in Phoenix will be better organized and more effective in using resources as a result of CPOP.	8	90	7	3
The main purpose of CPOP is to get city agencies to respond better and more effectively to community problems.	8	82	5	13
CPOP will be able to overcome the apathy of community residents and get them to participate in programs aimed at improving their community.	7	79	16	5
I expect crime will go down in (my) communities as a result of CPOP.	7	74	13	13

[1] Scale from 1 ("completely disagree") to 10 ("completely agree").

Respondents also believed that there was support for CPOP from the leadership of city agencies and the communities. Of those who responded to the statement "The leadership of city agencies is strongly committed to making CPOP work," 79 percent agreed that they were committed. Of those who responded to a similar statement about the leadership in communities, 85 percent believed that they were committed.

Table 6.4
Support for Implementation and Leadership

Statement	Median	% Agree	% Neutral	% Disagree
So far, the city has done a very good job in getting CPOP implemented.	8	81	3	16
So far, the right individuals have been involved in getting CPOP implemented.	7	83	11	6
The right decisions have been made about how to get CPOP going.	7	70	22	8
The leadership of city agencies is strongly committed to making CPOP work.	8	79	15	6
The leadership in the communities are strongly committed to making CPOP work.	8	85	12	3

Finally, when respondents were asked how much they supported CPOP, 87 percent stated they supported CPOP either completely (55%) or very much (32%). Only 13 percent said their support was moderate and no one responded "not very much" or "not at all."

Citizen Participation

While there was support for what CPOP was trying to accomplish and for the way it was being implemented, there also were areas of concern, many of which were related to the extent of citizen participation. Sufficient citizen participation is central to community empowerment and to community crime prevention. Without this participation it would be difficult to produce any change. In addition to generating participation, who is participating is also important. Unfortunately, in the early months of CPOP, there were a limited number of "grass-roots" citizens involved.

The typical person involved in the initial forums (excluding staff) was 50 years old, with 15 years of school completed. Fifty-eight percent were female and 42 percent were male. Sixty-one percent were white, 24 percent African American, nine percent Hispanic, three percent American Indian, and three percent other. Their occupations were quite varied. The most prevalent was a member of a non-profit agency (n=7, 22%); followed by retired (n=4, 13%), city employee (n=4, 13%), nurse (n=3,9%), teacher (n=3, 9%), business (n=3, 9%), faith (n=2, 6%), and homemaker (n=2, 6%); and one person each in the following: security guard, secretary, and warehouse worker. Thus, the picture that emerged, at least of those who were interviewed, was of a white, middle-aged, college-educated person.

The most important concern raised by respondents was about the level of participation. Fifty-six percent of respondents agreed that not enough people were involved in CPOP to really make much of a difference to communities. There appeared to be a concern that not enough grass-roots individuals were involved. One respondent said: "We are not seeing a lot of grassroots individuals. CPOP is a little top heavy with people who are active to begin with—too many professionals." This is supported in part by the demographic characteristics of respondents that we interviewed.

There also was concern that information about CPOP was not reaching the community; only 15 percent of respondents stated that they believed people knew what CPOP was all about. This lack of awareness is a factor that may also influence participation. As a result, while a number of people believed implementation should continue in the direction it was going, many recommended that the implementation of CPOP could be improved by generating more participation and reaching more of the community. This was reflected in comments that were made by a number of respondents. The following are typical comments:

- Reach more of the community—tap more resources such as seniors and schools.

- Put the word out about the mission to the community, business, and agencies.

- Get people involved who really know what's going on. We need people at various levels.

- More public awareness. Reach communities through churches, TV, and evening news. Communication is essential.

- Need to get the confidence of the community. Convince the community that the money spent will benefit them.

Finally, one person suggested that it was important to address:

- How to build incentive so people will participate. How to lead them towards knowing processes for successful empowerment as a citizen.

CONCLUSIONS

In this conclusion we first discuss the prospects of successful community crime prevention for CPOP, then for Project Intervention, and finally the prospects for community crime prevention in general. Clearly, greater citizen involvement is needed in order to make progress toward achieving the goals of CPOP. This fits in with the question of whether an indigenous neighborhood or community organization is essential to community crime prevention. CPOP had not been able to establish a strong community base at the beginning of its second year because just what was meant by "community" had not yet been resolved. At the end of the first year of operation, CPOP was still focusing on the entire city of Phoenix, but there were not enough people involved to carry the message to the entire city. The literature identifies how difficult it is to empower communities in poor, high-crime areas. However, CPOP did not focus on or target low income neighborhoods or communities. In its initial phase, it aimed to create a sense of community citywide. This is difficult to do in a city that has a wide diversity of ethnic and income communities. In fact, the framework published by the Office of Substance Abuse Prevention states that it is essential to recognize the cultural differences among the many ethnic groups that exist and to tailor the partnership to fit the varying needs of these groups (OSAP, 1991). CPOP had not done this by the beginning of 1996.

The process through which the partnership was being implemented may have caused some of those who were participating to lose faith in what could be accomplished. While it was emphasized that building a partnership is a long term process that cannot provide immediate results, there was frustration that no progress was being made. As we noted in the literature review, it is important for people to see the possibility of success in order for them to continue to participate.

It was clear when we wrote this chapter that, in order for CPOP to achieve its goals, changes needed to be made in how it was being implemented. Major changes were made in the structure of CPOP at the beginning of 1996. For the first year of operation, the partnership was run by the City of Phoenix. In March of 1996, the partnership was transferred to the Arizona Prevention Resource Center, a branch of Arizona State University. The reasons given for the transfer were to increase CPOP's chances for success and to allow the city to participate more as a full partner. Plans were being made for the city manager and department heads to participate in CPOP meetings. This was promoted as a way to be sure that decisionmakers (people who can implement the recommended changes) would be there to hear the discussions and would be prepared to help implement them. What appeared to be a result of the transfer was a shift from a bottom-up, or grass-roots approach, to a "top-down" strategy, which is the opposite of what the literature concludes is needed. It appeared as though power was being taken away from the people. However, after the initial shock of the transfer subsided, communications improved and prospects for success seemed brighter. Nevertheless, serious problems remained, including a change of project directors. While this would not necessarily be a fatal blow to the partnership, it upset CPOP considerably because the original project director was a charismatic figure with good community ties.

There is better news regarding the other CCP project we evaluated, Project Intervention. Some of the theory upon which community crime prevention is built was supported by our research in the six Project Intervention sites. In particular, the importance of a stable neighborhood, a strong indigenous neighborhood organization, a focus on more than a single goal, such as crime prevention and a sense of community neighborliness, all seem to have led to more crime reduction in the more successful Project Intervention sites. Outside support by the state government and community policing also were key ingredients in the more successful sites.

Of course, serious problems remained even in the more successful PI sites. The most serious is the fact that the amount of financial support from Project Intervention was far too small to do much more than make a small impact on the massive housing, job, and crime problems these communities faced. Several of the people whom we interviewed stressed this point. An even more serious problem remained in the job training area. It was difficult to get people, particularly males, to participate in the job training programs for a number of reasons. For some (mostly young males) they considered the kinds of jobs available to them to be demeaning and lacking in pay. The director of the job training component in the Urban League Program in Tucson told us:

> We don't have a problem finding jobs—there are plenty of them; but we have a problem getting people. Our referrals often don't show up for a job. They have a confidence problem and when they get to be 30 or 40 years old, it is hard to break them out of the routine of partying and doing drugs.

Drug rehabilitation programs, a number of people told us, were sorely needed; but drugs alone are not the problem. Many of the residents who wanted to find jobs did not have appropriate clothes to go to interviews. Many of the women needed day care, and a number did not have the means of transportation to get to the job training site or to work. Many young males had tattoos they had to remove and some did not want to do this. Much of the job training centered on how to talk and carry themselves during a job interview. Moreover, a large percent of the residents needed to take "English as a Second Language" and GED courses before they could qualify for job training. The end result was that the majority of the people who participated in the job training programs were women. But even they had a hard time because their husbands or boyfriends did not want them to participate in activities for which they did not get paid.

The major conclusions that arise from our work are:

- It is much more difficult—but not impossible—to develop successful programs in poor, high-crime areas than in middle-class areas.

- Successful programs require more than giving individuals or communities the responsibility to fight crime, drugs, and gangs; external help, primarily financial support, is also needed.

- Even though external financial support helps, programs cannot succeed without local, indigenous initiatives.

- Small successes are important and should be emphasized to maintain indigenous participation and to foster a belief that success can occur.

- Projects need to focus on economic conditions as well as crime prevention because the two are intricately related.

- Community policing is an important component, especially in poor neighborhoods.

- Communities that have high levels of residential turnover and low levels of home ownership are not likely to respond to communitarian strategies; the better strategy includes order maintenance and economic assistance.

- Community crime prevention takes a long time and is not the "magic bullet," but it can help.

- Because we do not yet know how to "cure" communities or individuals of crime, it does not mean we should stop trying.

NOTE

[1]   The Center for Substance Abuse Prevention is the current name for what was previously known as the Office of Substance Abuse Prevention.

INTRODUCTION TO CHAPTER 7

Traditionally, crime prevention has brought to mind the community-based approaches that have dominated the earlier chapters. What many people fail to recall is that the physical design orientation to crime prevention in the late 1960s and early 1970s also focused on design of businesses and schools. Indeed, one of the early applications of Crime Prevention Through Environmental Design (CPTED) was extended to schools. In recent years there has been a great growth of concern over crime and victimization in, on, and around school campuses.

The next chapter deals with victimization and crime prevention on college campuses. Interest in campus crime has received more attention recently due to media focus on a few high profile offenses, civil litigation against schools for not providing adequate protection, and legislation mandating the reporting of crime on campus. What these events suggest is that college campuses are over-run with crime and victimization, and that schools need to take immediate, concerted action to protect their students, staff, and campuses. Unfortunately, there has been relatively little research on the extent of the victimization problem or the response of students and schools to crime on campus.

Fisher and her associates present the results of a national survey of college students, focusing on both victimization and crime prevention initiatives taken on campus. Their results show that victimization is a rare event on campus and that most victimizations involve theft. While victimization is not a rampant problem, they point out that students should take precautions. At the same time, the results offer insight to what schools should be doing to address the problem as it exists. Once again, this paper offers a basic problem-oriented, situational prevention approach. The authors suggest that schools build an internal system of information collection, analysis, and response. They also note that students appear to make choices about crime prevention activities based on their experiences, perceptions, and available resources. Students, therefore, can benefit most by being given the information they need to make the appropriate choices, rather than having the school make decisions for them.

7

The On-Campus Victimization Patterns of Students: Implications for Crime Prevention by Students and Post-Secondary Institutions[1]

Bonnie S. Fisher
The University of Cincinnati

John J. Sloan III
The University of Alabama—Birmingham

Francis T. Cullen
Chunmeng Lu
The University of Cincinnati

INTRODUCTION

Safety and security on college and university campuses have risen to the top of Congressional and state-level policy concerns and have fueled students' and parents' demands for the implementation of additional crime prevention strategies on campus. Several events prompted these actions. First was a flurry of civil lawsuits, starting in the mid 1980s, by student victims or their families against post-secondary institutions for damages due to on-campus victimizations. The courts in several cases found colleges liable for a foreseeable on-campus victimization and ordered these institutions to pay considerable amounts in damages (see Smith & Fossey, 1995). Second were student right-to-know efforts around the country, that Howard and Connie Clery led after a fellow student brutally murdered their daughter at Lehigh University in 1986. These efforts succeeded in pressuring Congress and 20 state legislatures to mandate that these institutions publicly report their crime statistics and campus crime prevention and security procedures (Griffaton, 1995; Lu, 1996). Media coverage of campus crime rounds out the events that elevated campus crime to the top of lawmakers' agendas and that continues to capture Congressional attention (Lively, 1996; Schmidt, 1996). In the last few years the media (especially *The Chronicle of Higher Education*) has drawn a spotlight to campuses suggesting that on-campus crimes—especially violence—are markedly increasing. Their anecdotes portray the campus as a place rife with violence and disorder, and a place where students are not only packing books but also packing guns (Lederman, 1993, 1994a, 1994b, 1995; Matthews, 1993).

If these claims are correct and campuses are dangerous places where violent crime is widespread and increasing at an alarming rate and where students are arming themselves, the implications for the types and content of crime prevention programs, services, and measures offered by post-secondary institutions may be more than merely providing educational programs, victim services, and restricting access to buildings. The implications for students, too, may be more than merely attending crime prevention seminars or locking doors. If these claims are incorrect, then there may be a misunderstanding by students, their parents, and campus administrators as to the incidence and the types of crimes that happen on campuses. A possible mismatch between the type and frequency of on-campus crimes, the frequency and content of crime prevention programs and services implemented, and the types of crime prevention measures students take may exist. As a result, students may not be protecting themselves in a way that reduces their vulnerability to frequently occurring crimes, and campus administrators may not be properly or effectively addressing campus crime problems that may also leave students at risk and the school potentially liable.

To understand more adequately what types of crime prevention programs, services, and measures may benefit college and university students, this chapter examines the incidence and nature of on-campus incident-level information collected during the 1993-1994 academic year from a random sample of 3,742 students at 12 randomly selected four-year colleges and universities in the United States. We begin the chapter with a brief discussion of the crime prevention challenges campuses face because of students' lifestyles. To give the reader a sense of crime prevention activities on campuses today, we then turn to a description of what various colleges and universities have implemented to help prevent crime on their campuses and of what students have done to reduce their risk of victimization. Next, we present the results of our analyses that examined the frequency and nature of on-campus victimizations, the crime prevention behaviors of students, and the crime prevention programs, services, and measures implemented or adopted by selected schools. We end the chapter with a discussion of the need for more campus crime prevention, the implications for the content of crime prevention efforts, and the limits of crime prevention.

THE CAMPUS AS A COMMUNITY:
ITS CRIME PREVENTION CHALLENGES

Some individuals run a greater risk of victimization than others. Researchers have shown that certain lifestyle and routine activity characteristics significantly predict an individual's risk of criminal victimization: demographic characteristics (e.g., young, under 30), college-educated, males, white, high income), being an attractive target (e.g., the ownership of valuable consumer goods), engaging in public activities (e.g., going to bars, spending time away from the residence), lacking in guardianship (e.g., not engaging in safety precautions), and being close to offenders (see Miethe & Meier, 1994). College students' lifestyles and activities while on campus at times are characterized by these high-risk factors.

First, the college population is youthful—those under 18 to 24 years old made up 62 percent of the undergraduate population (more than 7.5 million students), and 25- to 34-year olds made up 46 percent of the graduate population (close to 780,000 students) in the fall of 1993 (U.S. Department of Education, 1995). Results from the 1993 National Crime Victimization Survey (NCVS) showed that these age categories had among the highest violent victimization rates compared with other age categories. Those who ranged in age from 16 to 19, for example, had the second highest violent victimization rate (116.8 per 1,000 persons in this age group), followed by those aged 20 to 24 (97.7 per 1,000), and then those aged 25 to 34 (60.9 per 1,000) (Bureau of Justice Statistics, 1996). Results from the 1992 NCVS showed that those aged 20 to 24 years old, for example, had the highest theft victimization rate (106.9 per 1,000 students in this age group), followed by 16- to 19-year-olds (94.8 per 1,000), and by 25-to 34-year-olds (73.4 per 1,000) (Bureau of Justice Statistics, 1994).[2]

The shear number of college students and the property that they bring with them—purses, wallets, backpacks, portable computers, compact disc players and compact discs, bicycles, and motor vehicles—provide an ample supply of suitable targets for would-be offenders. The number of targets changes every term, especially in the fall, when a new supply of suitable targets arrives on campus.

Second, many students attend entertainment events on campus (e.g., dances, parties, athletic games, movies, museums, concerts, or plays). Many students, those who are under the legal drinking age and those who are of legal drinking age, couple these functions with alcohol and/or drug use. In a recent national survey, 80 percent of those 17- to 25-year-olds reported using alcohol in the past year and just more than 60 percent reported using alcohol in the past month. Both percentages were the second highest users compared with all the other age groups. The drugs of choice among this age group were marijuana and hashish, with close to 23 percent reporting usage during the past year and 11 percent reporting usage during the last month—the highest percentage among all age groups (U.S. Department of Justice, 1994).

Third, although the above figures do not reflect all college students, the college years are notorious for the recreational use of, and experimentation with, alcohol and drugs (Powell, Pander & Nielsen, 1994). Our earlier work reported that college students spend an average of two nights per week partying on or near campus (Fisher, Sloan & Cullen, 1995). Studies have also shown that binge drinking is common among college students. These studies also have revealed that students who are not binge drinkers at schools with high binge rates are more likely than students at schools with lower binge rates to experience problems including being hit, pushed, or assaulted and experiencing an unwanted sexual advance (Wechsler et al., 1994). Other researchers have also reported that binge drinking is associated with a higher incidence of physical and sexual assault (Wechsler & Isaac, 1992). Powell, Pander, and Nielsen (1994) argued that the use of alcohol and drugs could lead to crimes ranging in seriousness from simple acts of vandalism to aggravated assault, sexual assault, or rape.

Fourth, students are often poor guardians of themselves. Some students may study or attend a party into the very early morning hours and then walk to their residence or motor vehicles alone, or take shortcuts through isolated, poorly lighted areas to arrive home faster or get to an early morning class. Students could be attractive targets for would-be robbers or rapists lurking in the shadows of poorly lit areas or seeking refuge in dense vegetation (Fisher & Nasar, 1995).

Students also are often poor guardians of their property. Walking away from their belongings or leaving the door to a dormitory room or office unlocked or propped open is common for students, if only for a minute to obtain a drink of water, go to the restroom, or go into someone else's room.

The campus setting and calendar do not provide guardianship at all times for various reasons. Many college campuses are park-like settings with permeable boundaries. Campuses are typically accessible during all hours; they are "open" 24 hours a day, seven days a week, 365 days a year. There are long periods, such as spring break or summer break, when most of the students are not on campus, thus leaving those who remain and their property vulnerable to criminal victimization.

Finally, the student and his or her property are only part of understanding the crime prevention challenges of the campus. Their proximity to the perpetrator or perpetrators also adds to these challenges. Siegel and Raymond (1992) reported that close to 80 percent of victimizations committed against students were by fellow students. They also reported that students who had committed multiple crimes since enrolling in college reported the most frequent drug and alcohol use of all other students, and reported using alcohol and drugs at the time their most serious crime was committed. For those students who live in university-operated housing, proximity to the offender may raise some concern, especially with respect to physical and sexual assaults, vandalism, and threatening and harassing behavior.

Other scholars have suggested that campus employees, especially those who have access to master keys, may be possible perpetrators of theft and that people not related to the campus commit many thefts on campus (see Smith & Fossey, 1995; Powell, Pander & Nielsen, 1994). We, however, could not find any data summarizing employee or nonstudent thefts against students or any studies that examined this phenomenon.

The unique lifestyle and routine activity characteristics of the campuses' largest group of people—students—create an environment in which different types of victimization may frequently occur at different places on campus or at the same place—"hot spots of crime"—at any hour of the day by a variety of perpetrators (see Fisher & Nasar, 1995; Wilkins, 1996). This scenario poses challenges for both personal-level and institutional-level crime prevention efforts. Coupled with this is the challenge of developing and implementing crime prevention programs, services, and measures for a highly transient youthful population who may live on or off campus, and who may spend an hour or more on campus one to seven days a week for a varying tenure that may last a day or two to many years until a degree is completed. Campus administrators cannot ignore these challenges as they compete to attract and recruit students, maintain enrollments, reduce their liability, and fall under the scrutiny of concerned parents and students, campus-safety interest groups, and state and federal legislation.

RESPONSES BY POST-SECONDARY INSTITUTIONS TO ON-CAMPUS CRIME

Colleges and universities have considerable discretion over the type and number of crime prevention strategies they employ to reduce opportunities for victimization. Following is an overview of on-campus crime prevention strategies that schools have implemented to make their campuses safer.[3] Common strategies employed by schools include: educational information and programs, access control and target-hardening measures, crime prevention and victim services, and campus-wide efforts.

Educational Information and Programs

Many colleges and universities provide printed information concerning ways to reduce the risk of personal and property victimization and a description of their security policies and procedures following the mandates of the Student Right-to-Know and Campus Security Act of 1990 (Lu, 1996). Distributing this information is accomplished in several ways: requiring new students to attend a crime prevention seminar (e.g., Georgia Tech and the University of Arkansas); distributing crime prevention pamphlets and brochures at high volume student-pedestrian sites on campus such as the student union or restroom stalls (e.g., Xavier University and The Ohio State University); and posting information electronically on World Wide Web home pages or maintaining an on-line discussion forum of campus safety issues for those who have access to the Internet (e.g., New York University and the University of Denver).

Access Control and Target-Hardening Measures

Because the campus is "open" 24 hours a day, many schools use various means to control access to classroom buildings, residence halls, department offices, and laboratories. While some schools have an "open-door" policy as to the main entrance—students and visitors can come and go as they please—other schools restrict access through various strategies. For example, some schools like Northern Illinois University require all students to show identification for entry so that security monitors allow only residents and their guests access to the residence hall; student residents must sign in all guests and escort guests continuously while in the dormitory. At other schools, like Willamette University and Wellesley College, residence halls are locked 24 hours a day and access is limited to those who have keys or to those who have been issued electronic key cards. Other schools not only limit access to residence halls but also keep classroom buildings locked when classes are not in session. Here, students can gain access by obtaining an "After Hours Pass" from their professors. At Brown University, access to buildings is controlled by installing alarms on doors and windows to keep them from being propped open. Finally, some schools use surveillance cameras as a means to monitor access to the campus and its buildings. At Columbia University, selected academic buildings have key card access and alarm monitoring systems combined with video surveillance 24 hours a day.

Crime Prevention and Victim Services

Campuses also offer various crime prevention and victim services for students. To deter theft, some schools, including Columbia University, have an engraver that students can borrow to mark all of their valuable property with a unique identification number (typically their social security number) that is registered with campus law enforcement. Others have registration services for motor vehicles and bicycles. At Purdue University, for example, students who park in university-designated parking lots must register their cars with the campus parking authorities. If the car is stolen, this fact can be broadcast to campus and local law enforcement officials. Campus escort services operating after dark are commonly offered by schools, and some schools have available shuttle bus services or "campus taxis" that take students to their destinations on or near the campus. Most schools provide counseling and mental health services after any type of victimization. The University of Missouri-St. Louis, for example, offers a "rape hot line" for students to call to report a rape, a victim counseling service, and medical services for rape victims at the campus women's center.

Campus-Wide Efforts

Some campuses (e.g., the University of Alabama at Birmingham and Carnegie Mellon University) have created campus "crime watch" programs to watch for opportunities for crime and for suspicious persons. Linked with campus police or security by telephone and fax, members alert each other of reported incidents and work with campus officials to help identify and apprehend suspects.

Schools have also modified the physical environment to reduce the opportunities for victimization. The University of Alabama at Birmingham, for example, undertook an extensive effort during 1993-1994 to remove overgrown vegetation, cut back trees and bushes, and remove potential hiding places on campus for offenders (see Sloan et al., 1995). UAB also routinely checks and upgrades overhead street and pathway lights, as well as those in parking lots and decks. The University of South Florida annually performs security surveys to evaluate the safety of their buildings and grounds to identify strengths and weaknesses of the present security systems, to identify crime risks, to develop and rank solutions to reduce crime risks, and to strengthen security (Richards, 1996).

Although crime prevention efforts by schools are apparently widespread, little is known about the crime prevention efforts of college students including to what extent they engage in crime prevention behaviors and what types they do adopt. Related to understanding students' crime prevention behaviors is understanding the nature and extent of their on-campus victimization. Both pieces of information have implications for the need for additional crime prevention efforts, the content of crime prevention efforts, and the limits of crime prevention.

COLLEGE STUDENTS' CRIME PREVENTION BEHAVIORS: EXTENT AND TYPES

Very little is known about the extent and types of crime prevention measures actually used by college students while on campus, in part because researchers are just beginning to examine the extent and the nature of on-campus victimization among students (see Fisher et al., 1995). Sloan et al. (1995) recently completed a two-year panel study of campus victimization at the University of Alabama at Birmingham. Their case study sheds some light on these issues.

Sloan et al. (1995) asked student members of their panel about the extent to which they engaged in crime prevention behaviors while on the UAB campus. Across the two-year period of the study, very few students reported that they "always" practiced crime prevention behaviors while on the campus, and there was little change in reported activities over time. Among the most popular forms of crime prevention were two types of target-hardening and risk management behaviors: More than 90 percent of the students reported that they "always" locked their cars, motorcycles, or bicycles when leaving them unattended, and close to 70 percent of the students reported that they "always" kept their keys in hand in a defensive manner when walking to their cars. Other risk management behaviors were not as popular as carrying keys defensively. For example, one-half of the students reported leaving their property unattended while on campus, and were thus ripe for theft victimizations. Carrying protection devices was not as popular among the students as the two behaviors above mentioned. Close to 70 percent of the students at both time periods reported that they "never" carried a personal protection device (e.g., weapon, mace, or pepper-spray) while on campus. Most of the students did not use crime prevention services offered by the school. For example, close to 90 percent of the students indicated that they had "never" used the campus escort service. Overall, Sloan et al. (1995) concluded that students routinely failed to engage in crime prevention behaviors while on campus.

Unlike the abundance of information concerning what schools are doing to prevent crime on their campuses, little is known about what students do to reduce their chances of victimization. We now turn to the description of the methods of the current study. We then present the results of our analyses in an attempt to discern the patterns of on-campus student victimizations and the extent and the nature of crime prevention efforts undertaken by students and by post-secondary institutions in our sample.

METHODS

Our analyses are part of a larger analysis of the nature and incidence of college student victimization. We collected data for the study using a structured-telephone interview modeled after the redesigned National Crime Victimization Survey (Bureau of Justice Statistics, 1996). Using this interview, we collected detailed information about the victimization incident, including its type and location (whether it occurred on or off campus and the specific location where the incident occurred), time of day it occurred, and the number and perceived characteristics of the offender(s). Our bounding period was "since school began in the fall 1993."

We also asked all the students about their crime prevention activities while on campus, and of those who lived on campus, we asked them to indicate the presence of specific types of on-campus residence crime prevention measures. From this information, we developed a fairly complete assessment of the incidence and of the nature of students' victimizations and the type of crime prevention activities used at the individual level. To supplement institution-level crime prevention information obtained from the students, we also surveyed campus officials at the sampled schools to assess the extent and nature of the crime prevention programs and services available on campus.[4]

Sampling Design

The population of schools for this study included all four-year institutions (N=2,142) appearing in the Department of Education's *State Higher Education Profiles* (1993) compilation of post-secondary institutions. We stratified all the schools on two variables: total student enrollment and location. The four sizes of enrollment categories were: 1,000-2,499; 2,500-9,999; 10,000-19,999; and 20,000 or more. We did not include schools with less than 1,000 students because most of them were religious schools (e.g., bible colleges or yeshivas), or specialty medical schools, and only six percent of post-secondary students in the United States were enrolled in these schools (U.S. Department of Education, 1993). School location was divided into three categories: urban, suburban, and small town/rural based on location designations found in *Peterson's Guide to Four-Year Colleges and Universities*.

Using the 4x3 matrix (size of enrollment by location), we randomly selected one school from each stratum. We then contracted with the American Student List Company to generate a random sample of the names and telephone numbers of undergraduate and graduate students enrolled at each school. The size of the sample from each school was computed using the formula for a simple random sample. Completed interviews were obtained from 3,472 undergraduate and graduate students enrolled as full-time or part-time students when school began in the fall term of 1993. Our overall response rate was 71 percent.

Sample Characteristics

More than 87 percent of the sample members were full-time students. Most of the sample members were seniors (25%), followed by first-year students (21%), juniors (20%), sophomores (17%), graduate students (15%), and certification program students (2%). More than one-half (56%) of the sample members were women. About three-fourths (76%) of the sample members were white, 13 percent were African American, eight percent were Asian-Pacific Islanders, and one percent said they were Native Americans (3% of the sample members refused to tell us their race). Seventy-three percent of the sample members were between 17 and 24 years of age and 17 percent were between 25 and 34 years of age. About 40 percent of the students lived on the campus. Among these students, close to 87 percent said they lived in a traditional dormitory while the remainder lived in married student housing, fraternities or sororities, or co-op type housing.

ANALYSIS AND RESULTS

In this section of the chapter, we report the results of our analyses. We begin by examining the extent and nature of on-campus victimizations. Following this, we report the on-campus location where the victimization occurred, the spatial and temporal distribution of on-campus student victimizations, and the perceived characteristics of the offender(s). We then report on the crime prevention activities of students while on campus and the types of crime prevention measures available in on-campus residences. We end this section by reporting on the extent and nature of crime prevention programs and services provided by the schools.

The Extent and Nature of On-Campus Victimizations

For all crimes that occurred on campus, Table 7.1 shows that 23 percent of the students experienced at least one victimization within the bounding period and of the students who were victimized, 30 percent experienced more than one victimization (the latter statistic is not in Table 7.1). Looking across the victimization sectors, Table 7.1 shows that personal sector victimization was the most common among the students; 12 percent of the students experienced a personal sector victimization. Other types of victimizations were not as common: eight percent experienced a living quarters sector victimization, six percent experienced harassment (either verbal or telephone call), five percent suffered a vandalism victimization, and a mere one percent were the victims of some type of threat.

Within the personal victimization sector, students were more than four times more likely to experience a crime of theft than to experience a crime of violence while on campus. Among the crimes of theft, personal larceny without contact was the most commonly experienced victimization; close to 11 percent of the students reported having been the victim of theft compared with a little over two percent of the students reported having been the victim of violence. Among living quarters sector offenses, burglary was most common, with 3.5 percent of the students experiencing either a completed or an attempted burglary. Threat of physical assault was the most common type of threat, although a somewhat rare event. Finally, among harassments, about four percent of the students experienced a verbal harassment, making it the most common form of harassment.

Almost all (93%) of the on-campus victimizations happened during the school year and not during a scheduled break (e.g., Christmas break) when few students typically are on campus (table not shown, see Fisher et al., 1995).

Table 7.1
On-Campus Victimization Counts, Percents, Rates per 1,000 Students and Percent and Number of Victims by Sector and Type of Crimes

Type of crime	Percent and number of victims	Percent and number of victims	Rate per 1,000 students
All Crimes	23.0% (799)	100.0% (1127)	324.3
Personal Sector	12.5 (434)	65.1 (520)	149.8
Crimes of Violence[1]	2.6 (89)	12.9 (103)	29.7
Rape[2]	0.4 (13)	1.8 (14)	4.0
Sexual Assault[3]	1.2 (41)	3.9 (44)	12.7
Robbery	0.0 (1)	0.0 (1)	0.3
Assaults	1.2 (43)	3.9 (44)	12.7
Aggravated Assault	0.3 (9)	0.8 (9)	2.6
Simple Assault	1.0 (34)	3.1 (35)	10.1
Crimes of Theft	10.7 (370)	37.0 (417)	120.1
Personal Larceny w/ contact	0.5 (18)	1.6 (18)	5.2
Personal Larceny w/o contact	10.1 (351)	37.4 (380)	109.4
Motor Vehicle Theft	0.1 (2)	0.2 (2)	0.6
Motor Vehicle Burglary	0.5 (17)	1.5 (17)	4.9
Living Quarters Sector	3.8 (131)	12.9 (145)	41.5
Burglary	3.5 (120)	11.5 (130)	37.2
Living Quarters Larceny	0.3 (12)	1.3 (15)	4.3
Vandalism Sector	5.1 (177)	16.8 (189)	54.4

Table 7.1 (*continued*)

Type of crime	Percent and number of victims	Percent and number of victims	Rate per 1,000 students
Threat Sector	1.1 (37)	5.5 (44)	12.7
Robbery	0.0 (1)	0.0 (1)	0.3
Physical Assaults[4]	1.0 (35)	3.1 (35)	10.1
Simple Assaults	0.2 (7)	0.6 (7)	2.0
Vandalism	0.0 (1)	0.0 (1)	0.3
Harassment Sector	6.2 (214)	20.3 (229)	66.0
Verbal	3.6 (125)	11.8 (133)	38.3
Telephone	2.6 (92)	8.5 (96)	27.6

[1]   Both completed and attempted victimizations are included in the counts. Rape, sexual assault, and aggravated assault include attempts as per their respective definitions and footnote 1 in Table 1, *Criminal Victimizations in the United States, 1993*.

[2]   The percentage of males who reported being raped was .32 (n=5), and the rate was 3.25 per 1,000 males (5/1541). The percentage of females who reported being raped was .36 (n=7), and the rate was 4.66 per 1,000 females (9/1931).

[3]   The percentage of males who reported being sexually assaulted was 1.04 (n=16), and the rate was 10.38 per 1,000 males. The percentage of females who reported being sexually assaulted was 1.29 (n=25), and the rate was 14.5 per 1,000 females.

[4]   Respondents' description of the incident did not allow us to classify the assault as a simple or aggravated assault.

The Spatial and Temporal Distribution of On-Campus Victimizations

The two most common locations for on-campus victimizations were the students' living quarters and inside a school building (e.g., the library, a laboratory, or a classroom building) (table not shown, see Fisher et al., 1995). For example, 22 percent of all personal sector crimes occurred in the living quarters and 42 percent occurred in a school building (most of which involved personal larceny). A closer look at personal sector crimes reveals an interesting pattern: violent crimes were more likely to occur in students' living quarters (43%) while thefts were more likely to occur in a school building (45%).

More than one-half (51%) of the threats occurred in the students' living quarters and 75 percent of the harassments also occurred there. One exception to this pattern was vandalism where the most common location for victimization was a parking lot or parking deck.

We also found very little variation in the time of day when the victimization occurred. The most common time for students' victimizations was between the hours of 6 a.m. and 6 p.m. That is, daytime hours appear to be "hot times" for student victimizations (see Wilkins, 1996). Exceptions to this pattern were the time period during which the most number of rapes and assaults occurred: between the hours of 2 a.m. and 4 a.m. and between the hours of 9 p.m. and 12 a.m., respectively (table not shown, see Fisher et al., 1995).[5]

Characteristics of Offenders

Most of the victimizations involved a single offender: 80 percent of the violent victimization, 79 percent of the harassments, 76 percent of the threats, 74 percent of the living quarters crimes, and 51 percent of the vandalism (table not shown, see Fisher et al., 1995). The vast majority of lone offenders were male *and* were perceived as a student by the victim. Further, a significant proportion of the lone offenders were perceived by their victim to have been drinking and/or on drugs during the victimization.

Multiple offender victimizations were not common, except for vandalism (49% of the victimizations). The multiple offenders' pattern was similar to the single offender pattern: a majority of the offenders were males, and were perceived by the victim as students and to have been drinking, taking drugs, or both.

Crime Prevention Activities by On-Campus Residents While On Campus

Prior research on the crime prevention activities of students has shown that most students did not routinely engage in behaviors that would reduce their chance for victimization (see Sloan et al., 1995). This study, however, was limited to a single institution, and thus the generalizability of the results is limited. Accordingly, we were interested in examining the extent to which Sloan et al.'s results held true for a larger sample of students enrolled at multiple institutions.

The results presented in Table 7.2 indicate that, by and large, students rarely engaged in crime prevention activities. For example, a large majority of the students in our sample indicated they had "never" attended non-mandatory campus sponsored crime prevention workshops. Additionally, a large proportion also indicated they rarely used avoidance strategies like avoiding areas of campus during the day or at night.

Table 7.2
Crime Prevention Activities by Students While on Campus
(percent and number)

Type of Crime Prevention Activity	Always	Frequently	Sometimes	Never
General Information				
Attended non-mandatory campus sponsored crime prevention workshop	0.82% (28)	2.24% (77)	15.07% (517)	81.87% (2809)
Avoidance Strategies				
Avoided specific areas of campus during the day	1.52 (52)	1.78 (61)	4.64 (159)	92.06 (3153)
Avoided specific areas of campus at night	11.62 (393)	9.09 (308)	20.93 (709)	53.37 (1977)
Risk Management				
Carried mace, pepper-spray, a screamer, etc. (not including a firearm)	11.04 (379)	4.66 (160)	6.73 (231)	77.56 (2662)
Carried a firearm	0.38 (13)	0.64 (22)	1.08 (37)	97.90 (3359)
Carried keys in hand in defensive manner	10.05 (345)	10.75 (369)	23.33 (801)	55.88 (1919)
Asked someone to walk you to your destination after dark	8.93 (305)	10.16 (347)	24.04 (821)	56.87 (1942)
Used campus sponsored crime prevention services like campus escort	0.85 (29)	2.16 (74)	10.70 (367)	86.30 (2960)
Target Hardening				
Asked someone to watch your property while you are away	14.31 (489)	17.07 (583)	44.50 (1520)	24.12 (824)
Locked door of dorm room, room in fraternity/sorority, or room in co-op while remained in building[1]	28.09 (393)	16.94 (274)	29.09 (407)	25.88 (362)
Locked motor vehicle when parking on or near campus[2]	90.80 (2408)	3.47 (92)	2.83 (75)	2.90 (77)
Locked bicycle/took front wheel when parking on or near the campus[3]	75.55 (720)	4.20 (40)	3.04 (29)	17.21 (164)

[1]   Only those students who lived in a traditional dorm, married student housing, a co-op, or a fraternity/sorority on campus are included.
[2]   Only those students who have access to a motor vehicle during the school year are included.
[3]   Only those students who have access to a bicycle during the school year are included.

It was also the case that few students engaged in risk management behaviors. For example, more than three-fourths (77%) of the students reported that they "never" carried mace, almost all of them (98%) indicated that they "never" carried a firearm while on campus, more than one-half (56%) of the students reported that they "never" carried their keys in a defensive manner, 57 percent said that they "never" asked another person to walk with them to their destination after dark, and 86 percent indicated that they "never" used services like campus escort.

Finally, when it came to using target hardening measures, our results showed that students were more likely to use this strategy than either avoidance or risk management strategies but their use of the former was occasional. For example, close to 69 percent of the students indicated that they "sometimes" or "never" asked someone to watch their property while they were away. Among the students living in on-campus housing, a majority (55%) reported that they "sometimes" or "never" locked the door(s) to their living quarters while they remained in their dorm, fraternity, sorority, or co-op.

Target hardening measures were popular among the students who had access to a car and/or bicycle during the school year. Nearly all of the students (90%) who reported having access to a motor vehicle said that they locked the vehicle when parking it on or near the campus, and over 75 percent of the students who had access to the use of a bicycle during the academic year indicated that they either locked the bicycle or dismantled the front wheel of the bicycle when parking it on or near the campus.

On-Campus Residence-Level Crime Prevention Measures

As shown in Table 7.3, the most frequent type of crime prevention available in on-campus housing involved access control. Some 40 percent of the students residing on campus indicated that there was a security guard on duty at their residence; 36 percent indicated that the residence used students to monitor access to the building; 30 percent of the students indicated that the residence provided card key access to the building or to their room. Finally, among students who did not live in graduate or married student housing, 30 percent indicated that their residence hall had a "sign-in/sign-out" policy for visitors. Only eight percent of the students indicated their residence used surveillance cameras in the lobby, while nearly 44 percent of the students indicated their residence used additional locks (e.g., deadbolt locks).

Institutional-Level Crime Prevention Activities

As the results in Table 7.4 show, all of the schools reported that they offered rape awareness programs, general crime prevention education, and alcohol and drug awareness programs. However, far fewer of the schools organized a "crime watch" program or offered self-defense classes. Additionally,

Table 7.3
On-Campus Residence-Level Crime Prevention Measures[1]

Type of Measure	Percent of students who said "yes" (n)
Access Control	
Card key access to building or room	29.74% (406)
Residents sign-in/sign-out policy	11.72 (160)
Visitors sign-in/sign-out policy[2]	30.40 (415)
Security guards on duty	40.37 (551)
Student monitor to show key or ID[3]	36.40 (497)
Telephone entry or electronic door	25.42 (347)
Surveillance Control	
Surveillance camera in lobby or hallways, or outside camera	8.64 (118)
Target Hardening	
Additional locks	43.66 (596)
Other[3]	4.47 (61)

[1]   The responses are from students who indicated that they lived on campus (n=1355).

[2]   This question was not asked of those respondents who lived in graduate or married student housing.

[3]   Other responses included such measures as: motion sensors, lock-up time, and inside doors or main gate locked at night.

few schools required participation by their students in the different programs. For example, only one-third of the schools required students to participate in the school's alcohol awareness program.

Turning to institution-level crime prevention services, the results in Table 7.4 shows that only two services—on-campus escort services after dark and the availability of a property engraver—were universally offered by the schools. The next most common services offered (in descending order of frequency) included: emergency "blue light" telephones, motor vehicle registration, bicycle registration, counseling for crime victims, daytime on-campus escort service, and nighttime off-campus escort service.

Table 7.4
Crime Prevention Activities Offered by Sample Schools
(percent and number)

Type of Strategy	Any Participation	Mandatory Participation[1]
Educational Programs		
Rape awareness	100.0% (12)	25.0% (3)
General crime prevention education	100.0 (12)	0.0 (0)
Alcohol awareness	100.0 (12)	33.3 (4)
Drug awareness	100.0 (12)	16.7 (2)
Crime watch	41.7 (5)	0.0 (0)
Self-defense classes	33.3 (4)	0.0 (0)
Services		
On-campus escort available after dark	100.0 (12)	
Engraving of property	100.0 (12)	
Emergency "blue light" telephones	91.7 (11)	
Counseling for crime victims	75.0 (9)	
Bicycle registration	75.0 (9)	44.4 (4)
Motor vehicle registration	83.3 (10)	70.0 (7)
On-campus escort available during the day	50.0 (6)	
Off-campus escort available after dark	25.0 (3)	
Surveillance and Security Measures		
Security desk(s) in dormatory	66.7 (8)	
Security inspections or evaluations for campus housing and other campus buildings	66.7 (8)	
Security check(s) at campus entrance(s)	25.0 (6)	
Surveillance cameras in dorms, class buildings, or other campus locations	25.0 (6)	

Table 7.4 *(continued)*

Type of Strategy	Any Participation	Mandatory Participation[1]
Physical Design		
Upgrade campus lighting	75.0 (9)	
Reduced hiding places (i.e., cut back shrubbery, etc.)	75.0 (9)	
Fenced boundaries around the campus	25.0 (3)	
Other		
Banned sale and consumption of alcohol at athletic contests	66.7 (8)	
Banned consumption of alcohol in campus housing	33.3 (2)	

[1]   Includes only those schools that indicated that they offered the respective program or service. The "don't know" and "no answer" responses were not included in the calculations.

The type of surveillance and security measures used by the schools varied with just over two-thirds (67%) of the schools having security desks in their campus dormitories and doing a security inspection or evaluation of campus housing or buildings, while one-fourth of the schools reported that they had installed surveillance cameras in the dorms or at other places on campus, or that the school had a security check at the campus entrance(s).

Physical design measures were employed by many of the schools. Seventy-five percent of the schools reported they had upgraded campus lighting and had reduced hiding places by cutting back shrubbery and other vegetation. One-half of the schools reported they had conducted a security inspection of campus buildings and one-third of the schools indicated that they had a fenced boundary.

Finally, most of the schools had addressed alcohol usage on campus by banning its use at sporting events (67%), while one-third of the schools had also banned the consumption of alcohol in on-campus residences.

DISCUSSION AND CONCLUSION

Overall, students' victimizations were relatively rare, and when they occurred, they were relatively minor in nature, typically involving theft of property from the students and occurring in either students' living quarters or while they were in a school building. We also found that student victims were likely to be victimized by a lone offender who was perceived by the victim as a fellow student; offenders were also perceived by most victims to have been under the influence of alcohol, drugs, or a combination of the two. Finally, our results indicated that students did not routinely engage in either avoidance or risk management strategies to reduce their chances of victimization, but were more likely to engage in certain forms of target hardening activities like locking doors, vehicles, or bicycles than in the other two types of crime prevention.

These empirical patterns have implications for crime prevention on college campuses. Below, we address two issues: First, is more crime prevention on campuses necessary? Second, when campus crime prevention is undertaken, what should its content be?

Is More Crime Prevention Necessary?

In light of the current concerns over crime on campus, college and university administrators must be sensitive to media depictions of student victimization as "widespread and violent" (e.g., Matthews, 1993). They must also comply with various state- and federal-level initiatives designed to disseminate information about crime and crime prevention activities on their campuses. As was previously discussed, schools have implemented a variety of institutional-level crime prevention strategies. At the same time, crime prevention consumes resources—money and time—that might be allocated to competing needs within any given institution. The challenge for any school, therefore, is to use resources judiciously in an attempt to ensure a safer environment for its students.

One consideration is whether student victimization is a serious problem or has been exaggerated. Our data provide no definitive answers, but they may be useful in setting some broad parameters in assessing this issue. As noted, slightly less than one-quarter of the sample reported being victimized at least once, with nearly 70 percent of these victims experiencing a theft-related offense. Based on these results, it would seem that the threat posed by crime on most campuses is far less than the media would portray. Thus, in any given academic year, most students will be safe from crime and very few will suffer a physical attack.

From another vantage point, however, our data suggest that student victimization is a problem that warrants attention. Again, the incidence of victimization in the sample for our study's bounding period was not high: less than one-quarter of the students were victimized in a six-month period. But if this rate were calculated for the four or five years students typically spend at a school, a clear majority of the students would experience some crime victimization during their college tenure. Moving to the aggregate level, relatively modest prevalence rates, when calculated over a large student base, can produce high numbers of crimes. For example, with the victimization incidence rate of 23 percent found in our study, a school of 10,000 students would experience 2,300 crimes in a single six-month period. Even if most of these crimes are nonserious, the sheer number of illegal acts might be cause for genuine concern.

Furthermore, although serious victimizations are rare, they do occur and can have potentially devastating effects. How preventable these serious crimes are remains an important research question, however, precisely because they are relatively rare events. Still, it would be imprudent of us to suggest that crime prevention measures not be employed that focus specifically on these offenses—at least not until the ineffectiveness of these measures can be definitively shown. Indeed, in the case of serious crimes, it can be argued that even small savings in crime through prevention efforts can be justified when juxtaposed to the harm victims suffer.

In summary, our data caution against the current tendency to portray student victimization as a social problem of enormous proportions. College campuses, however, are not ivory towers fully free from petty thefts and, occasionally, serious crime victimizations. Administrators thus need to take a balanced perspective on student victimization. In particular, we would caution against seeing student victimization as a crisis, and then blindly allocating more and more resources to crime prevention in an effort "to do something about the problem." Instead, we would recommend that administrators take a more sustained and judicious approach in which they pay more attention to how crime prevention resources should be allocated and how best to make students more effective co-producers of safety on campus.

The Content of Crime Prevention

To allocate crime prevention resources more effectively, campuses might benefit by implementing information systems that can identify not only how much victimization occurs on campus but also where and when different types of crime occur most frequently. This approach, which criminologists call identifying the "hot spots" for crime, would allow administrators to target security and other crime prevention resources in a more focused way (see Sherman, Gartin & Buerger, 1989; Wilkins, 1996). In theory, this approach yields more "bang for the buck" by allocating crime prevention resources where they potentially will do the most good.

Identifying such "hot spots," however, requires implementing an information system capable of accurately measuring the spatial and temporal distribution of crime on campus. One information source is the crime reports recorded by the campus security/police department. These "official statistics" ideally would be supplemented with a campus victimization survey that would detect offenses not reported to the campus authorities. Although victimization surveys are potentially costly to conduct, omitting victimization data is risky since the crime patterns revealed by this data source will overlap with, but not be identical to, those revealed by official statistics. Victimization surveys can also provide additional information about such things as the victim's activities before the incident, crime prevention behavior before and after the incident, perceived offender(s) characteristics, and needed victim services. This type of information can be useful to administrators when tailoring crime prevention efforts and campaigns, and victim services to effectively use their limited resources.

The uneven spatial and temporal distribution of crime found in our data have implications for what should be the content of the crime prevention information that schools share with students. To begin with, we do not have evidence from our study that broadly worded appeals to students to take crime prevention seriously have no value in raising their consciousness about crime. We do know, however, that despite the presence of campus crime prevention resources at the schools we surveyed, many students did not routinely engage in crime prevention activities. How might this situation be changed so that students become more sensitized to co-produce safety in their environment?

One way to approach this question is to consider students as exercising "rational choice" in deciding whether to allocate their time and psychic energies to crime prevention. In our study, the students seemed, more or less, to make choices that maximized their returns from crime prevention. Thus, we found that students indicated that they engaged in target hardening activities for "big ticket" items, such as locking their automobiles or their bicycles, but they were less likely to do so for other types of property that usually were of less value. In short, they invested their crime prevention where it seemed to matter the most.

Our data suggest, however, that students' rationality may be limited by their lack of specific information about their victimization risks. Although it may generally make sense to protect more valuable possessions, our data suggest that many theft-related victimizations—the predominant form of crime on campuses—involve other types of property and could have been prevented had students taken better precautions. In many instances, these precautions would have been as simple as students asking someone to watch their property while they were away for a few minutes or locking their door while in the residence hall. In turn, students might have been prompted to take these simple precautions if they were given *specific* information that many such crimes occur; that is, the "rationality" of crime prevention might have been clarified. With more serious crimes, such information as the roles that alcohol and drugs play in terms of the offender's behaviors may also be used to inform students about acting in their best interest to reduce their chances of becoming a victim to violence.

In this same vein, information on the spatial and temporal distribution of crime on campuses might reveal that particular sites on campus—for example, a residence hall or library—have especially high rates of victimization, especially for certain types of crime. In the case of the library, administrators might post reminders to students to be careful about leaving their property unattended. In effect, the goal would be to prompt students to use their crime prevention "resources" in places where, and during times when, the risks were empirically high.

At the University of Alabama at Birmingham, for example, the undergraduate library recently experienced a large number of thefts of property. In response, the library staff adopted a situational approach to crime prevention; they posted a reminder sticker on every table, carrel, and study room in the library informing the students of this fact and reminding them not to leave their property unattended. In effect, the library was identified as a "hot spot" for theft, and the campus authorities undertook a specific program to make users aware of that fact. In this case, specific information, rather than global appeals to participate in crime prevention, was employed to sensitize students to where they needed to be most on guard against theft crimes.

Finally, crime prevention information might benefit from sharing another finding of our study: most criminals on campus, it seems, are other students, who often are under the influence of alcohol or drugs. This insight suggests that students should keep in mind that the most likely people to steal their books, possessions in their room, or physically attack them are fellow students. Furthermore, situations in which students come into contact with others who are "drunk" or "high" are likely to increase the risks of victimization.

The Limits of Crime Prevention

We end with a word of caution: although we see crime prevention as a worthy enterprise, it is not a panacea for the student victimizations that occur on campuses. From the broader criminological literature, there is extensive research showing that while crime prevention can help to make social environments safer, it is only one factor in determining the risk of crime victimization (see Miethe & Meier, 1994). In particular, college administrators should pay attention to the factors that lead students—or those who come on to campuses from the larger community—to become *offenders*. Thus, the "root causes" of crime, that can involve the individual traits and lifestyle characteristics of students and the situations they encounter on campus at different locations, are factors that must be understood and addressed by any comprehensive strategy to make colleges and universities safer.

Furthermore, administrators should beware that even well-intentioned crime prevention efforts—leaving aside, for example, efforts that are politically inspired and largely symbolic in content—may prove unproductive and ineffective. Even in the best of circumstances, reducing crime is difficult—an enterprise in which success is often punctuated with disappointments. The challenge, then, is for administrators to develop crime prevention programs that are based on the existing research and are shaped by the specific victimization patterns and offending characteristics besetting their schools. In this way, crime prevention can move from broadly-based appeals to be careful about crime, to programs whose resources are invested strategically to make the specific campus in question safer. This approach may require tedious data collection and analysis, but it has the decided advantage of being the "best bet" to reduce the on-campus victimization of students.

In short, crime prevention efforts on campus are more than just "implanting" the latest generic crime prevention program, measure, or service. Researchers have convincingly argued theoretically and shown empirically that such an approach does not necessarily result in reducing crime; in fact, the opposite may happen, and indeed it has happened (Rosenbaum, 1987, 1988).

NOTES

[1] Supported under award 93-IJ-CX-0049 from the National Institute of Justice, Office of Justice Programs, U.S. Department of Justice. Points of view in this document are those of the authors and do not necessarily represent the official position of the U.S. Department of Justice.

[2] In the 1993 NCVS results, property crimes include thefts. The former are now considered household-level crimes and not individual-level crimes, and as a result, are reported as rates per 1,000 households and not as rates per 1,000 individuals. In the 1992 NCVS, thefts were considered individual-level crimes, and rates per 1,000 individuals were reported.

[3] Almost all of the information used in this section was obtained from the Internet using the NETSCAPE program and the search engines YAHOO and EXCITE. We searched using the terms "campus crime," "student victimization," "campus security," and "campus law enforcement." We were able to visit the home pages of those colleges and universities that had created a World Wide Web home page and gather information about the types of crime prevention programs, services, and measures offered or adopted by the respective school.

[4] For detailed information about the methods of the larger analysis (e.g., the individual-level and incident-level instruments) see Fisher et al. (1995).

[5] Robbery is not discussed because one on-campus robbery precludes any discussion of a temporal pattern.

North East Multi-Regional Training
-Instructors' Library-
355 Smoke Tree Plaza
North Aurora, IL 60542

INTRODUCTION TO CHAPTER 8

Victimization in elementary and secondary schools has also become a major source of concern and frustration in recent years. Media reports of violence and weapons in schools, the growing level of violence among juveniles, and claims that part of the failure of schools to adequately educate their students is due to disruption in the schools all add to a feeling that something must be done to make the schools safe. Most of the suggested responses to in-school victimization revolve around harsh discipline, strict control of the environment, and building a fortress against the outside world. Calls for installing metal detectors, conducting locker searches, hiring security guards, implementing more liberal suspension and expulsion policies, and imposing harsher punishments are not uncommon.

Mandatory attendance at school also contributes to the need to do something about in-school victimization. Requiring attendance at school means that society unwittingly brings together the three conditions for crime set forth in the routine-activities perspective—suitable targets (students and their belongings), motivated offenders (other students and/or gang members), and an absence of guardians (high student/teacher ratios). The school, therefore, becomes a prime site for crime.

Unfortunately, there has been little systematic study of the extent of victimization in schools or the responses of students to victimization. The next paper examines the extent of in-school victimization experienced by junior and senior high school students in a large midwestern county. Lab and Clark note that, while most students are not victimized, a significant proportion report becoming victims at school, and an even greater percentage know of others who have been victimized on school property. In response to the direct and indirect victimization, students report feeling unsafe at school, are fearful of being victimized, avoid school and places at school, and carry weapons to school for protection.

The results of this study are similar to those of other investigations. What is noteworthy is that students make rational choices based on their experiences with and perceptions of victimization at school. Their responses, however, are more inappropriate than appropriate. Avoiding school means that the student will not receive the education he or she needs to be successful later in life. Carrying weapons can result in more serious confrontations, expulsion, or legal trouble for the youth, even if it is brought for protection. Feeling unsafe and fearing victimization at school distracts the individual from the educational process. While these responses may make the students feel better, they work against the educational mission of the school. What is needed are crime prevention interventions that work in harmony with the school's mission while providing a safe environment.

8

Crime Prevention in Schools: Individual and Collective Responses[1]

Steven P. Lab
Bowling Green State University

Richard D. Clark
John Carroll University

Evidence continues to mount that crime in schools is a critical concern in contemporary America, despite cautions from historians that similar problems have existed for centuries (Newman & Newman, 1980). Approximately 40 percent of high school seniors have reported some type of theft victimization and more than 15 percent have reported being threatened at school (Maguire & Pastore, 1995:253). Victimization may elicit a variety of responses in people. Among the possible responses are fear of crime, fear of specific places, avoidance behavior, and the carrying of weapons. While research has focused on the general public, there has been little attention paid to the responses of students in school. This paper explores the relationship between in-school victimization and student responses.

LITERATURE REVIEW

Victimization in School

The National Institute of Education's Safe School Study (1978) stands as the benchmark for research on school crime. Responses from more than 31,000 junior and senior high students revealed that 11 percent were theft victims in an average month, 1.3 percent were physically attacked per month, and an additional .5 percent experienced a robbery victimization at school. In addition, victimization was more prevalent in junior high school settings. Gottfredson and Gottfredson (1985), reanalyzing the Safe School Study data, found that the amount of victimization is "a serious national problem" (1985:183) although it is better described as a situation of "some chronic disciplinary problems in many schools" rather than as "an acute crisis in school discipline or an increasing rebellion against order" (1985:183). To put this another way, the percentage of victimizations is small but, given the millions of children in school, that percentage translates into significant numbers of victims.

More recent national data on school victimization come from surveys of high school students. In 1994, 36 percent of the nation's seniors reported one or more thefts (less than $50) at school in the previous 12 months and 18 percent reported thefts of property worth more than $50. Twenty-seven percent claimed some type of damage to their own property. Twelve percent reported injury without a weapon, five percent injury with a weapon, 15 percent were threatened with a weapon, and 24 percent were threatened without a weapon (Maguire & Pastore, 1995:253). These percentages are almost identical to victimization figures from 1982. The 1989 National Crime Victimization Survey included a School Crime Supplement (NCVS:SCS) that gathered victimization data from 11,446 junior and senior high school youths. The NCVS:SCS uncovered only 66 robberies (.6%), 304 assaults (2.9%), and 1,256 thefts (12.2%) in school over a 6 month time period. While these data suggest that the victimization prevalence is low, extrapolating to population parameters would present large numbers of victims (Lab & Whitehead, 1992). Indeed, Walker, Colvin, and Ramsey (1995) estimated that there were more than three million acts of violence or theft in schools in 1994 and that more than 100,000 weapons found their way into school every day in the United States.

Two recent national surveys of students in grades three through 12 (Metropolitan Life Survey of the American Teacher, 1993, 1994) also provide insight to the problem of in-school crime. One-fourth of the student respondents reported having been in a physical fight at school, while almost 20 percent reported being threatened with a knife or gun, and 44 percent had been in an angry confrontation while at school (Metropolitan Life Survey, 1994). Theft offenses were also frequent problems with close to one-half of the students reporting at least one such victimization (Metropolitan Life Survey, 1993). Focusing on just the high school respondents, 38 percent claimed to have been the victim of at least one violent act in or around their school.

In summary, the research on school crime is limited, but it does indicate that in-school victimization is a matter of concern. While no consensus exists on the size of the problem, the results of every investigation reveal that a large number of students are victimized at school. The fact that students are required to attend school should make the issue of in-school victimization a priority concern for students, parents, educators, and the criminal justice system.

Responses to Victimization

Individuals can respond to victimization in many ways, such as enhanced fear, avoidance behavior, and carrying weapons. Research on victimization has produced contradictory findings on the relationship between victimization and fear of crime (Akers et al., 1987; Langworthy & Whitehead, 1986; Lawton & Yaffe, 1980; Lee, 1983; Liska, Lawrence & Sanchirico, 1982; Skogan & Maxfield, 1981; Yin, 1980). Suggested reasons for findings of no relationship are that victimization is a rare event, individuals rapidly forget victimization experiences, and most victimizations are simply not that serious, injurious, or life-threatening (Skogan & Maxfield, 1981). Although much of this research has focused on the elderly rather than on youths (see e.g., Akers et al., 1987), there is sufficient basis to argue that youthful victimization leads to youthful fear (McDermott, 1983).

The NCVS:SCS asked students about fear of being attacked at school or on the way to or from school. In response to these questions, 78.6 percent reported never fearing attack at school, and 85.8 percent responded similarly in relation to transit to school. At the same time, 5.3 percent and 4.3 percent responded fearing attack sometimes or most of the time at school or in transit, respectively. Lab and Whitehead (1992) found that the strongest predictor of students' fear of crime at school was in-school victimization.

One of the most often identified responses to crime is avoidance behavior. Various authors, in attempting to outline general avenues for response to crime and fear, suggest that avoidance is the key response used by individuals (DuBow et al., 1979; Furstenberg, 1972; Gates & Rohe, 1987; Lavrakas et al., 1981; Skogan, 1981). Two empirical attempts to identify citizen responses to crime and fear of crime (Lab, 1990; Lavrakas & Lewis, 1980) both uncover avoidance as a distinct alternative. Various other analyses demonstrate high levels of avoidance among urban respondents (Kelling et al., 1974; Lavrakas et al., 1981; Skogan & Maxfield, 1981), as well as in general population surveys (Garofalo, 1977; Maxfield, 1984, 1987).

While avoidance is seen as a viable reaction to victimization and fear, there has been little recognition that avoidance is difficult in various settings. Most research has failed to investigate avoidance from places where respondents are required to be, such as school. Using the NCVS:SCS, Lab and Whitehead (1992, 1994) and Ringwalt et al. (1992) found some evidence of selective avoidance, with students choosing to avoid places such as restrooms, hallways, and other school locations. Others avoided school altogether by deciding to "drop out" of school. Other recent research also suggests that students use avoidance, despite the requirement that they attend school. In a national survey of students in grades three through 12, Metropolitan Life found students stay home to avoid threats of violence (12%) and avoid certain areas of school (11%) (Metropolitan Life Survey, 1993, 1994).

Research has also looked at the relationship between victimization and other behavioral responses. The 1987 National Crime Survey data indicate that about seven out of 10 violent victims took some sort of self-protective measure, including attempts to reason with the offender, flight, screaming for help, physical retaliation, or resorting to use of a weapon (Shim & DeBerry, 1989). The use of a weapon is perhaps the most extreme measure taken and some researchers have found a relationship between victimization and gun ownership (Hill, Howell & Driver, 1985; Whitehead & Langworthy, 1989). While the mass media and anecdotal reports suggest that the presence of weapons is becoming an epidemic in schools, there has been relatively little empirical evidence to support this claim. The NCVS:SCS found that only 1.1 percent of the respondents reported bringing weapons to school. On the other hand, surveys restricted to urban samples uncover greater numbers of weapons in schools (Sheley et al., 1995).

This paper reports on the level of victimization and students responses to crime in junior and senior high schools.

DATA AND METHODS

This research was conducted in Lucas County, Ohio. Lucas County, which encompasses the city of Toledo, is fairly representative of similar sized counties in the United States. The 1990 census reports a population of 462,361 with a distribution of 82 percent white, 15 percent African American, and 52 percent female. Lucas County is largely urban (95% live within the confines of an urban area), with a median income of $28,245 and 15 percent of its population living below the poverty line. Its unemployment rate ranged from 7.9 percent for men to nine percent for women, with more than 10 percent of the population receiving some form of public assistance. Like many counties its size, its largest employers are involved in manufacturing, retail trade, health services, and educational services.

In 1994, the City of Toledo had a crime rate that was higher than other SMSAs in the State of Ohio. However, the rate was lower than that of many other cities whose population was over 250,000. Thus, the crime rate for Toledo appears to be comparable to other cities of a similar size.

A total of 44 schools allowed us to survey their students—31 public and 13 private schools. The 31 public schools represent 89 percent of the public junior and senior high schools in the county. Fifteen public junior and 16 public senior high schools participated. From the Catholic school system, we were able to secure data from eight (of 33) elementary schools (24%), that contain grades seven and eight, and four (of six, 67%) of the high schools. It must be noted that the Catholic schools that contain seventh and eighth graders also contain students in grades one through six. Thus, these schools are not equivalent to the public junior high schools that contain only seventh, eighth, or ninth graders. Finally, we were able to survey students in the largest, non-Catholic private school in the county.

In February of 1994, we anonymously surveyed over 11,000 students in grades seven through 12. The selection of the students for the survey was completely random and conducted by the schools. Each school received a packet of questionnaires for every teacher in their system who taught a class that included students in grades seven through 12. Within each packet was our survey, a second survey dealing exclusively with drug issues, and a teacher's guide that explained each survey. The two surveys were alternated in each packet so that when the teacher distributed the survey in the class, one-half of the students would receive our school victimization questionnaire and one-half would receive the drug abuse survey.

The questionnaire contained items on respondent demographics, school discipline and control procedures, victimization both at school and on the way to and from school, fear and avoidance behaviors, gang activity, possession of weapons for protection, and several other topics. The questionnaires were printed on computer scanable forms. Consequently, all questions were closed ended so that the students were presented with a finite set of responses from which to choose. Students were asked to answer all questions in relation to "since school started this year." Based on the date of survey administration, the data represent a roughly six month time frame.

Over 11,000 usable questionnaires were returned by the students. Questionnaires with missing school codes, inaccurate grade levels, or information that was inconsistent or clearly erroneous were eliminated. This resulted in 11,085 usable questionnaires that represented approximately 35 percent of the students in the participating schools. A comparison of grade level distribution, sex distribution, and race distribution for each school against official data for the school revealed only minor variation.

RESULTS

Victimization

Direct Victimization

Students were asked about their own experiences as a victim of three types of offenses: robbery, theft, and physical assault. Besides just the occurrence of victimization, we attempted to ascertain the level of loss or injury through simple follow-up questions. Students were asked "how many times did anyone take money or other things directly from you by force, weapons, or threat of force AT THIS SCHOOL?". A significant percentage of students reported being the victim of a robbery at school over the prior six months (Table 8.1). Indeed, 12 percent reported at least one such incident, with more than one-half of those reporting more than one. Broken down by grade level (data not shown), students in lower grades are disproportionately robbery victims. The data show that the level of victimization steadily drops from the seventh to the twelfth grade. This reflects the fact that younger students are easier targets for face-to-face crimes. Of the robbery victims, 53 percent reported at least one loss of greater than $10.

Table 8.1
Percent of Students Victimized at School

Frequency	Robbery	Theft	Assault
Never	88.2	60.8	87.1
Once	5.6	20.6	6.9
2-3 times	2.6	12.2	3.2
4-5 times	1.0	2.6	0.8
6+ times	2.6	4.0	2.0

Theft was probed as having something stolen from a "desk, locker, or some other place AT THIS SCHOOL." The data show that theft is a much more common form of victimization than robbery. Almost 40 percent of the students reported that they had been the victim of a theft at school (Table 8.1). Further, more than 15 percent reported being victimized more than once. Unlike robbery, grade level does not have as great an impact, due primarily to the fact that the lack of a face-to-face confrontation in theft offenses makes the older students just as vulnerable as younger ones. In addition to the high level of victimization, approximately 37 percent of the theft victims reported at least one loss in excess of $10.

The assault question asked "how many times did anyone physically attack or hurt you AT THIS SCHOOL?". Thirteen percent were assaulted at least once, with almost one-half of those being victimized more than once (Table 8.1). Victimization by grade again shows a decreasing level as the grade increases. This reflects the changing level of vulnerability as students age. A large percent of the assaults appear to be serious and require some form of medical treatment (33% of the victimizations).

Indirect

Individuals can be affected by crime, even though they are not directly victimized, through their knowledge of a crime problem. A large body of research has shown that indirect victimization affects many more individuals than does direct victimization. Such "indirect victimization" can lead to altered attitudes and behavior. Our survey probed indirect victimization by asking about the victimization of others at school.

Three questions dealing with assault, robbery, and theft probed the students' perception of victimization of others at school. The questions were similar in format to those used in the earlier direct victimization questions. In general, the students reported high rates of victimization in the schools. Fifty percent reported that both assaults and thefts are committed at least one to two times a month against other students, and 30 percent reported the same for robberies (Table 8.2). These figures show that students perceive a large problem with victimization against students in the school.

Table 8.2
Victimization of Other Students at School

Frequency	Assault	Robbery	Theft
Never	14.7	19.8	8.7
Almost never	20.4	24.0	17.8
1-2 times a month	26.2	13.9	19.7
1-2 times a week	11.4	6.4	12.0
Almost every day	7.3	5.9	11.9
More than once a day	5.0	3.3	5.7
Don't know	14.9	26.7	24.1

Victimization Summary

A significant percent of students experience thefts, robberies, and assaults at school. The percent of students responding that they were victimized ranged from 40 percent for theft to 13 percent for assault to 12 percent for robbery. While a majority of students are not directly victimized, the level of victimization is still high. Based on more than 11,000 respondents, the actual number of offenses ranges from at least 1,300 robberies to more than 4,400 thefts. Considering that this is based on a sample of less than one-third of the total junior and senior high students in Lucas County, the actual figures would be much higher. Moreover, many of the victimizations that do occur tend to be serious in nature as measured by the amount of loss or injury.

Responses to Victimization

Individuals can respond to victimization, both direct and indirect, in a variety of ways. Perceptions of safety at school, fear of victimization, taking avoidance behavior, and the carrying of weapons for protection are potentially all influenced by victimization. The student survey included a variety of questions to tap these domains.

Perceptions of School Safety

Students were asked whether they felt it was safe to bring money or other valuables to school, and whether it was safe to store these items at school. The results suggest that slightly more than one-half of the students feel safe in bringing money and valuables to school (52.2%). At the same time, more than one-half say that it is *not* safe to store valuables in their locker. Only 35 percent report that it is safe to store valuables in lockers.

In terms of overall school safety, 26.5 percent of the students report that their school is "very safe," with another 24.8 percent reporting them as "safe." More than 16 percent report their school as "unsafe" or "very unsafe." While not a majority, a significant number of students see their school as a threatening place. One must add to this figure any students who do not come to school at all (and therefore are not in this data) due to fear of the school environment. The data suggest the fear that occurs is evenly distributed across grades.

Fear of Victimization

Fear, independent of actual victimization, can itself be debilitating. Students may be unable to concentrate on studies or may opt to stay away from school if they are fearful of victimization at school. Fear was probed through two questions dealing with being fearful of assault both at school and in transit to school. Table 8.3 shows that 11.3 percent of the students fear an attack at school "sometimes" or "most of the time" and 70.3 percent never fear an attack. Fear is concentrated in the lower grades (data not shown), with seventh (14.2%) and eighth (13.8%) grades evincing the highest level of fear, and eleventh (9.7%) and twelfth (6.0%) grades reporting the lowest level of fear. The decreasing level of fear as one moves into later grades may be due to the reduced vulnerability felt by older students.

Table 8.3
Percent of Students Fearing Attack

Frequency	At School	To and From School
Never	70.3	76.2
Almost never	18.4	13.0
Sometimes	8.4	7.7
Most of the time	2.9	3.1

A similar level of fear appears when considering fear in transit. A significant percent of students (10.8%) reported "sometimes" or "most of the time" being fearful, while 76.2 percent are never afraid (Table 8.3). As was the case with fear in school, fear on the way to and from school is more prevalent in the lower grades, although the difference is minimal.

Avoidance Behavior

Another potential response is avoidance behavior. An avoidance response may result from both victimization (direct or indirect) as well as from any resultant fear. Students were asked how many times they stayed home from school because of concerns over assault and theft. For the county, nine percent reported staying home at least once due to fear of attack. Avoiding school out of fear of assault is concentrated in the lower grades. More than 10 percent of the students in seventh, eighth, and ninth grades stayed home at least once due to a fear of assault. In contrast, only 4.6 percent of the twelfth graders stayed home due to fear.

Similar to assault, relatively few students stayed home from school due to a fear of theft—only five percent did so. Moreover, avoidance behavior due to a fear of theft is more evenly distributed throughout the grade levels, ranging from 3.1 percent in eleventh grade to 6.3 percent in eighth grade.

Besides avoiding school altogether, students may be more selective in their movements. The survey inquired as to whether students avoided certain locations associated with school due to a fear of victimization. Among the locations probed were buses, school entrances, stairways, the cafeteria, restrooms, and the parking lot. The results suggest that there is no one location that is viewed as more dangerous. The percentage of students who avoid certain locations range from eight percent for "restrooms" and "other areas on school grounds," to four percent for "certain school entrances." Perhaps most interesting, 7.7 percent of the students report that they avoid "extra-curricular activities" due to a fear of victimization. While these percentages are small, they represent hardships and/or missed opportunities for a significant number of students.

Weapons

Another alternative response to victimization and fear involves carrying weapons for protection. Students were asked if they brought a variety of weapons to school for protection. Included in the list of weapons were guns, knives, razor blades, nunchucks (sic), brass knuckles, and mace. Since in many cases only a small number of students reported carrying a certain weapon, Table 8.4 provides information on carrying "any" weapon and a variety of individual weapons to school "for protection." Twenty-four percent of the students report carrying weapons to school for protection. Knives were the most prevalent weapon carried (15.8%), followed by "something else," (13.7%) and mace (10.1%). Only 8.4 percent of the students reported that they carried a gun to school for protection.

Table 8.4
Percent Ever Carrying Specific Weapons

Weapon	%
Any	24.1
Gun	8.4
Knife	15.8
Brass Knuckles	8.2
Razor Blade	7.8
Spiked Jewelry	9.7
Mace	10.1
Nunchucks	5.7
Something Else	13.7

Bringing a weapon to school was distributed fairly evenly throughout the grade levels (data not shown). The percentage of students who responded they "ever" brought a weapon to school for safety ranged from 19 percent in twelfth grade to 28 percent in eighth grade. Of those students who reported ever carrying any weapon for protection, 67 percent said that it made them feel safer.

Influences on Protective Behaviors

In an attempt to evaluate the impact of in-school victimization on the various student responses, the data were submitted to ordinary least square (OLS) regression techniques. Four separate responses were identified as dependent variables—avoidance (measured as the number of times students stayed home due to fear of victimization), weapons (an additive scale of number of times students carried different weapons to school), fear of attack at school, and school safety (perceptions of a school's safety). Both direct and vicarious victimization, as well as several basic demographic variables were used as predictors.

The resultant equations in Table 8.5 account for a significant amount of the variance in the dependent variables. More than one-third of the variance in avoidance (34.2%) and perceptions of school safety (33.9%), as well as 23 percent of the variance in fear of attack and 40 percent of the variance in carrying weapons for protection are accounted for by the predictor variables. Of particular note is the high R^2 for avoidance, in which students who are not in school may be staying away as a response to real or potential victimization. The inclusion of these students could possibly result in an even stronger result.

The most important predictors tend to be the victimization variables, with direct victimization being the most consistently strong predictor. Vicarious victimization measures are also strong predictors of protective actions, particularly feelings of safety and fear. The most notable exception to the general dominance of victimization is the strong impact of self-reported gang membership on carrying weapons for protection. Gang membership is the strongest predictor of weapon use.

Table 8.5
Standardized Regression Coefficients for Student Responses to Victimization

Variable	Avoidance	Weapons	Attack	Safety
Sex	−.004	−.072*	.031*	−.005
Race	−.019	−.006	.050	−.063*
Gang Membership	−.094*	−.306*	−.008	−.066*
Grade	.018	.038*	−.027*	.005
Public/Private	−.006	−.006	−.080*	−.124*
Robbery Victim	.252*	.219*	.094*	.060*
Theft Victim	.122*	.065*	.112*	.035*
Assault Victim	.293*	.163*	.215*	.051*
Vicarious Assault	−.014	.051*	.135*	.230*
Vicarious Robbery	.076*	.126*	.058*	.175*
Vicarious Theft	−.024	−.007	.051*	.109*
R^2	.342	.403	.230	.339

* indicates significance at the .05 level

Key: Sex—male=1, female=2
       Race—nonwhite=1, white=2
       Gang—member=1, nonmember=2
       Public/Private—public school=1, private school=2

DISCUSSION

The student survey data provide insight into the actual level of victimization in the schools, as well as perceptions about victimization and the general school environment. These results can be compared to other studies of in-school victimization. At first glance, the levels of victimization appear somewhat higher than in the Safe School Study or the NCVS:SCS data. This is probably due to a number of factors. First, the present study focused on a single, largely urbanized county, while the other studies were national in scope and contained a larger rural/suburban component. Second, juvenile crime has been on the increase in recent years (particularly since the late 1980s) and, therefore, the recency of this data should reflect that increase. Third, differences in the data collection and reporting techniques from study to study may account for some of the variance.

At the same time, the present results are similar to or are more modest than some findings from other analyses. The Metropolitan Life Surveys (1993, 1994) and Johnston et al. (1993) uncover higher levels of violence and theft than found in these data. They also report higher levels of avoidance behavior and fear. Reports of carrying weapons to school also vary around the 24 percent mark found in this study (Gallup, 1993; "Violence Related Attitudes," 1993). For almost all of the minor discrepancies, the difference can be attributed to methodological variation (i.e., different time frames, sampling variations, question construction).

The victimization and response results from Lucas County are similar in scope to that found in other analyses. What differences do emerge can easily be attributable to differences in study methodology and the time period of the study. Consequently, there is every reason to believe that the present study will provide insight to in-school victimization problems beyond the study site.

The results of the regression analyses suggest that protective responses by students (avoidance, carrying weapons, and heightened fear) are highly related to in-school victimization and should be responsive to efforts at reducing such victimization. Interestingly, Lab and Whitehead (1994), using the NCVS:SCS, found an inverse relationship between avoidance and in-school victimization. They suggest that students who did not avoid school subjected themselves to an increased risk of victimization, and that "it may be prudent for students to avoid certain dangerous places" as a means of self-protection (Lab & Whitehead, 1994). The reasons for the differences between the results of the two studies are not clear, but may be attributable to the methodologies employed.

IMPLICATIONS FOR CRIME PREVENTION

What has not yet been addressed is the appropriateness of the self-protective measures employed by students. We would suggest that each of the measures addressed in this paper is more *inappropriate* than appropriate. Each of the responses works against the primary mission of the schools—education. Fear of victimization and assessments that the school is not safe may shift the attention of the student to immediate physical well-being and away from learning. While fear may be a useful tool in generating self-protection, to the extent that it detracts from normal and/or needed activity, it becomes more debilitating than enriching. Avoiding school altogether, or avoiding certain places in school, may mitigate the amount of level of harm an individual experiences. At the same time, avoidance may mean missing class, going hungry due to avoiding the cafeteria, being uncomfortable because the restrooms are unsafe, or simply missing out on the extra-curricular activities that help make school more enjoyable and enriching. Finally, bringing weapons to school opens the door to more serious problems for the students and the school. In every case, where self-protection may be enhanced, the education of the individual is harmed. The self-protective measures uncovered in this paper are more *debilitating* than empowering.

The easiest and often typical responses of schools to victimization and fear is an increase in physical control over the students, visitors, and the environment. Actions such as conducting locker searches, hiring security guards, installing metal detectors, using drug sniffing dogs, and imposing harsh penalties for rule violation may not solve the problem. While such actions may reduce victimization, they may increase the level of fear in students by creating the perception that the school is unsafe. Rather than alleviate the problems, these actions may contribute to the adoption of debilitating self-protection measures.

An alternative approach to dealing with in-school victimization and debilitating student self-protective measures is to alter the environment of the school. Educators have suggested that schools need to engender order that relies more on consent than on coercion (Gaddy, 1988; Lunenburg, 1991). In essence, the argument is that the school needs to shift from attempts at imposing order to working with students, staff, administration, and the public in building a group response to school problems. This reflects what we in criminal justice refer to as developing a "normative" approach to law and control. Lab and Clark (1996) demonstrate that schools with lower levels of victimization are those that rely more on responses that include students as part of the solution, as opposed to seeing a need to simply control and discipline students.

What then are we suggesting as the direction for crime prevention in schools? In general, there is a need to build responses that are conducive to learning and education, rather than to control and coercion. A number of directions should be pursued. First, as suggested above, schools should include students in the identification of problems and potential solutions, and implementation of the solutions. This is not unlike the basic ideas underlying community-oriented policing, wherein the police rely on the public to identify the problems and participate in addressing the issues. Unlike the police who have recognized that they cannot solve problems alone, too many schools and administrators still believe that coercing compliance is the appropriate way to address problems.

Second, schools need to look toward interventions that avoid making the school look like an armed camp or a battlefield. This means that guards, metal detectors, dogs, locks, and alarms should be made secondary to peer mediation programs, student courts, student and parent participation in rule setting, conflict resolution, and similar programs. Success with the latter types of intervention will negate the need for the former.

Third, while many commentators argue that the school reflects the community in which it sits, schools must take action independent of whatever efforts may occur outside their doors. For example, weapons are not manufactured at school and gangs do not appear just in the school setting. Weapons must be available to youths outside of school before they can be brought to school and the gangs exist independent of the schools. Schools implementing programs such as those suggested above will contribute to changes that potentially impact on the entire commmunity, not just the school. The fact is that schools are faced with problems that also confront the larger community. Consequently, solving the problems in school may contribute to changes outside the school. Rather than engender an armed camp atmosphere, prevention efforts should focus on more constructive responses to crime and victimization.

CONCLUSION

This paper has demonstrated that the extent of victimization in schools, while not as rampant as often portrayed in the media, is large enough to cause concern among the public, school administrators, and students. Even more problematic is the extent to which students respond to both direct and indirect victimization in debilitating ways. While fear, avoidance, and carrying weapons are logical responses to victimization, they are not conducive to the educational mission of schools. Unfortunately, common school responses to victimization and crime may exacerbate student feelings that they need to take such self-protective actions. We suggest that schools need to alter their approach to solving crime related problems from the typical coercive/control responses to approaches that produce an environment more supportive of the school's educational mission.

NOTE

[1]   This research was supported under award #93-IJ-CX-0034 from the National Institute of Justice, Office of Justice Programs, U.S. Department of Justice. Points of view in this paper are those of the authors and do not necessarily represent the official position of the U.S. Department of Justice.

INTRODUCTION TO CHAPTER 9

In the next paper, Tim Hope shifts our attention from the more recognized crime prevention issues and moves into the debate on making more fundamental changes in society as a means of combatting crime. The economic realities of modern communities serve to concentrate crime, unemployment, disenfranchisement, broken families, a lack of political power, and other problems into enclaves in which crime is often allowed to flourish, provided it does not threaten the rest of society. This situation presents a number of problems. Foremost for traditional crime prevention is the inability to identify leaders and constituents in those areas who are willing and able to organize the residents for crime prevention.

Indeed, the structural inequality that exists in society may inhibit the development of interventions that can effectively deal with social problems. As a consequence of inequality, the larger community can choose various responses to address the crime problem in different neighborhoods. These can range from providing a gentle helping hand in low crime communities, to increased criminal justice intervention with offenders, to working with "at-risk" individuals, to symbolically sealing off the problem areas from the rest of the community. The most fundamental point at which a change could occur would entail efforts to alter the economic structure that contributes to crime. Hope notes that it takes a great deal of political will to deal with these root causes of the crime problem. Instead, "governments . . . place their faith in the mechanisms of social control—to bolster the fugitive utopia of the truly advantaged while increasing the containment of the truly disadvantaged."

Hope's paper clearly offers a different perspective for crime prevention. Rather than deal with problems at a situational level, his analysis suggests that more basic social changes need to be considered. In one sense, crime and victimization are no longer the problem. They are merely symptoms of a problem. It therefore becomes our task to identify the root cause (in this case structural inequality) and seek methods for dealing with that issue. Successfully solving the root problem would eliminate the symptoms and erase the need to address the surface concerns of crime, victimization, and fear.

9

Inequality and the Future of Community Crime Prevention

Tim Hope
Keele University

Some years ago, the American criminologist Lamar Empey wrote:

> For most people, the idea of crime prevention is attractive. To the traditionalist, it bespeaks a kind of fugitive Utopia in which the citizenry is protected from the ravages of human predation by a vigilant and efficient system of social control. To others, the utopian society would be one in which each individual is given a stake in conformity and thereby rendered unlikely to become delinquent or criminal (Empey, 1977:92).

The polarity between the external control of deviant behavior and the internalization of social norms lies at the heart of crime prevention discourse. Yet for some time now, the pursuit of social control has dominated crime prevention policymaking and practice (O'Malley, 1992). Underpinning crime prevention has been the coercive power of the agencies of criminal justice to supervise and deter behavior, even if the primary mechanisms for delivering this power are now seen as the multifarious agencies of civil society (Home Office et al., 1990)—and the preferred techniques, those that modify the environments of everyday life (see Clarke, 1995; Felson, 1994). At the same time, the pursuit of social and economic policy by other parts of government has not helped, and may even have undermined, the capacity of the "intermediate institutions" of civil society—including the family, school, and the local community—to provide a new generation, especially of the disadvantaged, with a stake in conformity sufficient to promote internalized self-controls over unlawful actions and, particularly, over the victimization of others.

This fundamental paradox may be having a disastrous impact on community life in economically disadvantaged areas, not the least of which is fostering the growth of crime and disorder. It is the poor who suffer most, and whose meager resources for communal self-regulation have been progressively undermined. In this chapter, I want to sketch how this paradox has arisen in contemporary Britain, concluding with some possible futures for community crime prevention in light of the scenario drawn from the contemporary evidence about the distribution of crime.[1]

PROBLEMS WITH THE PRESENT PARADIGM

Much community crime prevention effort during the past two decades has sought, by one means or another, to generate *informal social control*—that is, the self-regulation of crime within the community without invoking the direct intervention of the state. In earlier approaches, particularly in the work of Clifford Shaw and Henry McKay, community social control was held to emerge from the development of indigenous institutions, with the active involvement of residents in building local organizations, including schools, social clubs, churches, political groups, trade unions, friendly and co-operative societies, and so on. Such organizations would provide both community self-help, linkages to wider economic resources, and, particularly important for the control of crime, also serve as agencies through which adults would socialize with youth (Bursik & Grasmick, 1993; Hope, 1995a).

During the 1970s, however, this institution-building approach to community development and socialization gave way to a more specifically behavioral approach emphasizing the *surveillance* of crime and disorder (Cohen, 1985; Hope, 1995a). This model sought to encourage a sense of community defense amongst residents so that they would be able to exert control over criminal behavior in their neighborhood. A range of means were suggested to achieve these ends—for example, the creation of "defensible space" and improved dwelling security, estate clean-up and maintenance programs directed at vandalism and disorder, local housing management initiatives, neighborhood watch, community policing, and, most importantly for the public sector, the active involvement of residents in the affairs of their communities. While the common thread running through these programs has been to organize communities so that they will be able to solve their own problems (cf. Kornhauser, 1978), these have been defined, primarily, as the threat of predation to private life and property (Currie, 1988; Hope, 1995a; Wilson, 1985).

This is not the place for an exhaustive review of the achievements or failings of the considerable effort invested in crime prevention in high crime communities over the past two decades.[2] However, I want to highlight three general problems that have afflicted many recent efforts to organize poor communities to exercise this kind of control over local crime.

Implanting Control

First, there is what has become known as the *implant problem*. It would seem that, almost universally, anti-crime activities are least likely in low-income, heterogeneous, deteriorated, renting, high-turnover, high-crime areas (Skogan, 1988b). Mutual suspicion and lack of trust in high-crime communities undermine community anti-crime efforts, particularly those like Neighborhood Watch that require members to exchange information about themselves (Podolefsky & DuBow, 1981). The implant problem is double-sided: not only will few people be inclined to participate if there are no available opportunities to do so, but people also may not voluntarily organize themselves to attain the collective goal of defense in which trust is absent (Hope, 1995a).

One feature that may deter residents of high-crime areas from organizing against crime is perhaps less any general sense of anomie than the particular *social fragmentation* of their communities. An unfortunate consequence of the general failure to define "disorganization" in social disorganization theory (Bursik, 1988; Kornhauser, 1978) has been to foster an image of high-crime neighborhoods as atomized collections of isolated households. Yet, typically, ethnographic research in most kinds of communities—including high-crime areas—has often found strong primary links between residents and has repeatedly failed to find evidence of widespread interpersonal isolation (see Hope, 1995a). Nevertheless, while there may be neighborliness, there may no *neighborhood-ism*—no sense of membership of the community as a whole. Taken from survey data, Table 9.1 shows a high degree of neighborly trust coexisting with a substantial absence of community cohesion in four English social housing areas with above average rates of crime (see Foster & Hope, 1993, Table 3).

Although residents still see their neighbors and local friends as a source of mutual support, such networks may not extend across residential areas—more likely, the community is fragmented into small groups who know little about each other and have very little incentive to get involved with those "strangers" amongst their fellow residents, whom they perceive, alternatively, to be potentially dangerous (cf. Merry, 1981). In other words, there may be a lack of "closure" in the social networks that span a neighborhood (Coleman, 1990). And, in the absence of closure, it becomes difficult for a community to maintain social norms (Coleman, 1990) or to organize itself collectively (Granovetter, 1973).

Neighborhood Stigma

The second problem that has arisen in the experience of community crime prevention is the effect of *neighborhood stigma*. For instance, the residents of "problem" estates in Britain are acutely aware of the stigma attaching to them by virtue of where they live (Reynolds, 1986)—a stigma that affects how they are perceived in the wider community. While the effects of stigma might once have been thought to have been experienced through the allocative and dispositional decisions of welfare state professionals in housing, welfare, and juvenile justice (Gill, 1977), nowadays its consequences may be even more profound, especially in the context of a "free" housing market in which area reputation becomes an important element of market valuation. Once acquired, stigma may not only become difficult to shake-off, but may also set in motion a process that becomes self-fulfilling. As a community's reputation deteriorates, existing residents try to move and those prospective residents with any choice as to where to live go elsewhere. Importantly, migration into and out of the community is selective—those with personal resources, from whom community activists and leaders might once have been drawn, tend to move away; those with many personal problems, including a desperate need for housing, are the only ones willing to move in. This problem—at one time known as the problem of the "sink estate"—has been apparent in Britain certainly since the postwar expansion of mass public housing (Wilson, 1963).

Table 9.1
Neighbourliness and Community on Four English
High Crime Council Housing Estates (percentages)

	Estate 1	Estate 2	Estate 3	Estate 4
Talk to, or are friendly with, two or more neighbours	51	60	52	67
Friends with two or more households on estate	63	67	57	55
Neighbours now keep watch on property when out	62	69	66	55
"Most people on estate go their own way" (percent agree)	73	62	53	60
Household members do not belong to any voluntary organisation	60	65	65	55
Household members belong to one or more organisations that meet on the estate	14	10	8	19
BASE	578	480	242	382

The market stigmatization of poor neighborhoods entails a cruel irony. Not only does it affect decisionmakers' allocation of resources, but it also conditions residents' own actions, even when they are able to muster the ability to organize themselves to bid for more resources. Logan and Molotch (1987) draw attention to the "iron law of community upgrading." That is, indigenous community groups are swayed by the powerful incentives of the market to preserve, if not increase, the "exchange value" of their neighborhood as it is judged by outsiders (Skogan, 1988b)—whether by government agencies bestowing resources, commercial investment interests, or prospective residents (see Taub et al., 1984). Given these incentives, it may not be surprising that the activists in community groups generally want to discourage those whom they perceive to be lowering the value of their neighborhood (Logan & Molotch, 1987:145). In particular—and quite realistically in terms of the way that neighborhood stigmatization operates—those who seem to be deviant or troublesome come to be seen by their neighbors as the cause of the estates" unpopularity and lowered value. Stigmatized neighborhoods in a market society face the dilemma of excluding their troublesome members, or being themselves excluded.

Residential Mobility

A third problem for community crime prevention is that of *residential mobility*. The theory of the link between community social disorganization and crime emphasizes the destabilizing and disintegrative consequences of social mobility for attempts to build community cohesion (Bursik & Grasmick, 1993). The effect of selective mobility was vividly illustrated in our evaluation of the effect of a decentralized housing management initiative (the Priority Estates Project) on one public housing estate in the English city of Hull (Hope, 1995b; Hope & Foster, 1992; Foster & Hope, 1993). In a part of the estate in which the local housing authority had installed fencing, extended gardens, and generally created more "defensible space," resident satisfaction improved, feelings of territoriality increased, and tenant turnover and the rate of burglary reduced considerably. Similarly, in another part of the estate, despite an increase in poverty, the efforts of PEP seemed to have encouraged tenant involvement and a sense of empowerment, and to have stabilized the level of burglary, despite its increase elsewhere. Nevertheless, the rate of turnover here remained high and constant—an exchange of about one-quarter of the residents over three years. Moreover, in a further part of the estate, the arrival of younger, poorer residents precipitated a cataclysmic departure of the previous population—some 44 percent left in the space of three years—and a concentration of victimization in their particular residential area (Hope, 1995b).

Summary

Paradoxically, the implantation of informal social control into high-crime communities depends on there being most of the ingredients of community already present. The assumption of the past two decades has been that what was needed was to find a way of unlocking the latent communal sentiment that had been impeded—whether by housing design, poor management, anonymity, or lack of community organization—from expressing itself. Yet our experience now suggests that this supposedly latent community is no longer, or only tenuously, present. And if it does exist, it is only at the very private level of neighborliness. Not surprisingly, high-crime communities are likely to be unstable, socially fragmented, and riven with deep mistrust, not only from the wider society but also of itself.

CRIME AND INEQUALITY

The political discourse on "social exclusion" is in part an attempt to respond to two structural trends in post-industrial society: structural unemployment and the spatial concentration of poverty. Analysts such as William Julius Wilson in the United States have cast the debate about the "underclass" in spatial form—that the development of "ghetto" culture is fostered specifically by structural conditions that have concentrated poor people in certain neighborhoods (Wilson, 1987). It is this *concentration effect* of poverty that brings about and sustains cultural adaptations or behaviors regarding work, family, education, and crime (Sampson & Wilson, 1995)—and ultimately of participation within the polity—that others have associated with personal morality, or the perverse incentives of the welfare system (see also Lash & Urry, 1994; Morris, 1994).

Authoritative research carried out in Britain for the *Joseph Rowntree Foundation Inquiry into Income and Wealth* (JRF, 1995) has demonstrated a considerable growth in economic inequalities since the 1970s—a widening of the gap between rich and poor (Hills, 1996). In particular, this research shows an increasing spatial polarization of income and wealth, producing both a greater spatial segregation between better-off and poorer areas (Green, 1996), and a growth in spatially-concentrated poverty amongst communities within urban areas (Noble & Smith, 1996). It now turns out that the distribution of the victimization of private citizens between residential communities is likewise highly inequitable and has also become more spatially concentrated since the 1970s (Trickett et al., 1992; Trickett et al., 1995b).

A minority of crime victims, living in a minority of residential communities, suffer a substantially disproportionate amount of crime victimization. Table 9.2 suggests that one-fifth of the victims of household property crime who live in the top decile of areas, whose residents have the highest average rates, have *more than one-third* of the national total of household property crime (which itself constitutes just under one-half of all victimization recorded in the BCS). More than one-half of all property crime—and more than one-third of all property crime victims—are likely to be found in just one-fifth of the communities of England and Wales. Conversely, the least affected half of the country only experiences 15 percent of the crime, spread between one-quarter of victims. Respective shares of violent crime victimization are even more sharply drawn (Hope, 1996; Trickett et al., 1992).

Table 9.2
Local Area Distribution of Household Property Crimes
in England and Wales (percentages)

Area crime incidence rate rankings	Share of victims	Share of incidents
highest 10%	19	33
highest 20%	37	50
highest 50%	77	85
lowest 50%	23	15

Household property crimes include: burglary, theft from dwelling, other household theft, and criminal damage.

"Areas" are geographic clusters of BCS respondents aggregated by parliamentary constituency.

Source: 1992 British Crime Survey (weighted data)

The distribution of victims (i.e., prevalence) between areas differs significantly from random, and does so more dramatically the higher the victimization incidence rate. Yet consistently fewer people in each area are victimized than would be expected if crime were distributed randomly across areas (Trickett et al., 1992). Relative to their crime rates, proportionately fewer victims are victimized more frequently in the higher-crime areas, while the comparatively smaller number of victims in the lower-crime rate areas suffer less victimization than their counterparts in the higher-crime areas. Thus in high-crime areas, there is a *double concentration effect*—a spatial concentration of victims, being victimized at a greater frequency rate than in lower-crime rate areas. Further analysis of the British Crime Survey suggests that these concentration effects increased during the 1980s, with growing inequalities in the rate of victimization emerging between the neighborhoods and regions of England and Wales (Trickett et al., 1995a).

In addition to the frequency of victimization, there are two other features of the crime profile of high-crime areas. First, the concentration effect is most marked for the more serious offenses, particularly burglary and robbery (Hope & Hough, 1988). Second, it is also the case that residents in these areas perceive the level of disorder (Skogan, 1990) to be far more serious than in lower crime areas.[3] Both serious victimizations and less serious disorderly incidents in public seem to go hand-in-hand in the highest crime residential areas.

Recent multivariate statistical models of integrated data from the British Crime Survey and the decennial census indicate fairly conclusively that area characteristics are correlated with individual and household victimization risks (particularly for property crime), net of, and in addition to, other individual or household characteristics. From these analyses, a number of features of high property crime rate areas consistently stand out (Ellingworth et al., 1995; Osborn & Tseloni, 1995; Osborn et al., 1992; Osborn et al., 1996; Sampson & Groves, 1989; Sampson & Wooldredge, 1987; Trickett et al., 1995a; Trickett et al., 1995b):

- the *lack of economic resources* of neighborhood residents
- the predominance of *rental housing tenure*
- their *demographic structure*, including the size of the child, teenage, young adult, single parent household, and one-person household populations in the area

Importantly, the risk of victimization is increased for individual households not only if they live in areas with these characteristics, but also if they possess them themselves (Ellingworth et al., 1995; Osborn & Tseloni, 1995; Osborn et al., 1996; Trickett et al., 1995). Thus, notwithstanding the attractions to offenders of more affluent neighborhoods and targets for which there is also some support in these analyses, both the distribution of victimization and the characteristics of high-crime communities also suggest that crime victimization may be concentrating in residential areas alongside the concentration of poverty.

THE UNDERMINING OF COMMUNITY

Not surprisingly, residents in the highest-crime areas have high levels of worry about being victimized, low levels of satisfaction with their area, and little sense of community cohesion (Hope & Hough, 1988; Skogan, 1990)—none of which are likely to lead to community responses to crime, as noted above. In further analysis of the British Crime Survey, Sampson and Groves (1989) identified three aspects of community life in such areas that may undermine the ability of a community to control its own crime: first, the capacity of residents to supervise neighborhood teenage peer groups; second, the extent and strength of local social networks; and, third, the degree of organizational participation among residents. Each of these features has been increasingly undermined since the 1980s.

Young Male Peer Groups

High-crime areas are both economically disadvantaged and have concentrations of teenagers and young adults. The great weight of delinquency research tells us that much local crime and incivility involves local male youth in groups. Consistently, studies of delinquent development have shown that young men reach the peak of delinquent activity at the end of their period of compulsory schooling, or over the transition from school to work. Criminal activity declines in adulthood thereafter. Criminologists have typically ascribed the reasons for such "maturation" out of crime to the growth of a personal stake in conformity and a concomitant removal from delinquent peer activities (Sampson & Laub, 1993)—in which the risks or costs of crime start to outweigh the rewards. Notwithstanding punishment, the risks incurred by persistent involvement in crime after the mid-teenage years stem primarily from social approbation—failure to hold or secure a well-paid or steady job, failure to attract a marriage partner and care for a family, and moral censure from the local community. The rewards from conformity are the conventional ones of personal worth, material reward, collective participation, and social esteem.

If these resources for conformity to lawful behavior, or adherence to community norms, are removed, there seems little incentive for young men to grow out of crime, or to lose a taste for disorder. Hagan (1993) has termed this a process of *criminal embeddedness* that has been supported by analyses of classic longitudinal data sets of offender development (Hagan, 1993; Sampson & Laub, 1993). Criminal embeddedness is the converse of embeddedness in the conventional labor market. And high-crime communities may have features that embed more youths, more deeply, in crime and disengage them further from employment-based sources of conformity (Hagan, 1994; Sullivan, 1989). Thus, Loeber and Wikstrom (1993) found that boys living in areas of low socio-economic status were more likely than boys from other areas not only to engage in criminal activity, but also to engage more frequently, and in more serious offenses.

The failure of low-skilled young men to enter the job-market interacts with the availability of opportunities for illegitimate activities, including networks of others involved in offending, disposal of stolen goods, and other illegal activities such as drug-dealing. Continuing involvement in these activities embeds youths further into crime in their localities (Hagan, 1994). The impact of a concentration of benefit-dependent, low-skilled, poor youths on a community was evident in our study of the Priority Estates Project (Hope & Foster, 1992). Unemployed young people were able to find accommodation on one of the estates studied but had little benefit entitlement to support independent living, leading them to become involved in crime and drug-dealing to support themselves. In particular, the 18- to 25-year-olds formed a "demographic link" between delinquent teenage groups on the estate—who would hang out with them—and the local network of older adults involved in distributing stolen goods. Their arrival on the estate resulted in a bridging of the delinquent and criminal cultures, and widening and deepening of the local network of those involved in crime, which the remainder of the community found increasingly difficult to ignore or resist (Foster & Hope, 1993).

The crucial, collective factors that may embed young men in accelerating rates of local crime may include a lack of either formal or informal access to entry-level jobs in primary employment markets (McGahey, 1986), and the economic and social segregation of the community (Sullivan, 1989). Government welfare and employment policies may ameliorate or exacerbate the magnitude of the problem of young males' joblessness. In Britain, changes in social security benefit rules and training provisions may be helping the development of such criminogenic communities. While the government's intention to curtail the social security benefit entitlement of 16- to 17-year-olds in 1986 may have been to increase the incentives of young adults to seek training, its simultaneous failure to deliver quality jobs or places on training programs—despite a guarantee of a place for all—has created a substantial number of young people who have little means of attaining independent living. It is likely that many of those slipping through the jobs/training net will be youth already most susceptible to delinquency—and to trouble and exclusion from schooling—by virtue of their poor school performance or adverse home background (Graham & Bowling, 1995).

Finally, as is well-known, their communities may be becoming progressively detached from the economic mainstream, leading to disinvestment from employers, and a collapse of primary labor markets and routes into secure employment. As shown particularly in Sullivan's (1989) study of youth in Brooklyn neighborhoods, the ease of initial access to the primary labor market may be crucial in forestalling criminal embeddedness (Hagan, 1994). Thus, if as seems likely, low-skilled young people are increasingly to be found in high-crime areas, then the societal failure to provide a viable economic future for them will have the effect of retaining them at home and further reinforcing the concentration of poverty in their communities, and their consequent embeddedness in crime. Welfare and benefit traps may act as a multiplier in the process. Their only alternatives, then, may be homelessness on the streets—which has increased dramatically in recent years (Carlen, 1996), intermittent presence in the homes of parents or female contemporaries (Campbell, 1993) or, if they are "lucky," the offer of unlettable accommodations on an unpopular estate without, of course, the financial means to support themselves (Foster & Hope, 1993).

Families and Social Networks

High-crime communities have above average rates of both single-parent and single-adult households, and of children and teenagers. Female-headed households with dependent children are likely to experience considerable social isolation. Single-adult households often neither have the time nor the social contacts to invest in getting to know other residents. The absence of familiarity breeds fear and mistrust, and undermines the community's ability to work collectively together. Their isolation also renders them vulnerable as victims—

divorced or separated women, often in single parent households, consistently have very high levels of victimization from crime (Maxfield, 1987; Smith & Jarjoura, 1989) and threatening behavior (Tseloni, 1995).

Collectively, a large number of single-parent or adult-only households provide the community with relatively few adults capable of exercising meaningful guidance or supervision of local youth. The problem of family disruption for crime is not necessarily an individual one—many divorced or single-parent families may be able to guide their children adequately (Riley & Shaw, 1985). The community concentration of family disruption may be firstly, a problem for communities—particularly if it means an absence of a network of parents and significant adults who are able to give each other mutual support and reinforcement in guiding the behavior of local teenagers (Sampson, 1993; Sampson & Wilson, 1995); and secondly, a problem for individual families, who cannot draw on this reservoir of support in guiding their own children (Furstenberg, 1993).

The ecological concentration of high proportions of teenagers, young adults, and single-parent and lone-adult households is likely, in large measure, to have been a consequence of major transformations in the British housing market, especially those that have affected the provision of social housing. The operation of housing allocations, transfers, and discounted-purchase systems within social housing are no less market processes than those within the private sector—and have become more so in recent years (Forrest & Murie, 1988). The application of these specifically market-oriented policies have accompanied a progressive and rapid "residualization" of social housing—remaining tenants have become relatively poorer automatically, and new household formation in social housing—obviously involving younger adults—is restricted to those who are poor, homeless, or in other need, including the housing of children. Government and housing association survey data show that the concentration of poverty in social housing has increased dramatically since the early 1980s (Page, 1993:31). And because so much social housing in England is still concentrated on "estates" rather than spatially dispersed, the economic polarization of tenure "shows up on the ground as a concentration of people with low incomes in particular neighborhoods" (JRF, 1995, Volume 1:29).

Organizational Participation

Community organizations serve two purposes of social cohesion. On the one hand, they help in the *horizontal integration* of the community—they serve to express the mutual inter-dependencies among residents, providing a means and opportunity for mutual support and collective problem-solving. On the other hand, they facilitate the *vertical integration* of the community to wider economic and political resources (Hope, 1995a; Sampson, 1987). Without representational bodies, communities are disadvantaged in gaining additional resources for economic development, welfare support, or local policing. Increasingly, in a market-oriented society, those communities that are unable to bid for public resources for special projects and facilities may be losing the ability to call upon scarce external resources in their struggle to preserve social order in their neighborhoods.

The problem is symbiotic. On the one hand, without representation, the community cannot capture resources. On the other hand, without representatives to articulate demand, local agencies are disinclined to develop approaches to meet the specific needs of the community as a whole. Much of the experience of the administration of the welfare state in Britain has been that of the varying capacities of differing income groups to acquire disproportionate shares of benefits. Now, as increasing amounts of public resources necessary for urban investment are being allocated competitively through quasi-markets, social network fragmentation may be disabling the residents of high-crime communities from organizing themselves collectively to compete for area-based resources.

Resident involvement in local voluntary activities is a function of personal commitment, time, and resources. Members of economically secure, stable households are more able to generate the additional personal resources necessary for voluntary activity. However, it is precisely this group who are being drawn away from poor neighborhoods. In the United States, Wilson (1987) has argued that the problem of ghetto poverty concentration is partly due to the departure of middle-class black people from the inner city, leaving only the poor behind. In Britain, government policies of preferential sales of council homes to tenants may have been performing the same siphoning function (Forrest & Murie, 1988). The consequence of social selectivity in housing choice is that poor neighborhoods are not only increasingly concentrated in the social housing sector, but are also simultaneously deprived of the resources for community organization and leadership. And, as Wilson (1987) further argues, the removal of a "social buffer" of more stable and able residents not only deprives a community of those who can build community organizations, but also of positive role models for young people. Thus, the socializing purpose of community organization—that Clifford Shaw saw at the heart of the effort to counter social disorganization (Hope, 1995a)—is being undermined by the forces of the new competitive urban market.

FUTURES IN COMMUNITY CRIME PREVENTION

What are the prospects for community crime prevention given this scenario? In concluding, I want to sketch very briefly three alternative futures, some of which are already emergent as crime prevention strategies.

The Market Solution?

One possibility is simply to accept the imperatives of the market. This leaves to the government the task of ensuring that the emergent "market" in community safety does not fail. If the market has inequitably distributed between communities the social capital necessary to generate self-regulation over deviance then, in practice, the crime prevention task will involve a bifurcated strategy. On the one hand, for low-crime communities, the task becomes that of helping them to preserve their position. Recognizing that, if needed, they can generate resources for ensuring community safety in addition to those provided by the state (in the form of policing), the role of government would be to ensure that such communities were not impeded from attaining these ends, and that community resources were not dissipated. For example, Home Office analysts Laycock and Tilley (1995), in recognizing the success of the Neighborhood Watch organization in low-crime communities, argue that the role of the police should be to sustain its development in order to keep crime rates low. Facilitating these communities' ability to purchase extra prevention in the form of private security, or in recruiting volunteer patrols, would also form part of this approach.

On the other hand, it might be argued, if young men in high crime communities were choosing careers in crime then it would be the government's duty to meet the additional "demand for punishment" that was being generated in these areas. Thus, if the government was to arrange matters so that its apprehensive, incarcerative, and deterrent services worked efficiently, then, assuming these penalties bore on every individual criminal equally, the additional risk in high-crime communities would be met by an increase in the supply of punishment. Risks might then begin to reduce. Of course, for the government not to make disproportionate losses it would be prudent to ensure that the threat of punishment outweighed the actual delivery of arrest and incarceration, and that this was communicated effectively to high risk groups and communities. But if the costs of punishment escalated, the government would have to assess the marginal benefit achieved.

Much then might depend upon the extent to which the costs of unpunished crime spilled-over into the wider society, or could be contained—and borne—within the communities in which crime was being generated. That is, how much "externality" crime generated for high and low risk communities respectively.[4] On the one hand, it might be argued that if host communities did not bear much of the full costs of the crime their members were generating, then they would have less incentive themselves to take additional measures of crime prevention on behalf of society as a whole—for example, through parental discipline, the exclusion of troublesome families, or in bringing offenders to book. On the other hand, it might be argued that low crime communities also had less direct incentive to support crime prevention efforts that were primarily directed at reducing the risk in high crime areas, leaving the burden to be born by the state, or to go unaddressed.[5] Whatever the outcome, such actuarial calculations would become part of the governance of crime prevention by virtue of the logic of "prudentialism" (O'Malley, 1992) inherent in the market approach to dealing with inequality in the community distribution of community safety.

The Welfare Solution?

Another possibility is a "welfare" approach aimed at the alleviation and reduction of harm. In many respects, such an approach would be a simple extension of individualized welfare strategies. The approach would be aimed at doing something to or for "at-risk" individuals. In as much as high-rate individuals are seen as the "cause" of epidemics of crime in communities, the preventive approach would seek to limit the spread of the epidemic; for example by "inoculating" high-risk groups, such as "first-time victims," against the actuarial likelihood that they will be further victimized (Farrell & Pease, 1993), or by treating, isolating, or incapacitating those (high rate offenders) who are held responsible for spreading the disease. Reducing the frequency of victimization and offending by targeting preventive benefits (or penalties) on high-risk groups in the highest crime communities has appeal both on utilitarian grounds—by scheduling preventive resources so as to maximize the reduction in the national crime rate relative to effort expended (cf. National Board for Crime Prevention, 1994), and in terms of personal welfare by addressing specific needs.

The welfare approach requires both the conceptual and practical disaggregation of communities—high-crime areas are now just convenient locales in which prevention is to be concentrated. And there is no community-effect as such, other than the processes of social selection that bring high-risk groups together. Even then, the strategy depends upon its targeting efficiency, which in turn depends upon being able to predict high-risk groups. Yet research into criminal careers has failed on the whole to predict high-rate offenders, and so far the prediction of repeat victims has proven just as elusive (Osborn et al., 1996). The strategy requires prevention to *dis-embed* high-risk individuals from the social contexts that may be sustaining their risk, yet there is little guarantee that individuals could be so isolated or that others would not become high-risk in their stead. While the approach has some merit in addressing individual needs—especially of victimized groups—this does not necessarily mean that aggregate crime rates would be reduced.

The Institutional Solution?

Much of the foregoing analysis has suggested that the areal concentration of poverty has coincided with the areal concentration of crime victimization, and that crime may be the cost of structural inequality (Blau & Blau, 1982). Structural change and the redistribution of income and wealth notwithstanding, it is also clear that the contemporary patterns and experiences of concentrated poverty have severely undermined the capacity of poor neighborhoods to sustain or connect with social institutions capable of resisting the disassociative pressures of structural inequality and providing their members with a stake in conformity. The undermining of the community has engendered a victimizing culture in its place, biting hardest on the young and the economically marginal.

Political ideologies of the free market seem unable to recognize the socializing capacity of the institutions of the family, education, employment, and community, often preferring to see them merely as mechanisms for developing individual economic capital (Hutton, 1996). Yet without the social capital that such institutions generate, it becomes harder to sustain the bonds of community that in the absence of which victimization becomes an everyday response to the harsh problems of life. Facing this issue, Elliott Currie has argued that it is necessary to:

> . . . reaffirm the legitimacy of the . . . traditional idea of community *reconstruction* as the bedrock of community crime prevention; the idea that we confront crime most effectively by building communities that work, by strengthening local institutions so that they can better do their job of socialization, nurturance and support, by building stable community roles in work and family life into which we may guide the coming generations (1988:285).

Yet the outstanding issue remains that of political will, for the concentration of victimization we have been talking about here also implies its increasing containment in relatively few communities. And it is the temptation of governments, not seized by any sense of injustice on behalf of the disadvantaged, to place their faith in the mechanisms of social control—to bolster the fugitive utopia of the truly advantaged while increasing the containment of the truly disadvantaged. It remains to be seen how even the most prudent of governments calculate the relative advantage to the public good that is gained by addressing the "secession of the successful" (Robert Reich quoted in McKenzie, 1994) in preference to the exclusion of the disadvantaged. In the absence of a commitment to social justice, the alternative route of encouraging stake-holding in conformity may seem merely an old-fashioned piety from a less hard-headed era.

NOTES

[1]   Much of the supporting evidence in this paper is summarized in Hope (1995a, 1995b, 1996, and forthcoming) and Foster and Hope (1993), to which the reader is invited to refer for more detail.

[2]   I have attempted to review some of this literature elsewhere (Hope, 1995a), and the Safe Neighborhoods Unit has also produced a comprehensive overview of crime prevention initiatives in British public housing areas (Department of the Environment, 1993).

3   Analysis of residents' responses in the British Crime Survey to perceptions of disorder—i.e., graffiti, litter, teenagers on the streets, public drinking, etc.—shows that area victimization rates are much higher in areas where these problems are perceived as frequent or rated more seriously (Hope & Hough, 1988).

4   See Field and Hope (1990) for a discussion of the effects of externality costs in the consumption of crime prevention.

5   As one large British insurance company stated in an advertising campaign for domestic insurance: "only certain areas in the country qualify for special low-risk status . . . low risk areas are those that in our experience have a lower than average level of claims. Which means we can cut the costs of your insurance without cutting the cover. After all, *why should you subsidize higher risk areas?*" (Sun Alliance, 1995, reference P383AA, emphasis added).

INTRODUCTION TO CHAPTER 10

As noted in the opening chapter, crime prevention faces a number of challenges, including the necessity to compete in the political arena with alternative issues and concerns. Unfortunately, too often prevention efforts are secondary to more punitive, crime control approaches. This final paper addresses a political problem that faces all of criminal justice and social science—that being that too often the uninformed, poorly informed, and the "I don't want to be informed" make the key decisions and control public policy. Lavrakas illustrates this situation by examining the actions of national legislators and the news media as they relate to crime prevention. He argues that the lack of understanding by those in power serves to perpetuate the very problems they claim to be solving.

While the natural implication would be to blame "politics" for the existing crime policies, Lavrakas attributes much of the problem to the media. He does so for two basic reasons. First, the news media are typically not educated about criminal justice and crime policy. Second, the media do not hold politicians accountable for their actions or rhetoric. As a consequence, the public does not receive the information it needs to make informed decisions and the politicians can continue posturing for the uninformed public. What the public receives is a sanitized version of what is taking place through "sound bites" of catchy phrases. Lavrakas calls for educating the media (and politicians) about crime prevention, as well as demanding that more research be conducted on prevention initiatives. While not a panacea for removing politics from crime prevention, this suggestion would open the door for more informed decisionmaking and, possibly, place prevention on the level with deterrence and incapacitation.

10

Politicians, Journalists, and the Rhetoric of the "Crime Prevention" Public Policy Debate

Paul J. Lavrakas
The Ohio State University

On July 21, 1992, as the lead-in to the major in-depth story of that night's *CBS Evening News*, Dan Rather announced, "It's the job of the police to protect us from crime and to make us safe in our neighborhoods." Had this pronouncement been advanced 20 years ago, few might have questioned its validity. But since the enactment of the Omnibus Crime Control and Safe Streets Act of 1968, many billions of dollars have been spent on crime prevention programming, research, and evaluations in order to expand our concept of *how* public safety from crime is attained and maintained. Unfortunately, Mr. Rather, his writers, and producers—along with many other journalists— appeared not to have kept abreast of major developments in the fight against crime. And in not doing so, the media have contributed to the mostly bankrupt anti-crime public policies that politicians have been allowed for years to haphazardly devise and tout.

Since the 1960s, we have witnessed *no significant headway* in our nation's struggle to reduce the extent of serious crime and the extent of crime's impact on our nation's quality of life. This is not to say that no progress has been made, but by most informed accounts, the annual number and the seriousness of criminal victimization incidents has increased since the 1960s, with a proportionately greater increase experienced in the public's adverse reactions to crime (e.g., personal fear). Furthermore, it is likely that billions of dollars are spent annually by home and personal security industries on advertising and product development, and by consumers in a quest to enhance their own security, that of their families, their neighborhoods, and their businesses. Yet, despite this considerable commitment of resources by both the public and private sectors to "fight crime," no meaningful improvement has been realized. Why has this happened?

In my view, a large part of the blame falls on politicians and the news media, both of whom appear to be sorely misinformed about what must be done to achieve meaningful improvement in the level of safety experienced by the citizenry. I say that politicians and journalists appear to be misinformed because if one reviews the discourse that surrounds the public policy debate about crime in the past few decades, one will conclude that neither most politicians nor most journalists appear to have a clue about what effective "crime fighting" is. In a nutshell: they appear unaware of, or at least unwilling to act upon, the reality that *a society cannot reduce crime without preventing it* and that *reactive measures do not prevent crime*.

A recent example is the 1994 federal anti-crime legislation that was debated by Congress and signed by President Clinton in September, 1994. This legislation allocated less than one-fourth of the funding to crime prevention measures, many of which were supported more for political reasons than because they were expected to actually be effective against crime. Furthermore, the giant prison allocation in the 1994 bill is itself an indicator of the basic failure of past anti-crime policies. Despite these failures, elected officials are allowed to pontificate to an ill-informed public about how they—the politicians—are helping to reduce our crime problems with these types of expenditures.

POLITICIANS AND JOURNALISTS

Too often the roles of elected officials and the news media are ignored in studies of "anti-crime" policy. However, it is my contention that the "business as usual" role of both politicians and journalists actually *interferes substantially* with our nation's ability to make meaningful progress in "fighting crime."

In saying this, I am suggesting that the vast majority of anti-crime public policy "solutions" that are funded at the federal level are ineffectual when it comes to actually reducing crime problems. A vicious cycle occurs: as politicians put more and more money into programs that do not work, crime problems escalate and the message is sent that more and more harsh and severe attacks on crime and criminals are needed.

In advancing this critique, I do not regard myself as a bleeding-heart liberal who blames society for the crimes that are committed, for example, by disadvantaged youth. I hold each and every criminal offender responsible and culpable for her or his own actions and their consequences. However, if our anti-crime public policy were far less reactive and more proactive, I am certain that we could slowly begin to see a society-wide improvement.

If politicians were held much more accountable for the successes and failures of the programs they fund, they might be more motivated to sponsor programs that are likely to have real effects on crime, rather than only having politically expedient "public relations" effects.

That politicians are not held accountable for what I consider to be the misguided anti-crime policies we have witnessed during the past 30 years is due, in part, to the poor performance of the news media. The media profess to serve society as our watchdog on government by making public the deliberations and actions of elected and appointed officials and, thereby, educating the citizenry and holding these officials accountable. However, for the most part, what I see is lazy journalism that reports on form much more than substance; one that turns away criticism of the nature that I am advancing with empty arguments, such as "we don't make news, we only report it . . ."

A CONCEPTUAL FRAMEWORK FOR ADVANCING AND ANALYZING ANTI-CRIME POLICY

My basic premise in this chapter is that neither politicians—at least as manifested by the legislation they pass and by their public comments—nor journalists understand what effective "crime fighting" entails. They do not understand what crime *prevention* actually means, and how it differs from crime *control*. And, in not understanding that crime must be "prevented," not merely "controlled," in order for crime to be "reduced," elected officials and journalists inadvertently perpetuate the very crime problems against which they profess to be working.

What is lacking for both politicians and the news media is a conceptual framework that would provide them with an understanding of which "anti-crime" policies and measures are likely to be effective against crime in a free society and which are not. I have proposed such a framework in the past to help plan anti-crime programs and public policy (e.g., Lavrakas, 1985; Lavrakas, 1995: Lavrakas & Bennett, 1988). This framework also provides a structure for analyzing the discourse that makes up the anti-crime public policy debate as is done later in this paper.

Of note, Lab (1992) correctly observed that prior to his own textbook, *Crime Prevention: Approaches, Practices and Evaluations*, first published in 1988, no scholarly treatise had been devoted exclusively to the topic of crime prevention. Granted there were some books titled "crime prevention" (e.g., Washnis, 1976), but these were limited mostly to describing what the police did to react to crime and to encourage citizens to secure their homes. Thus, despite what many may assume, there has not been a long history of critical thinking about what "preventing crime" really means. Lavrakas and Bennett (1988) described a framework for guiding the implementation of citizen and community anti-crime measures. This framework consisted of a hierarchy similar to the public health model of prevention that differentiates among primary, secondary, and tertiary levels of preventive action. It can be noted that although Lab (1992) and Brantingham and Faust (1976) advanced a "conceptual model of crime prevention" with similarly labeled levels, the substance of their models is quite different from the framework described herein, and those conceptualizations do not appear as explicitly proposed to aid policy formulation as does the more "public health" type model described below.

As background to the framework that I discuss below, I first propose to the reader that it is helpful to think about the rhetoric that accompanies public discourse on anti-crime policy as falling into three broad types of categories: (1) reactive policies/measures, (2) preventive policies/measures, and (3) symbolic policies/measures. What politicians and journalists call "fighting crime" can include any of these measures, as the phrase is used carelessly to include any effort that sounds as though it is against crime. The problem is that some of the policies and measures can reasonably be expected to be effective in reducing the crime problems facing the nation, at least in principle, whereas others cannot.

Reactive measures, including those that traditionally have been used by law enforcement agencies to control crime, e.g., arresting suspected offenders, do just that—they control crime, but do not reduce it. The *symbolic measures* are those politically expedient gestures that politicians have used to placate an irate, but typically uninformed citizenry; such as measures in the 1994 crime bill that ostensibly try to reduce illegal immigration by trying to penalize illegal immigrants once they are here. These symbolic measures let politicians sound "tough" even though the measures cannot reasonably be expected to have an actual impact on crime's magnitude or severity. It is only *preventive measures* (e.g., recreation programs for youth; citizen neighborhood patrols coordinated with local law enforcement agencies; increased outdoor lighting around residences; and many others) that provide a means whereby crime can be logically *reduced*.[1]

However, this reality has not been understood by the news media or, apparently, by many politicians. Thus, we find the media reporting about everything that politicians claim needs to be done to address the crime problem, as though every one of these measures is an effective anti-crime strategy. Rather than exercising proper discretion and labeling empty political rhetoric about crime for what it is, the news media tend to report it uncritically. In this way, politicians are not held accountable and the public learns nothing about the emptiness of many of the crime-related pronouncements of its political leadership. Rather than advancing the citizenry's knowledge about what is likely to be effective in reducing crime, and thereby helping to empower the public to hold their elected officials accountable, the news media mostly distribute "easy news" about crime that does nothing to help anti-crime policy.

The following is a theoretical framework for thinking about ways to *prevent*, and thereby *reduce*, crime. The premise that underlies this framework is that citizens are at least partially, if not primarily, responsible for their own safe daily existence and that of their families and local communities. A corollary of this premise is that in a democracy, the police and other criminal justice agencies should *not* be viewed as the primary mechanism through which crime can be *prevented*, although I believe they should play an important and central role (cf. Lavrakas, 1985, 1995). This corollary follows, in part, from my assumption that as a free society we are—and I hope we will be able to remain—*unwilling* to hire so many criminal justice personnel so as to saturate our public and private areas in order to stop all or even most instances of criminality from occurring. And, if we do not want to live in a highly militarized and restricted society that relies upon its police to "prevent" crime, then very significant changes must occur in how our leaders, citizens, and the media think about *crime prevention*.

For their part, the police did not perceive and/or acknowledge soon enough their limitations in the struggle to prevent crime. To this day, too many rank and file police personnel are ignorant about how crime is likely to be prevented, even though many of these same individuals behave as though they are "crime prevention experts." On a more positive note, the majority of U.S. police chiefs and sheriffs appear to have begun to "see the light" by acknowledging the need for collaboration with a host of other agencies and institutions outside their departments to marshal viable comprehensive local crime prevention efforts (Lavrakas & Rosenbaum, 1989).

To begin reasoned deliberations about what is needed, one should have a framework to conceptualize what "prevention of crime" and "crime prevention" really mean. As noted above, the crime prevention framework I advance consists of a hierarchy similar to the public health model of prevention that differentiates among primary, secondary, and tertiary levels of preventive action.

Primary Prevention

Primary crime prevention is *proactive and preventive in the most basic sense*, in that it encompasses strategies that occur prior to anyone even contemplating the commission of a crime. Primary crime prevention includes *all efforts that strive to keep individuals from developing into criminal offenders*. It aims at many of the so-called "root causes" of crime, such as poverty, lack of education, discrimination, hatred, the need for immediate gratification, and anomie (cf. Currie, 1988; Silberman, 1978; Wilson & Herrnstein, 1985).

Examples of primary crime prevention include efforts to raise the educational level of all members of society so as to make them qualified for noncriminal employment. Job training programs, particularly ones targeted at raising the marketable skill levels of members of the underclass (cf. Curtis, 1988), should be regarded as primary crime prevention. Companion to these efforts are ones that strive to provide equal opportunities for employment to all qualified individuals. In this vein, affirmative action programs meant to redress past hiring inequities logically can be viewed as a form of primary crime prevention to the extent that they succeed in developing positive social behaviors in program participants.

Beyond government-sponsored programs, but no less important, are the myriad efforts that other public and private sector institutions contribute. Religious denominations strive to impart and nurture prosocial moral values to their members and to society at large. Schools offer education and recreation programs to turn children away from crime. Health care professionals provide services that promote the physical and mental well-being of the populace. A multitude of voluntary service organizations try to help those who are unable, at least temporarily, to help themselves lead a better life. This is not "liberal pap" as some of our conservative demagogues would have the public believe. This is the way that crime is prevented at a primary level.

Primary crime prevention is the most important level at which the war on crime and drugs in a democracy must be fought. Unfortunately, American politicians and other so-called leaders have not provided the necessary vision to move the country in this needed direction. To date, there has been no truly comprehensive and coordinated effort to marshal a primary level crime prevention campaign in which the police, although important, are one of the players in a large cast of characters.

Secondary Prevention

Crime prevention at a secondary level refers to *proactive measures that prevent specific instances of, or opportunities for, potential threat from developing into instances of actual criminal victimization.* Secondary crime prevention measures are important as they are based upon the realistic premises that the potential for crime is ever-present and measures can and should be taken to strengthen the "resistance" of individuals and property from being victimized. Secondary crime prevention measures strive to minimize the likelihood that specific criminal acts will be initiated at a particular time and in a particular place.

It should be noted that a logical criticism of all secondary level measures is that they may merely "displace" crime from one time or place to another (cf. Maltz, 1972). Unlike primary crime prevention measures, secondary-level measures do not attack the forces and motives that lead individuals to commit crimes except in the crudest sense by "reducing opportunities" for crime. (It is in this latter context that secondary crime prevention measures include all those that have been labeled *opportunity-reduction* strategies.) It is assumed that, if the risk of apprehension and punishment is great enough, would-be offenders will be deterred from committing specific crimes. To the extent that there are few low-risk opportunities for crime, it is theorized that potential criminals will be diverted away from crime and toward activities that enhance society.

Examples of secondary crime prevention abound. When individuals voluntarily restrict their behavior, such as staying in their homes at night rather than going out to shop, they are eliminating the chance that they will be present in the outdoor neighborhood environment and "available" to fall victim to robbery or assault. This is secondary-level crime prevention because it is proactive and intended to minimize the likelihood that an individual will become a crime victim.

When residents "target-harden" their homes through the use of locks, security systems, and such, they are engaging in secondary crime prevention. By creating physical barriers to would-be offenders, target-hardening strategies aim to increase the effort and risk involved in the commission of a crime and thereby deter the would-be offender away from a specific target. Increasing the amount and intensity of outdoor lighting also is meant to reduce the perceived opportunity for committing an easy crime in as much as it increases the chances of being observed by someone who might call the police. The use of timers and indoor lighting to give the appearance of home-occupancy is thought to create a psychological barrier to the would-be burglar who does not want to confront a resident.

Organized community-level strategies, such as Neighborhood Watch and citizen patrols, can also be forms of secondary crime prevention—providing their effect is to increase the level of surveillance performed by law-abiding citizens and thereby discouraging offenders from finding easily victimized targets. These strategies are also thought to signal a higher degree of social control on the part of residents that is presumed to further deter would-be offenders.

Tertiary Prevention

There are other responses to crime that are *purely reactive* in that they strive to minimize the severity of loss when specific crimes are threatened or initiated. (An example in the public health field of tertiary-level prevention would be surgery, radiation, or chemotherapy for a cancer victim *after* the disease is manifest.) Tertiary crime prevention measures include self-protection strategies such as martial arts training or carrying a concealed weapon. Since these measures typically do not manifest themselves until after the onset of threat—such as, nowadays people do not carry handguns in plain sight to signal potential offenders that they are well-armed (which would be a secondary level of prevention)—they are preventive only in the sense that they may reduce the seriousness of the outcome of an attempted victimization for the potential victim (although in some cases a victim's own weapons may be turned against her or him and lead to greater harm).

WhistleSTOP, a community anti-crime program developed in the 1970s, is a tertiary level prevention effort. Carrying a high-pitched whistle to blow if one is threatened, or if one witnesses someone else being victimized, does nothing to reduce the likelihood of a specific criminal victimization attempt, but may "prevent" the offender from succeeding. Personal injury and personal property insurance serve the purpose of "loss reduction." That is, insurance is preventive at a tertiary level because, at best, it reduces the severity of one's financial loss to criminal victimization.

Deterrence

Where do the so-called deterrence measures—such as harsh and certain punishment for convicted offenders—fit into this framework? The rationale supporting these measures suggests that punishment sends a clear and powerful "signal" to would-be offenders about the certainty and seriousness of their punishment, and thereby deters (prevents) them from committing (more) crimes. However, decades of scientific research and practical experience shows the inadequacy of punishment in a free society to motivate pro-social behavior. Although it can be argued that punishment is justice served, it should not be argued that it is crime *prevention*.

Summary

Anyone developing a comprehensive crime prevention program must rely heavily upon the potential impact that law-abiding citizens can have on the amount of crime that exists in a given geographic area. Otherwise, a program would require far too many tax dollars to achieve the political support that is needed for its approval and implementation. In the American society of the late twentieth century and early twenty-first centuries, the resources that must be mustered to make meaningful headway in the war on crime and drugs are so massive that I believe the only hope is to tap the volunteer potential of the citizenry. This amount of untapped resources will dwarf the amount of tax dollars that our governing bodies can provide (cf. Lavrakas, 1989).

To improve the chances for success in increasing citizens' participation in crime prevention, a comprehensive plan must take into account the levels of crime prevention and the varied motives that lead citizens to get (and stay) involved in anti-crime behaviors. The discussion presented in this section has meant to acquaint the policy-oriented reader with the complexities that must be considered.

With this framework in mind, let me proceed to an analysis of the discourse from, and news coverage of, one of our federal government's legislative efforts to "fight" our nation's crime problems.

CONTENT ANALYSIS OF NEWS COVERAGE OF 1994 ANTI-CRIME BILL

The analytic approach I took for reviewing past anti-crime political rhetoric and journalistic coverage was a systematic and critical content analysis of the news coverage of the congressional debate that occurred in the summer of 1994 concerning the 1994 anti-crime bill. For this content analysis, I used coverage that appeared in the *New York Times* in 1994 between mid-July and the end of September. This covered the period from the first congressional

accord between the House and the Senate negotiators that was reached on the
1994 crime bill, through the eventual signing of the bill by President Bill Clinton in September, 1994. My choice of the *New York Times* was based on its
reputation as the nation's foremost and definitive daily news coverage of public
policy debates.

The *Times* carried 41 articles on the 1994 crime bill on 21 days of this
75-day period. In four-fifths of the days (81%) that an article on the crime bill
was carried, a news story about the bill received Page One placement, with the
article being the *Times'* lead story on eight of the 21 days. In all, of the 41
news stories and opinion pieces about the crime bill, all but two ran in August.
It was these 41 articles that served as the basis of my analysis.

In reviewing the evolution of the congressional debate on the crime bill in
August, 1994, it became quickly apparent to me that political rhetoric and
media reporting of the debate was framed as the "three Ps": Prevention,
Police, and Punishment. The Prevention side of the debate was associated with
various social programs that were aimed mostly at so-called "root causes" of
crime, such as job training and recreational programs directed at high-risk
youth and young adults. The Police side was primarily intended to provide
initial funding for the hiring of 100,000 additional police officers through the
end of the decade and for their deployment in community policing type programs. The Punishment side included a number of "get tough" measures, such
as several billion dollars to build more prisons, expanding the availability of
the death penalty for federal crimes, reduced privacy rights for accused and
convicted sex offenders, and more certain sentencing rules for offenders with
previous convictions.

Across the 41 news stories, prevention and punishment measures were
mentioned or discussed in 80 percent of the stories, whereas police measures
were mentioned or discussed in only 40 percent. This difference was due to
there being more disagreement in Congress over the prevention and punishment measures than about the police measures, and *as too often is the case, it
was the disagreement that became the main news story the* Times *chose to
report, not the substantive merit of the various "anti-crime" measures.*

From the 41 news articles, one can see that the then-Democratic majori-
ties in Congress were out maneuvered by the Republican minorities in both
houses, with the Republicans taking control of and framing the nature of the
debate. (At least that was the way the debate was presented in the *New York
Times,* and there is no reason to suspect the *Times* of a pro-Republican bias in
covering this, or any, policy debate.) The Republicans quickly jumped upon the
theme that the prevention programs were nothing more than misguided social
welfare and political "pork" for big city mayors that would do nothing good in
the fight against crime. Slogans like "hug-a-thug" were used by Republicans to
belittle these types of (primary) prevention measures. The battle over the value
of prevention programs was won by the Republicans in that there were nearly

three times as many negative references in the *Times'* news stories *about what was wrong with the prevention programs* as there were positive references as to why these prevention programs would/should be effective.

The Republicans also showed themselves to the champions of the punishment side of the debate, and again controlled the discourse over these types of alleged "crime fighting" strategies with there being *three times more positive references* in the news stories *about the value of the punishment programs* compared to the number of negative references about these programs as being ineffectual as anti-crime strategies.

Of note, few of the news stories mentioned anything positive or negative about the proposed enhancements to policing. Also, few stories mentioned pros or cons about the proposed ban on assault weapons, that was also a part of the debate.

However, the most compelling conclusion I draw from analyzing these 41 news stories is the *near total absence of informed opinion about which measures are likely to reduce the nation's crime problem and which are not*. In one instance, there was even an explicit reference to the absence of such substantive information when the *Times* quoted Congressman Henry Hyde (Rep-IL) in noting the dearth of expert testimony presented to aid Congress' deliberations. Hyde said, "Some of these social programs may be marvelous, but I would like to have some semblance of orderly process to have some experts testify who would say, 'Yes, we need this.'"

In reviewing the discourse reported in the *Times*, it can be seen again and again that the Democrats and those supporting the bill's prevention measures were completely inept in countering the political posturing of the Republicans, who consistently linked crime prevention with wasteful and failed liberal social engineering. Nowhere was there any report from criminal justice scholars providing expert perspectives on what the most effective allocation of funds to prevent crime might be.

Granted, it is possible that some of this type of dialogue may have been introduced by the supporters of the prevention measures, but if it was introduced, it apparently did not impress the *New York Times'* news staff enough to appear in their news coverage. Rather, it was only after President Clinton signed the 1994 bill into law that the *Times*, in its wrap-up article about the legislation, contacted a few prominent criminologists for expert perspectives on the likely effectiveness of the bill's measures to reduce the nation's crime problems.

Throughout the *Times'* coverage of the 1994 congressional debate, prevention and punishment were played off against each other in a "battle" between congressional forces. President Clinton and his congressional allies were portrayed as the advocates of the prevention measures, but they were hardly ever quoted as providing substantive arguments for why these types of programs were needed. In contrast, Bob Dole, Newt Gingrich, and their Republican allies were consistently quoted as labeling the prevention programs as worthless, even though they too were not held accountable by the *Times* to provide evidence that the prevention programs would not work.

In all, what the public was left with in the political discourse and the accompanying news coverage was a story about winning political strategy, not about effective anti-crime public policy.

As can be seen, the relevance of how one can and should "think about" crime prevention had little to do with the political rhetoric or the news coverage of the 1994 anti-crime bill that appeared in the *New York Times* that summer. When "prevention" was mentioned, it was done so in a superficial manner, merely using the word as a label for the strategies the Clinton administration backed and the Republicans in Congress opposed. Although not called "primary" prevention efforts, the bill contained anti-crime strategies aimed at so-called root-causes of crime, such as lack of employment and recreation opportunities to inner-city youth. Apart from this, no evidence was presented as to why these primary prevention programs should work or not, why some other prevention measures might or might not be more cost-effective, or why anything at all should be expected to successfully prevent crime and thereby reduce the amount and seriousness of the crime problem the legislation ostensibly was intended to address. In sum, applying the crime prevention theoretical framework I advanced earlier, I find the discourse and news coverage of the 1994 anti-crime legislation wholly lacking any meaningful structure or substance.

IMPROVING THE SITUATION:
IMPLICATIONS FOR NEWS COVERAGE

I have been an avid daily reader of the *New York Times* for nearly 20 years and I regard it as the most important single source of news in the world. However, I was appalled by the superficiality I found in my critical content analysis of the newspaper's coverage of the 1994 crime bill debate. I was equally appalled by the wholly partisan debate in Congress, one that was devoid of rhetoric about what might actually work in reducing the nation's crime problems. Instead, the debate focused almost entirely on what was politically expedient.

Furthermore, I do not share the view of Professor Frank Zimring, who was quoted by the *Times* (August 27, 1994:A6) as saying that:

> . . . to talk about [the crime bill's] efficacy is to miss the
> point. It is far more important as a symbolic denunciation
> and expression of concern than as a serious crime counter-
> measure.

I do not believe that one should put such a "happy face" on the travesty of governance that occurred that summer. Should we believe that a $30 billion legislative package cannot be effective in its anti-crime mission and also send an effective symbolic message, rather than being merely symbolic? Did we need Congress to allocate $30 billion to send a symbolic message?

In 1980, I joined the faculty of the Medill School of Journalism at Northwestern University and quickly learned that journalists are neither trained to understand the criminal justice system nor the processes that result in the level of criminal victimization the citizenry suffers. In most cases, legal and criminal reporters may have received formal training in how to cover the court systems. Apart from that, what most journalists assigned to legal and criminal beats know about their beat is what they learn in the course of reporting their assignments. Few have the time or interest to educate themselves about criminology. This lack of education and understanding about crime, and thus about crime prevention, keeps many journalists from thinking critically about the crime-related news stories on which they are reporting. Because of this, the news media mostly fail in their self-proclaimed mission to educate the citizenry about important public policy developments, such as those dealing with crime prevention, and they fail in their mission to serve as the nation's "watchdog" on government.

THE ROLE OF SCHOLARS IN THE DEBATE

I am not especially sanguine about the likely success of improving the public policy debate over crime—one that includes what I consider to be absurdities like the growing movement to promote the carrying of concealed weapons by the citizenry. It should be clear that I believe that before any improvement will come from the politicians, the news media must raise the quality of the news coverage they provide the nation vis-á-vis crime. It is simply not enough for the press to report anti-crime public policy debates as "games" with political strategies that one side wins and the other loses. All this amounts to is lazy journalism with the public ending up the loser since nothing effective is achieved regarding the reduction of the magnitude and severity of the nation's crime problem.

As discussed above, the news media must be educated and encouraged to better hold politicians accountable for their anti-crime posturing. The news media must take a more proactive role, such as that advocated by the new movement toward "civic" or "public" journalism. Yet, for this to happen, criminal justice scholars must take a more active role in teaching journalists to ask the right questions of politicians. Additionally, scholars must be more vigilant and critical of the media when they do not.

I do not believe that we can expect journalism programs to change their curricula to close this knowledge gap. Instead, if change is to occur, I suggest that it is criminal justice educational programs that need to begin to offer training in news coverage and the media. This would include, for example, short courses for editors and reporters to help them better understand the public policy implications of crime prevention. Such training could also be offered to government officials and their staffers who deal with anti-crime legislation and programs. In the extreme, one might envision a series of McGruff ads targeting politicians and journalists in order to teach them how to "Take a Bite Out of Crime."

In conclusion, I believe that we must do much more as a community of scholars to demand of politicians and government officials that there be much more testing of well-conceived and well-funded comprehensive crime prevention programs and strategies. Also, we must be more vigorous in the efforts we make to educate the news media and politicians about effective and ineffective anti-crime policies. To succeed at these tasks, I believe we must come to some agreement on a theoretical framework to help organize thinking about what is likely to be effective in preventing crime and what is not. The framework I have advanced here may not be the most useful for this purpose, but it is an example of what I believe is needed to empower our efforts to make crime prevention a success in the twenty-first century.

NOTE

[1]   Some have argued that many crime "prevention" measures simply displace crime, thus resulting in a zero-sum game at the societal level (cf. Maltz, 1972). This is a very complex issue that has never been studied to the extent that would be needed to know with confidence whether the amount of crime that might be displaced is equal to the amount that would have occurred had the prevention measures not been implemented.

North East Multi-Regional Training
-Instructors' Library-
355 Smoke Tree Plaza
North Aurora, IL 60542

North East Multi-Regional Training
-Instructors' Library-
355 Smoke Tree Plaza
North Aurora, IL 60542

Bibliography

Akers, R.L. (1997). *Criminological Theories: Introduction and Evaluation*, Second Edition. Los Angeles, CA: Roxbury.

Akers, R.L., A.J. LaGreca, C. Sellers & J. Cochran (1987). "Fear of Crime and Victimization Among the Elderly in Different Types of Communities." *Criminology,* 25:487-505.

Alston, J.D. (1994). "The Serial Rapist's Spatial Pattern of Target Selection." Burnaby, B.C.: Unpublished Master's Thesis, School of Criminology, Simon Fraser University.

Angel, S. (1968). "Discouraging Crime Through City Planning." Working Paper #75. Berkeley, CA: Center for Planning and Development Research.

Appleyard, D. (1981). *Livable Streets: Protected Neighborhoods*. Berkeley, CA: University of California Press.

Atkins, S., S. Hussain & A. Storey (1991). "The Influence of Street Lighting on Crime and Fear." Home Office Crime Prevention Unit Paper #28. London: Home Office Police Department.

Ayres, I. & J. Braithwaite (1992). *Responsive Regulation: Transcending the Deregulation Debate*. New York, NY: Oxford University Press.

Bandura, A. (1976). "Social Learning Analysis of Aggression." In E. Ribes-Inesta & A. Bandura (eds.) *Analysis of Delinquency and Aggression*. Hillsdale, NJ: Lawrence Erlbaum Associates.

Bardach, E. (1989). "Moral Suasion and Taxpayer Compliance." *Law and Policy,* 11:49-69.

Bartnicki, S.P. (1989). "Crime in Poland: Trends, Regional Patterns and Neighbourhood Awareness." In D.J. Evans & D.T. Herbert (eds.) *The Geography of Crime*. London: Routledge.

Bauer, Y. (1990). "The Evolution of Nazi Jewish Policy, 1933-38." In F. Chalk & K. Jonassohn (eds.) *The History and Sociology of Genocide: Analysis and Case Studies*. New Haven, CT: Yale University Press.

175

Baumeister, R.F., T.F. Heatherton & D.M. Tice (1994). *Losing Control: How and Why People Fail at Self-Regulation*. San Diego, CA: Academic Press.

Bayley, D.H. (1994). "International Differences in Community Policing." In D.P. Rosenbaum (ed.) *The Challenge of Community Policing*. Thousand Oaks, CA: Sage.

Belson, W.A. (1978). *Television Violence and the Adolescent Boy*. Westmead, UK: Saxon House.

Berry, B.J.L. & J.D. Kasarda (1977). *Contemporary Urban Ecology*. New York, NY: Macmillan.

Blau, J.R. & P. Blau (1982). "The Cost of Inequality: Metropolitan Structure and Violent Crime." *American Sociological Review,* 47:114-129.

Block, R. & S. Davis (1995). "The Criminology of Dangerous Places and Areas: The Environs of Rapid Transit Stations." Paper presented at 4th International Seminar on Environmental Criminology and Crime Analysis, Cambridge, England.

Braithwaite, J. (1989). *Crime, Shame and Reintegration*. Cambridge, MA: Cambridge University Press.

Brantingham, P.J. & P.L. Brantingham (1994b). "Surveying Campus Crime: What Can be Done to Reduce Crime and Fear?" *Security Journal*, 5:160-171.

Brantingham, P.J. & P.L. Brantingham (1991). *Environmental Criminology*. Prospect Heights, IL: Waveland Press.

Brantingham, P.J. & P.L. Brantingham (1984). *Patterns in Crime*. New York, NY: Macmillan.

Brantingham, P.J. & P.L. Brantingham (1978). "A Theoretical Model of Crime Site Selection." In M.D. Krohn & R.L. Akers (eds.) *Crime, Law and Sanctions*. Beverly Hills, CA: Sage.

Brantingham, P.J., P.L. Brantingham & D. Butcher (1986). "Perceived and Actual Crime Risks." In R.M. Figlio, S. Hakim & G.F. Rengert (eds.) *Metropolitan Crime Patterns*. Monsey, NY: Criminal Justice Press.

Brantingham, P.J., P.L. Brantingham & R. Fister (1979). "Mental Maps of Crime in a Canadian City." Paper presented at Academy of Criminal Justice Sciences Annual Meeting, Cincinnati, OH.

Brantingham, P.J., P.L. Brantingham & T. Molumby (1977). "Perceptions of Crime in a Dreadful Enclosure." *Ohio Journal of Science*, 77:256-261.

Brantingham, P.J. & F.L. Faust (1976). "A Conceptual Model of Crime Prevention." *Crime & Delinquency,* 22:284-296.

Brantingham, P.L. & P.J. Brantingham (1995). "Criminality of Place: Crime Generators and Crime Attractors." In M. Hough & J. Marshall (eds.) *Crime Environments and Situational Prevention, European Journal of Criminal Policy and Research,* 3:5-26.

Brantingham, P.L. & P.J. Brantingham (1994a). "La Concentration Spatiale Relative de la Criminalit." *Criminologie,* 27:81-97.

Brantingham, P.L. & P.J. Brantingham (1993). "Nodes, Paths and Edges: Considerations on Environmental Criminology." *Journal of Environmental Psychology,* 13:3-28.

Brantingham, P.L. & P.J. Brantingham (1984). "Burglar Mobility and Crime Prevention Planning." In R.V.G. Clarke & T. Hope (eds.) *Coping With Burglary: Research Perspectives on Policy.* Boston, MA: Kluwer-Nijhoff.

Brantingham, P.L. & P.J. Brantingham (1981). "Mobility, Notoriety, and Crime: A Study in the Crime Patterns of Urban Nodal Points." *Journal of Environmental Systems,* 11:89-99.

Brantingham, P.L. & P.J. Brantingham (1975). "Residential Burglary and Urban Form." *Urban Studies,* 12:273-284.

Brantingham, P.L., P.J. Brantingham & J. Seagrave (1995). "Crime and Fear at a Canadian University." In B.S. Fisher & J.J. Sloan (eds.) *Campus Crime: Legal, Social, and Policy Perspectives.* Springfield, IL: Charles C Thomas.

Brantingham, P.L., P.J. Brantingham & P.S. Wong (1991). "How Public Transit Feeds Private Crime: Notes on the Vancouver 'Skytrain' Experience." *Security Journal,* 2:91-95.

Breton, M. (1994). "On the Meaning of Empowerment and Empowerment-Oriented Social Work Practice." *Social Work with Groups,* 17(3):23-37.

Bryk, A.S. & S.W. Raudenbush (1992). *Hierarchical Linear Models: Applications and Data Analysis Methods.* Newbury Park, CA: Sage.

Buerger, M.E. (1994). "The Limits of Community." In D. Rosenbaum (ed.) *The Challenge of Community Policing.* Thousand Oaks, CA: Sage.

Bureau of Justice Statistics (1996). *Criminal Victimization in the United States, 1993.* Washington, DC: United States Department of Justice, Office of Justice Programs, Bureau of Justice Statistics.

Bureau of Justice Statistics (1994). *Criminal Victimization in the United States, 1992.* Washington, DC: United States Department of Justice, Office of Justice Programs, Bureau of Justice Statistics.

Bursik, R.J. (1988). "Social Disorganization and Theories of Crime and Delinquency: Problems and Prospects." *Criminology,* 26:519-551.

Bursik, Jr., R.J. & H.G. Grasmick (1993). *Neighborhoods and Crime: The Dimensions of Effective Community Control.* New York, NY: Lexington Books.

Cameron, M. & S. Newstead (1994). "Evaluation of Mass Media Publicity as Support for Enforcement." In D. South & A. Cavallo (eds.) *Australasian Drink-Drive Conference 1993, Conference Proceedings.* Melbourne: VicRoads.

Campbell, B. (1993). *Goliath.* London: Methuen.

Canadian Centre for Justice Statistics (1995). "Factfinder on Crime and the Administration of Justice in Canada." Juristat 15(10). *Statistics Canada Catalogue,* 85-002.

Capone, D. & W. Nichols (1976). "Urban Structure and Criminal Mobility." *American Behavioral Scientist,* 20:199-201.

Carlen, P. (1996). *Jigsaw—A Political Economy of Youth Homelessness.* Buckingham: Open University Press.

Casey, S. & A. Lund (1993). "The Effects of Mobile Roadside Speedometers on Traffic Speeds." *Accident Analysis and Prevention,* 24:507-520.

Cavallo, A. & A. Drummond (1994). "Evaluation of the Victorian Random Breath Testing Initiative." In D. South & A. Cavallo (eds.) *Australasian Drink-Drive Conference 1993, Conference Proceedings.* Melbourne: VicRoads.

Clarke, R.V. (1995). "Situational Crime Prevention." In M. Tonry & D.P. Farrington (eds.) *Building a Safer Society: Strategic Approaches to Crime Prevention.* Chicago, IL: University of Chicago Press.

Clarke, R.V. (1983). "Situational Crime Prevention: Its Theoretical Basis and Practical Scope." In M. Tonry & N. Morris (eds.) *Crime and Justice,* vol. 4. Chicago, IL: University of Chicago Press.

Clarke, R.V. (1980). "Situational Crime Prevention: Theory and Practice." *British Journal of Criminology,* 20:136-147.

Clarke, R.V. (ed.) (1992). *Situational Crime Prevention: Successful Case Studies.* Albany, NY: Harrow and Heston.

Clarke, R.V. & D.B. Cornish (1985). "Modeling Offenders' Decisions: A Framework for Policy and Research." In M. Tonry & N. Morris (eds.) *Crime and Justice,* vol. 6. Chicago, IL: University of Chicago Press.

Clarke, R.V. & M. Felson (1993). "Introduction: Criminology, Routine Activity, and Rational Choice." In R.V. Clarke & M. Felson (eds.) *Routine Activity and Rational Choice: Advances in Criminological Theory,* vol. 5. New Brunswick, NJ: Transaction Books.

Clarke, R.V. & P.M. Harris (1992). "Auto Theft and its Prevention." In M. Tonry (ed.) *Crime and Justice,* vol. 16. Chicago, IL: University of Chicago Press.

Clarke, R.V. & D. Lester (1989). *Suicide: Closing the Exits.* New York, NY: Springer-Verlag.

Clarke, R.V. & P. Mayhew (1994). "Parking Patterns and Car Theft Risks: Policy Relevant Findings from the British Crime Survey." *Crime Prevention Studies,* 3:91-107.

Clarke, R.V. & D. Weisburd (1994). "Diffusion of Crime Control Benefits: Observations on the Reverse of Displacement." In R.V. Clarke (ed.) *Crime Prevention Studies,* vol. 2. Monsey, NY: Criminal Justice Press.

Cohen, L.E. & M. Felson (1979). "Social Change and Crime Rate Trends: A Routine Activity Approach." *American Sociological Review,* 44:588-608.

Cohen, S. (1985). *Visions of Social Control.* Cambridge, England: Polity.

Coleman, J.S. (1990). *Foundations of Social Theory.* Cambridge, MA: Belknap Press.

Cornish, D.B. (1994). "The Procedural Analysis of Offending and its Relevance for Situational Prevention." *Crime Prevention Studies,* 3:151-196.

Cornish, D.B. & R.V. Clarke (1986). *The Reasoning Criminal: Rational Choice Perspectives on Offending.* New York, NY: Springer-Verlag.

Covington, J. & R.B. Taylor (1991). "Fear of Crime in Urban Residential Neighborhoods: Implications of Between and Within-Neighborhood Sources for Current Models." *The Sociological Quarterly,* 32:231-249.

Crenson, M.A. (1983). *Neighborhood Politics.* Cambridge, MA: Harvard University Press.

Cromwell, P.F., J.N. Olson & D.W. Avary (1991). *Breaking and Entering: An Ethnographic Analysis of Burglary.* Newbury Park, CA: Sage.

Cromwell, P.F. & D. Zahm (1991). "Mitigating Traffic to Control Crime: The Impact on Property Crime of Street Closings and Barricades." Paper presented at American Society of Criminology Annual Meetings, San Francisco, CA.

Currie, E. (1988). "Two Visions of Community Crime Prevention." In T. Hope & M. Shaw (eds.) *Communities and Crime Reduction.* London: HMSO.

Curtis, L. (ed.) (1987). "Policies to Prevent Crime: Neighborhood, Family and Employment Strategies." *The Annals of the American Academy of Political and Social Sciences,* 494:9-169.

Curtis, L.A. (1988). "The March of Folly: Crime and the Underclass." In T. Hope & M. Shaw (eds.) *Communities and Crime Reduction.* London: HMSO.

Department of the Environment (1993). *Crime Prevention on Council Estates.* Prepared for the Safe Neighbourhoods Unit. London: HMSO.

DuBow, F., F. McCabe & G. Kaplan (1979). *Reactions to Crime: A Critical Review of the Literature*. Washington, DC: U.S. Government Printing Office.

Duffala, D.C. (1976). "Convenience Stores, Armed Robbery, and Physical Environmental Features." *American Behavioral Scientist,* 20:227-246.

Eck, J.E. (1995). "A General Model of the Geography of Illicit Retail Marketplaces." In J.E. Eck & D. Weisburd (eds.) *Crime Prevention Studies,* vol. 4. Monsey, NY: Criminal Justice Press.

Eck, J.E. & W. Spelman (1992). "Thefts from Vehicles in Shipyard Parking Lots." In R.V. Clarke (ed.) *Situational Crime Prevention*. New York, NY: Harrow and Heston.

Ellingworth, D., D.R. Osborn, A. Trickett & K. Pease (1995). "Prior Victimisation and Crime Risk." Quantitative Criminology Group, University of Manchester (unpublished).

Ellul, J. (1965). *Propaganda: The Formation of Men's Attitudes*. New York, NY: Vintage Books.

Empey, L.T. (1977). "Crime Prevention: The Fugitive Utopia." In J.A. Inciardi & H.A. Siegel (eds.) *Crime: Emerging Issues*. New York, NY: Praeger.

Farrell, G. & K. Pease (1993). "Once Bitten, Twice Bitten." Crime Prevention Unit Paper 46. London: Home Office.

Fattah, E.A. (1991). *Understanding Criminal Victimization: An Introduction to Theoretical Victimology*. Scarborough, Ontario: Prentice-Hall, Canada.

Felson, M. (1995). "Those Who Discourage Crime." In J.E. Eck & D. Weisburd (eds.) *Crime Prevention Studies,* vol. 4. Monsey, NY: Criminal Justice Press.

Felson, M. (1994). *Crime and Everyday Life: Insight and Implications for Society*. Thousand Oaks, CA: Pine Forge Press.

Felson, M. (1986). "Routine Activities, Social Controls, Rational Decisions and Criminal Outcomes." In D. Cornish & R.V. Clarke (eds.) *The Reasoning Criminal*. New York, NY: Springer-Verlag.

Felson, M. (1983). *The Ecology of Crime. Encyclopedia of Crime and Justice*. New York, NY: Macmillan.

Felson, M., M.E. Belanger, G.M. Bichler, C.D. Bruzinski, G.S. Campbell, C.L. Fried, K.C. Grofik, I.S. Mazur, A.B. O'Regan, P.J. Sweeney, A.L. Ullman & L.M. Williams (1996). "Redesigning Hell: Preventing Crime and Disorder at the Port Authority Bus Terminal." In R.V. Clarke (ed.) *Crime Prevention Studies,* vol. 6. Monsey, NY: Criminal Justice Press.

Felson, R.B. (1993). "Predatory and Dispute-Related Violence: A Social-Interactionist Approach." In R.V. Clarke & M. Felson (eds.) *Routine Activity and Rational Choice: Advances in Criminological Theory,* vol. 5. New Brunswick, NJ: Transaction Books.

Ferraro, K.F. (1994). *Fear of Crime: Interpreting Victimization Risk.* Albany, NY: SUNY Press.

Field, S. & T. Hope (1990). "Economics, the Consumer and Under-Provision in Crime Prevention." In R. Morgan (ed.) *Policing Organised Crime and Crime Prevention.* British Criminology Conference 1989, vol. 4. Bristol: Bristol Centre for Criminal Justice.

Fisher, B.S. & J.L. Nasar (1995). "Fear Spots in Relation to Microlevel Physical Cues: Exploring the Overlooked." *Journal of Research in Crime and Delinquency,* 32:214-239.

Fisher, B.S., J.J. Sloan & F.T. Cullen (1995). *Understanding Crime Victimization Among College Students: Implications for Crime Prevention.* Final report submitted to the National Institute of Justice, Washington D.C.

Fleming, Z., P.L. Brantingham & P.J. Brantingham (1994). "Exploring Auto Theft in British Columbia." In R.V. Clarke (ed.) *Crime Prevention Studies,* vol. 3. Monsey, NY: Criminal Justice Press.

Forrest, R. & A. Murie (1988). *Selling the Welfare State: The Privatisation of Public Housing.* London: Routledge.

Foster, J. & T. Hope (1993). *Housing, Community and Crime: The Impact of the Priority Estates Project.* Home Office Research Study No. 131. London: HMSO.

Furstenberg, F. (1993). "How Families Manage Risk and Opportunity in Dangerous Neighborhoods." In W.J. Wilson (ed.) *Sociology and the Public Agenda.* Newbury Park, CA: Sage.

Furstenberg, F. (1972). "Fear of Crime and Its Effects on Citizen Behavior." In A. Biderman (ed.) *Crime and Justice: A Symposium.* New York, NY: Nailburg.

Gabor, T. (1994). *Everybody Does It.* New York, NY: Macmillan.

Gaddy, G.D. (1988). "High School Order and Academic Achievement." *American Journal of Education,* 96:496-518.

Gallup, G. (1993). *The Gallup Poll Monthly.* No. 339. Princeton, NJ: The Gallup Poll.

Garofalo, J. (1977). *Public Opinion About Crime.* Washington, DC: National Criminal Justice Information and Statistics Service.

Garofalo, J. & J. Laub (1978). "The Fear of Crime: Broadening our Perspective." *Victimology,* 3:242-253.

Garofalo, J. & M. McLeod (1988). *Improving the Use and Effectiveness of Neighborhood Watch Programs*. NIJ Research in Action. Washington, DC: National Institute of Justice.

Gates, L.B. & W.M. Rohe (1987). "Fear and Reactions to Crime: A Revised Model." *Urban Affairs Quarterly,* 22:425-453.

Gill, O. (1977). *Luke Street*. London: Macmillan.

Goldstein, H. (1990). *Problem-Oriented Policing*. New York, NY: McGraw Hill.

Goldstein, H. (1979). "Improving Policing: A Problem-Oriented Approach." *Crime & Delinquency,* 25:234-258.

Gottfredson, G.D. & D.C. Gottfredson (1985). *Victimization in Schools*. New York, NY: Plenum.

Gottfredson, M.R. & T. Hirschi (1990). *A General Theory of Crime*. Stanford, CA: Stanford University Press.

Graham, J. & B. Bowling (1995). *Young People and Crime*. Home Office Research Study 145. London: Home Office.

Granovetter, M.S. (1973). "The Strength of Weak Ties." *American Journal of Sociology,* 76:1360-1380.

Grasmick, H.G. & R.J. Bursik (1990). "Conscience, Significant Others, and Rational Choice." *Law and Society Review,* 34:837-861.

Green, A.E. (1996). "Aspects of the Changing Geography of Income and Wealth." In J. Hills (ed.) *New Inequalities: The Changing Distribution of Income and Wealth in the United Kingdom*. Cambridge, England: University of Cambridge Press.

Greenberg, S., W.M. Rohe & J.R. Williams (1985). *Informal Citizen Action and Crime Prevention at the Neighborhood Level*. Washington, DC: National Institute of Justice.

Greenberg, S.W., J.R. Williams & W.R. Rohe (1982). "Safety in Urban Neighborhoods: A Comparison of Physical Characteristics and Informal Territorial Control in High and Low Crime Neighborhoods." *Population and Environment,* 5:141-165.

Greene, J.R. & R.B. Taylor (1988). "Community-Based Policing and Foot Patrol: Issues of Theory and Evaluation." In J.R. Greene & S.D. Mastrofski (eds.) *Community policing: Rhetoric or Reality?* New York, NY: Praeger.

Griffaton, M.C. (1995). "State Level Initiatives and Campus Crime." In B.S. Fisher & J.J. Sloan (eds.) *Campus Crime: Legal, Social and Policy Perspectives*. Springfield, IL: Charles C Thomas.

Guba, E. & Y. Lincoln (1989). *Fourth Generation Evaluation*. Newbury Park, CA: Sage.

Hagan, J. (1994). *Crime and Disrepute*. Thousand Oaks, CA: Pine Forge Press.

Hagan, J. (1993). "The Social Embeddedness of Crime and Unemployment." *Criminology,* 31:465-491.

Hauser, P.M. (1974). "Contextual Analysis Revisited." *Sociological Methods and Research,* 2:365-375.

Hill, G.D., F.M. Howell & E.T. Driver (1985). "Gender, Fear, and Protective Handgun Ownership." *Criminology,* 23:541-552.

Hills, J. (1996). *New Inequalities: The Changing Distribution of Income and Wealth in the United Kingdom*. Cambridge, England: University of Cambridge Press.

Hindelang, M., M. Gottfredson & J. Garofalo (1978). *Victims of Personal Crime: An Empirical Foundation for a Theory of Personal Victimization*. Cambridge, MA: Ballinger.

Hirschi, T. (1969). *Causes of Delinquency*. Berkeley, CA: University of California Press.

Hirschi, T. & M.R. Gottfredson (eds.) (1994). *The Generality of Deviance*. New Brunswick, NJ: Transaction Books.

Holden, R.N. (1992). *Law Enforcement: An Introduction*. Englewood Cliffs, NJ: Prentice-Hall.

Home Office, Department of Education and Science, Department of Employment, Department of the Environment, Department of Health, Department of Social Security, Department of Trade and Industry, Department of Transport, and Welsh Office (1990) *Crime Prevention: The Success of the Partnership Approach*. Home Office Circular 44/1990. London: Home Office.

Homel, R. (1988). *Policing and Punishing the Drinking Driver: A Study of General and Specific Deterrence*. New York, NY: Springer-Verlag.

Homel, R., D. Caseldine & I. Kearns (1988). "Drink-Driving Countermeasures in Australia." *Alcohol, Drugs and Driving,* 4(2):113-144.

Hope, T. (forthcoming). *Crime Prevention and Community Safety*. Cambridge, MA: Cambridge University Press.

Hope, T. (1996). "Communities, Crime and Inequality in England and Wales." In T. Bennett (ed.) *Preventing Crime and Disorder: Targeting Strategies and Responsibilities*. Cambridge, England: Institute of Criminology.

Hope, T. (1995a). "Community Crime Prevention." In M. Tonry & D.P. Farrington (eds.) *Building a Safer Society: Strategic Approaches to Crime Prevention*. Chicago, IL: University of Chicago Press.

Hope, T. (1995b). "The Flux of Victimization." *British Journal of Criminology,* 35:327-342.

Hope, T. & J. Foster (1992). "Conflicting Forces: Changing the Dynamics of Crime and Community on a 'Problem' Estate." *British Journal of Criminology,* 32:488-504.

Hope, T. & M. Hough (1988). "Area, Crime and Incivility: A Profile from the British Crime Survey." In T. Hope & M. Shaw (eds.) *Communities and Crime Reduction.* London: HMSO.

Hough, J.M., R.V. Clarke & P.M. Mayhew (1980). "Introduction." In R.V. Clarke & P.M. Mayhew (eds.) *Designing Out Crime.* London: HMSO.

Hunter, A. (1974). *Symbolic Communities.* Chicago, IL: University of Chicago Press.

Hutton, W. (1996). *The State We're In.* London: Vintage Books.

Jackson, H. (1874). *On Epilepsy and Epileptiform Convulsions.*

Jacobs, J. (1961). *Death and Life of Great American Cities.* New York, NY: Random House.

Jamieson, K.M. (1994). *The Organization of Corporate Crime: Dynamics of Antitrust Violation.* Thousand Oaks, CA: Sage.

Jankowski, M.S. (1991). *Islands in the Street.* Berkeley, CA: University of California Press.

Jeffery, C.R. (1971). *Crime Prevention Through Environmental Design.* Beverly Hills, CA: Sage.

Johnston, L.D., P.M. O'Maley & J.G. Bachman (1993). *Monitoring the Future Study for Goal 6 of the National Education Goals.* Ann Arbor, MI: Institute for Social Research.

JRF (1995). *Joseph Rowntree Foundation Inquiry into Income and Wealth.* Volumes 1 and 2. York: Joseph Rowntree Foundation.

Kelling, G.L., T. Pate, D. Dieckman & C. Brown (1974). *The Kansas City Preventive Patrol Experiment: A Technical Report.* Washington, DC: The Police Foundation.

Kennedy, L.W. & D.R. Forde (1990). "Routine Activities and Crime: An Analysis of Victimization in Canada." *Criminology,* 28:137-152.

Klockars, C.B. (1985). *The Idea of Police.* Beverly Hills, CA: Sage.

Knoke, D. & J.R. Wood (1981). *Organizing for Action: Commitment in Voluntary Associations.* New Brunswick, NJ: Rutgers University Press.

Kohfeld, C.W. & J. Sprague (1990). "Demography, Police Behavior, and Deterrence." *Criminology,* 28:111-136.

Kornhauser, R.R. (1978). *Social Sources of Delinquency*. Chicago, IL: University of Chicago Press.

Krisberg, B. & J.F. Austin (1978). *The Children of Ishmael*. Palo Alto, CA: Mayfield.

Lab, S.P. (1997). *Crime Prevention: Approaches, Practices and Evaluations*, Third Edition. Cincinnati, OH: Anderson Publishing Co.

Lab, S.P. (1990). "Citizen Crime Prevention: Domains and Participation." *Justice Quarterly*, 7:467-492.

Lab, S.P. & R.D. Clark (1996). *Discipline, Control and School Crime: Identifying Effective Intervention Strategies*. Final Report. Washington, DC: National Institute of Justice.

Lab, S.P. & J.T. Whitehead (1994). "Avoidance Behavior as a Response to In-School Victimization." *Journal of Security Administration*, 17:32-45.

Lab, S.P. & J.T. Whitehead (1992). *The School Environment and School Crime: Causes and Consequences*. Final Report. Washington, DC: National Institute of Justice.

LaGrange, R.L. (1993). *Policing American Society*. Chicago, IL: Nelson-Hall.

Langworthy, R.H. & J. LeBeau (1992a). "The Spatial Evolution of a Sting Clientele." *Journal of Criminal Justice*, 20:135-146.

Langworthy, R.H. & J. LeBeau (1992b). "The Spatial Distribution of Sting Targets." *Journal of Criminal Justice*, 20:541-552.

Langworthy, R.H. & L.F. Travis, III (1994). *Policing in America: A Balance of Forces*. New York, NY: Macmillan.

Langworthy, R.H. & J.T. Whitehead (1986). "Liberalism and Fear as Explanations of Punitiveness." *Criminology*, 24:575-591.

Lash, S. & J. Urry (1994). *Economies of Signs and Space*. London: Sage.

Lavrakas, P.J. (1995). "Community-Based Crime Prevention: Citizens, Community Organizations, and the Police." In L.B. Joseph (ed.) *Crime, Communities, and Public Policy*. Chicago, IL: University of Illinois Press.

Lavrakas, P.J. (1989). *America's War on Drugs: Guest Centerpiece Essay*. Evanston, IL: Center for Urban Affairs and Policy Research Newsletter, Fall (14):4.

Lavrakas, P.J. (1986). "Evaluating Police-Community Anticrime Newsletters: The Evanston, Houston and Newark Field Studies." In D.P. Rosenbaum (ed.) *Community Crime Prevention: Does It Work?* Beverly Hills, CA: Sage.

Lavrakas, P.J. (1985). "Citizen Self-Help and Neighborhood Crime Prevention." In L. Curtis (ed.) *American Violence and Public Policy*. New Haven, CT: Yale University Press.

Lavrakas, P.J. & S.F. Bennett (1988). "Thinking About the Implementation of Citizen Anti-Crime Measures." In T. Hope & M. Shaw (eds.) *Communities and Crime Reduction*. London: HMSO.

Lavrakas, P.J. & D. Lewis (1980). "Citizen Participation in Neighborhood Crime Prevention." *Criminology*, 20:479-498.

Lavrakas, P.J., J. Normoyle, W.G. Skogan, E.J. Herz, G. Salem & D. Lewis (1981). *Factors Related to Citizen Involvement in Personal, Household, and Neighborhood Anti-Crime Measures: Executive Summary*. Washington, DC: National Institute of Justice.

Lavrakas, P.J. & D.P. Rosenbaum (1989). *The Crime Prevention Beliefs and Practice of U.S. Law Enforcement Chief Executives*. Washington, DC: National Crime Prevention Council.

Lawton, M.P. & S. Yaffe (1980). "Victimization and Fear of Crime in Elderly Public Housing Tenants." *Journal of Gerontology*, 35:768-799.

Laycock, G. & N. Tilley (1995). "Policing and Neighbourhood Watch: Strategic Issues." Crime Detection and Prevention Series Paper 60. London: Home Office.

Lederman, D. (1995, Feb. 3). "Colleges Report Rise on Violent Crime." *The Chronicle of Higher Education*, A31-A42.

Lederman, D. (1994a, Mar. 9). "Weapons on Campus." *The Chronicle of Higher Education*, A21-A22.

Lederman, D. (1994b, Feb. 2). "Crimes on the Campuses: Increases in Reported Robberies and Assaults." *The Chronicle of Higher Education*, A31-41.

Lederman, D. (1993, Jan. 20). "Colleges Report 7,500 Violent Crimes on Their Campuses in First Annual Statements Required Under Federal Law." *The Chronicle of Higher Education*, A32-43.

Lee, G.R. (1983). "Social Integration and Fear of Crime in Older Persons." *Journal of Gerontology*, 38:745-750.

Letkemann, P. (1973). *Crime as Work*. Englewood Cliffs, NJ: Prentice Hall.

Lewis, D.A., J.A. Grant & D.P. Rosenbaum (1988). *The Social Construction of Reform: Crime Prevention and Community Organizations*. New Brunswick, NJ: Transaction Books.

Lewis, D.A. & S. Riger (1986). "Crime as Stress: On the Internalization of a Social Problem." In E. Seidman & J. Rappaport (eds.) *Redefining Social Problems*. New York, NY: Plenum.

Lewis, D.A. & G. Salem (1986). *Fear of Crime*. New Brunswick, NJ: Transaction Books.

Ley, D. & R. Cybriwsky (1974). "Urban Graffiti as Territorial Markers." *Annals of the Association of American Geographers,* 64:491-505.

Liska, A.E., J.L. Lawrence & A. Sanchirico (1982). "Fear of Crime as a Social Fact." *Social Forces,* 60:760-770.

Lively, K. (1996, Apr. 26). "Drug Arrests Rise Again." *The Chronicle of Higher Education,* A37.

Loeber, R. & P-O.H. Wikstrom (1993). "Individual Pathways to Crime in Different Types of Neighborhood." In D.P. Farrington, R.J. Sampson & P-O.H. Wikstrom (eds.) *Integrating Individual and Ecological Aspects of Crime.* Stockholm: National Council for Crime Prevention.

Logan, J.R. & H.L. Molotch (1987). *Urban Fortunes: The Political Economy of Place.* Berkeley, CA: University of California Press.

Longshore, D., S. Turner & J.D. Stein (1996). "Self-Control in a Criminal Sample: An Examination of Construct Validity." *Criminology,* 34:209-228.

Lu, C. (1996). "The Extent and Patterns of Compliance with the Crime Awareness and Campus Security Act of 1990 Among Post-Secondary Institutions: A National Study." Ph.D. Dissertation. Cincinnati, OH: University of Cincinnati.

Lunenberg, F.C. (1991). "Pupil Control Ideology and Behavior as Predictors of Environmental Robustness." *Journal of Research and Development in Education,* 24:14-19.

Maguire, K. & A.L. Pastore (1995). *Sourcebook of Criminal Justice Statistics 1994.* Washington, DC: U.S. Department of Justice, Bureau of Justice Statistics.

Maguire, K. & A.L. Pastore (1994). *Sourcebook of Criminal Justice Statistics 1993.* Washington, DC: U.S. Department of Justice, Bureau of Justice Statistics.

Maguire, M. (1982). *Burglary in a Dwelling.* London: Heinemann.

Maltz, M.D. (1972). *Evaluation of Crime Control Programs.* Washington, DC: U.S. Government Printing Office.

Matthews, A. (1993, Mar. 7). "The Ivory Tower Becomes an Armed Camp." *New York Times Magazine,* 38-47.

Matthews, R. (1990). "Developing More Effective Strategies for Curbing Prostitution." *Security Journal,* 1:182-187.

Maxfield, M.G. (1987). "Household Composition, Routine Activity and Victimization: A Comparative Analysis." *Journal of Quantitative Criminology,* 3:301-320.

Maxfield, M.G. (1984). *Fear of Crime in England and Wales.* London: HMSO.

McDermott, J. (1983). "Crime in the School and in the Community: Offenders, Victims and Fearful Youth." *Crime & Delinquency,* 29:270-282.

McGahey, R.M. (1986). "Economic Conditions, Neighborhood Organization and Urban Crime." In A.J. Reiss & M. Tonry (eds.) *Communities and Crime.* Chicago, IL: University of Chicago Press.

McKenzie, E. (1994). *Privatopia.* New Haven, CT: Yale University Press.

McKenzie, R.D. (1921). "The Neighborhood." In A.H. Hawley & R.D. McKenzie (eds.) *On Human Ecology.* Chicago, IL: University of Chicago Press.

McPherson, M. & G. Silloway (1986). "The Role of the Small Commercial Center in the Urban Neighborhood." In R.B. Taylor (ed.) *Urban Neighborhoods: Research and Policy.* New York, NY: Praeger.

Merry, S.E. (1981). *Urban Danger: Life in a Neighborhood of Strangers.* Philadelphia, PA: Temple University Press.

Metropolitan Life (1994*). Violence in America's Public Schools: The Family Perspective.* New York, NY: Louis Harris and Assoc.

Metropolitan Life (1993). *Violence in America's Public Schools.* New York, NY: Louis Harris and Assoc.

Miethe, T. (1995). "Fear and Withdrawal from Urban Life." *Annals of the American Academy of Political and Social Science,* 539:14-27.

Miethe, T.D. & R.F. Meier (1994). *Crime and Its Social Context: Toward an Integrated Theory of Offenders, Victims, and Situations.* Albany, NY: SUNY Press.

Morris, L. (1994) *Dangerous Classes: The Underclass and British Citizenship.* London: Routledge.

Nalla, M. & G. Newman (1990). *A Primer in Private Security.* Albany, NY: Harrow and Heston.

Nasar, J.L. & B. Fisher (1993). "Hot Spots of Fear and Crime: A Multi-Method Investigation." *Journal of Environmental Psychology,* 13:187-206.

Nasar, J.L. & B. Fisher (1992). "Design for Vulnerability: Cues and Reactions to Fear of Crime." *Sociology and Social Research,* 76:48-58.

National Board for Crime Prevention (1994). *Wise After the Event: Tackling Repeat Victimisation.* London: Home Office.

National Institute of Education (1978). *Violent Schools Safe Schools: The Safe School Study Report to Congress.* Washington, DC: U.S. Government Printing Office.

Newman, J. & G. Newman (1980). "Crime and Punishment in the Schooling Process: A Historical Analysis." In K. Baker & R.J. Ruble (eds.) *Violence and Crime in the Schools.* Lexington, MA: Lexington Books.

Newman, O. (1972). *Defensible Space: Crime Prevention Through Urban Design.* New York, NY: Macmillan.

Nobel, M. & G. Smith (1996). "Two Nations? Changing Patterns of Income and Wealth in Two Contrasting Areas." In J. Hills (ed.) *New Inequalities: The Changing Distribution of Income and Wealth in the United Kingdom.* Cambridge, England: University of Cambridge Press.

Norstrom, T. (1981). *Studies in the Causation and Prevention of Traffic Crime.* Stockholm: Almqvist and Wiksell.

Office of Substance Abuse Prevention (1991). *The Future by Design: A Community Framework for Preventing Alcohol and Other Drug Problems through a Systems Approach.* Washington DC: U.S. Department of Health and Human Services, Public Health Service, Alcohol, Drug Abuse and Mental Health Administration.

O'Malley, P. (1992). "Risk, Power and Crime Prevention." *Economy and Society,* 21:252-275.

Osborn, D.R., D. Ellingworth, T. Hope & A. Trickett (1996). "Are Repeatedly Victimized Households Different?" *Journal of Quantitative Criminology,* 12:223-245.

Osborn, D.R., A. Trickett & R. Elder (1992). "Area Characteristics and Regional Variates as Determinants of Area Property Crime Levels." *Journal of Quantitative Criminology,* 8:265-285.

Osborn, D.R. & A. Tseloni (1995). "The Distribution of Household Property Crimes." The University of Manchester School of Economic Studies Discussion Paper #9530. Manchester: University of Manchester.

Page, D. (1993). *Building for Communities: A Study of New Housing Association Estates.* York: Joseph Rowntree Foundation.

Painter, K. (1994). "Street Lighting as an Environmental Crime Prevention Strategy." In D. Zahm & P. Cromwell (eds.) *Proceedings of the International Seminar on Environmental Criminology and Crime Analysis—1993.* Tallahassee, FL: Florida Statistical Analysis Center, Florida Criminal Justice Executive Institute.

Pate, A.M. (1986). "Experimenting with Foot Patrol: The Newark Experience." In D.P. Rosenbaum (ed.) *Community Crime Prevention: Does it Work?* Beverly Hills, CA: Sage.

Pease, K. (1994). "Crime Prevention." In M. Maguire, R. Morgan & R. Reiner (eds.) *The Oxford Handbook of Criminology.* Oxford, U.K.: Clarendon Press.

Perkins, D.D., P. Florin, R.C. Rich, A. Wandersman & D.M. Chavis (1990). "Participation in the Social and Physical Environment of Residential Blocks: Crime and Community Context." *American Journal of Community Psychology,* 18:83-115.

Perkins, D.D., J.W. Meeks & R.B. Taylor (1992). "The Physical Environment of Street Blocks and Resident Perceptions of Crime and Disorder: Implications for Theory and Measurement." *Journal of Environmental Psychology,* 12:21-34.

Perkins, D.D. & R.B. Taylor (in press). "Community Disorder Influences Fear of Crime." *American Journal of Community Psychology.*

Perkins, D.D., A. Wandersman, R. Rich & R.B. Taylor (1993). "Physical Environment of Street Crime: Defensible Space, Territoriality and Incivilities." *Journal of Environmental Psychology,* 13:29-49.

Platt, A.M. (1977). *The Child Savers: The Invention of Delinquency.* Chicago, IL: University of Chicago Press.

Podolefsky, A. & F. DuBow (1981). *Strategies for Community Crime Prevention.* Springfield, IL.: Charles C Thomas.

Powell, J.W., M.S. Pander & R.C. Nielsen (1994). *Campus Security and Law Enforcement,* Second Edition. Boston, MA: Butterworth-Heinemann.

Poyner, B. (1992). "Situational Crime Prevention in Two Parking Facilities." In R.V. Clarke (ed.) *Situational Crime Prevention: Successful Case Studies.* New York, NY: Harrow and Heston.

Poyner, B. (1983). *Design Against Crime: Beyond Defensible Space.* London: Butterworth.

Pyle, G.F. (1974). *The Spatial Dynamics of Crime.* Chicago, IL: University of Chicago Press.

Ramsay, M. & R. Newton (1991). "The Effect of Better Street Lighting on Crime and Fear." Home Office Crime Prevention Unit Paper #29. London: Home Office Police Department.

Reed, J. (1982). *One South: An Ethnic Approach to Regional Culture.* Baton Rouge, LA: Louisiana State University Press.

Reiss, A.J. (1986). "Why Are Communities Important in Understanding Crime?" In A.J. Reiss & M. Tonry (eds.) *Communities and crime.* Chicago, IL: University of Chicago Press.

Rengert, G.F. (1995). "Comparing Cognitive Hot Spots to Crime Hot Spots." In C.R. Block, M. Dabdoub & S. Fregly (eds.) *Crime Analysis Through Computer Mapping.* Washington, DC: Police Executive Research Forum.

Rengert, G.F. & T. Wasilchick (1985). *Suburban Burglary.* Springfield, IL: Charles C Thomas.

Reppetto, T.A. (1974). *Residential Crime*. Cambridge, MA: Ballinger.

Reynolds, F. (1986). *The Problem Estate*. Aldershot: Gower.

Richards, E.R. (1996). "The Security Survey: Creating a Proactive Foundation for Campus Crime Prevention." *Journal of Contemporary Criminal Justice*, 12:45-53.

Riger, S. (1985). "Crime as an Environmental Stressor." *Journal of Community Psychology*, 13:270-280.

Riley, D. & M. Shaw (1985). "Parental Supervision and Delinquency." Home Office Research Study #83. London: HMSO.

Ringwalt, C., P. Messerschmidt, L. Grahman & J. Collins (1992). *Youth's Victimization Experiences, Fear of Attack or Harm, and School Avoidance Behaviors*. Final Report. Washington, DC: National Institute of Justice.

Rosenbaum, D.P. (1988). "Community Crime Prevention: A Review and Synthesis of the Literature." *Justice Quarterly*, 5:323-394.

Rosenbaum, D.P. (1987). "The Theory and Research Behind Neighborhood Watch: Is It Sound Fear and Crime Reduction Strategy?" *Crime & Delinquency*, 33:103-134.

Ross, H.L. (1960). "Traffic Law Violation: A Folk Crime." *Social Problems*, 8:231-241.

Rossmo, D.K. (1994). "Targeting Victims: Serial Killers and the Urban Environment." In T. O'Reilly-Fleming & S. Egger (eds.) *Serial and Mass Murder: Theory, Research and Policy*. Toronto: University of Toronto Press.

Rowe, D.C., D.W. Osgood & W.A. Nicewander (1990). "A Latent Trait Approach to Unifying Criminal Careers." *Criminology*, 28:237-270.

Sampson, R.J. (1993). "The Community Context of Violent Crime." In W.J. Wilson (ed.) *Sociology and the Public Agenda*. Newbury Park, CA: Sage.

Sampson, R.J. (1987). "Communities and Crime." In M.R. Gottfredson & T. Hirschi (eds.) *Positive Criminology*. Newbury Park, CA: Sage.

Sampson, R.J. & W.B. Groves (1989). "Community Structure and Crime: Testing Social Disorganization Theory." *American Journal of Sociology*, 94:774-802.

Sampson, R.J. & J.H. Laub (1993). *Crime in the Making: Pathways and Turning Points Through Life*. Cambridge, MA: Harvard University Press.

Sampson, R.J. & W.J. Wilson (1995). "Toward a Theory of Race, Crime and Urban Inequality." In J. Hagan & R.D. Peterson (eds.) *Crime and Inequality*. Stanford, CA: Stanford University Press.

Sampson R.J. & J.D. Wooldredge (1987). "Linking the Micro- and Macro-Level Dimensions of Lifestyle-Routine Activity and Opportunity Models of Predatory Victimization." *Journal of Quantitative Criminology*, 3:371-393.

Schlossman, S. & M. Sedlak (1983). *The Chicago Area Project Revisited.* Santa Monica, CA: Rand.

Schmidt, P. (1996, June 14). "Lawmakers Told that Colleges Fail to Comply with Campus-Crime Law." *The Chronicle of Higher Education,* A37.

Shaw, C.R. & H.D. McKay (1942). *Juvenile Delinquency in Urban Areas.* Chicago, IL: University of Chicago Press.

Shaw, C.R. & H.D. McKay (1931). *Social Factors in Juvenile Delinquency.* Washington, DC: U.S. Government Printing Office.

Sheley, J.F., Z.T. McGee & J.D. Wright (1995). *Weapon-related Victimization in Selected Inner-city High School Samples.* Washington, DC: National Institute of Justice.

Sherman, L.W. (1990). "Police Crackdowns: Initial and Residential Deterrence." In M. Tonry & N. Morris (eds.) *Crime and Justice: A Review of Research,* vol. 12. Chicago, IL: University of Chicago Press.

Sherman, L.W., P. Gartin & M. Buerger (1989). "Hot Spots of Predatory Crime: Routine Activities and the Criminology of Place." *Criminology,* 27:27-56.

Shim, K.H. & M. DeBerry (1989). *Criminal Victimization in the United States.* Washington, DC: U.S. Department of Justice.

Siegel, D.G. & C.H. Raymond (1992). "An Ecological Approach to Violent Crime on Campus." *Journal of Security Administration,* 15(2):19-27.

Silberman, C.E. (1978). *Criminal Violence, Criminal Justice.* New York, NY: Random House.

Skogan, W.G. (1990). *Disorder and Decline: Crime and the Spiral of Decay in American Cities.* New York, NY: Free Press.

Skogan, W.G. (1988a). "Disorder, Crime and Community Decline." In T. Hope & M. Shaw (eds.) *Communities and Crime Reduction.* London: HMSO.

Skogan, W.G. (1988b). "Community Organizations and Crime." In M. Tonry & N. Morris (eds.) *Crime and Justice,* vol. 10. Chicago, IL: University of Chicago Press.

Skogan, W.G. (1981). "On Attitudes and Behavior." In D.A. Lewis (ed.) *Reactions to Crime.* Beverly Hills, CA: Sage.

Skogan, W.G. & M.G. Maxfield (1981). *Coping with Crime.* Beverly Hills, CA: Sage.

Sloan, J.J., B.S. Fisher & D.L. Wilkins (1995). *Crime, Fear of Crime and Related Issues on the Campus: Final Report.* Birmingham, AL: University of Alabama at Birmingham.

Sloan-Howitt, M. & G.L. Kelling (1990). "Subway Graffiti in New York City: 'Getting Up' vs. 'Meaning It and Cleaning It'." *Security Journal,* 1:131-136.

Smith, D.A. & R. Jarjoura (1989). "Household Characteristics, Neighborhood Composition and Victimization Risk." *Social Forces,* 68:621-640.

Smith, K.A. & K.A. Kinsey (1987). "Understanding Taxpaying Behavior: A Conceptual Framework with Implications for Research." *Law and Society Review,* 21:639-663.

Smith, M.C. & R. Fossey (1995). *Crime on Campus: Legal Issues and Campus Administration.* Phoenix, AZ: The Oryx Press.

Sparrow, M. (1994). *Imposing Duties: Government's Changing Approach to Compliance.* Westport, CT: Praeger.

Spelman, W. & J.E. Eck (1987). *Problem-Oriented Policing.* Washington, DC: National Institute of Justice.

Staples, L. (1990). "Powerful Ideas About Empowerment." *Administration in Social Work,* 14(2):29-42.

Stead, P.J. (1983)). *The Police of France.* New York, NY: Macmillan.

Sullivan, M.L. (1989). *Getting Paid: Youth Criminal Work in the Inner City.* Ithaca, NY: Cornell University Press.

Sun Alliance (1995). Reference P383AA.

Sutherland, E. & D. Cressey (1966). *Principles of Criminology,* Seventh Edition. New York, NY: J.B. Lippincott.

Sykes, G.M. & D. Matza (1957). "Techniques of Neutralization: A Theory of Delinquency." *American Sociological Review,* 22:664-670.

Tanioka, I. (1989). "The Informal Social Control of High School Student Behavior in Osaka, Japan: A Test of 'The Web of Informal Control' Theory of Delinquency Causation." Ph.D. Dissertation. Los Angeles, CA: University of Southern California.

Taub, R.P., D.G. Taylor & J.D. Dunham (1984). *Paths for Neighborhood Change.* Chicago, IL: University of Chicago Press.

Taylor, R.B. (1995a). "Changes on Baltimore Streetblocks, 1981 to 1994: Changes in Disorder and Decay." Paper presented at the annual meetings of the American Psychological Association, New York, NY.

Taylor, R.B. (1995b). "Measurement and Community Disorder." Paper presented at National Institute of Justice conference on "Measuring what matters." Washington, DC.

Taylor, R.B. (1995c). "Hierarchical Linear Models vs. Contextual Analysis in Environmental Criminological Research: Progress and Persistent Problems." Paper presented at the annual meetings of the American Society of Criminology, Boston, MA.

Taylor, R.B. (1987). "Toward an Environmental Psychology of Disorder." In D. Stokols & I. Altman (eds.) *Handbook of Environmental Psychology*. New York, NY: Wiley.

Taylor, R.B. & S. Gottfredson (1986). "Environmental Design, Crime, and Prevention: An Examination of Community Dynamics." In A.J. Reiss & M. Tonry (eds.) *Communities and Crime*. Chicago, IL: University of Chicago Press.

Taylor, R.B. & S.A. Shumaker (1990). "Local Crime as a Natural Hazard: Implications for Understanding the Relationship Between Disorder and Fear of Crime." *American Journal of Community Psychology,* 18:619-642.

Taylor, R.B., S.A. Shumaker & S.D. Gottfredson (1985). "Neighborhood-Level Links Between Physical Features and Local Sentiments: Deterioration, Fear of Crime, and Confidence." *Journal of Architectural Planning and Research,* 2:261-275.

Tedeschi, J. & R.B. Felson (1995). *Violence, Aggression and Coercive Action*. Washington, DC: American Psychological Association Books.

Thurman, Q.C., C. St. John & L. Riggs (1984). "Neutralization and Tax Evasion: How Effective Would a Moral Appeal be in Improving Compliance to Tax Laws? *Law and Policy,* 6:307-327.

Trickett, A., D. Ellingworth, T. Hope & K. Pease (1995a). "Crime Victimization in the Eighties." *British Journal of Criminology,* 35:343-359.

Trickett, A., D.R. Osborn & D. Ellingworth (1995b). *Property Crime Victimisation: The Roles of Individual and Area Influences*. International Review of Victimology.

Trickett, A., D.R. Osborn, J. Seymour & K. Pease (1992). "What is Different About High Crime Areas?" *British Journal of Criminology,* 32:81-89.

Tseloni, A. (1995). "The Modelling of Threat Incidence: Evidence from the British Crime Survey." In R.E. Dobash, R.P. Dobash & L. Noaks (eds.) *Gender and Crime*. Cardiff: University of Wales Press.

United States Department of Education (1995). "Digest of Education Statistics 1995." Washington DC: U.S. Department of Education, Office of Educational Research and Improvement.

United States Department of Education (1993). *State Higher Education Profiles,* Third Edition. Washington DC: U.S. Department of Education.

Violence Related Attitudes and Behaviors of High School Students—New York City, 1992 (1993). *Journal of School Health,* 63:438-440.

Walker, H.M., G. Colvin & E. Ramsey (1995). *Antisocial Behavior in School: Strategies and Best Practices*. Pacific Grove, CA: Brooks/Cole.

Wandersman, A., P. Florin, R. Friedman & R. Meier (1987). "Who Participates and Who Does Not and Why? An Analyses of Voluntary Neighborhood Organizations in the United States and Israel." *Sociological Forum,* 2:534-555.

Washnis, G. (1976). *Citizen Involvement in Crime Prevention.* Lexington, MA: Lexington Books.

Wechsler, H., A. Davenport, G. Dowdall, B. Moeykens & S. Castillo (1994). "Health and Behavioral Consequences of Binge Drinking in College: A National Survey of Students at 140 Campuses." *Journal of the American Medical Association,* 272:1672-1677.

Wechsler, H. & N. Isaac (1992). "'Binge' Drinkers at Massachusetts Colleges: Prevalence, Drinking Styles, Time Trends, and Associated Problems." *Journal of the American Medical Association,* 267:2929-2931.

Weigel, R.H., D.J. Lessing and H. Elffers (1987). "Tax Evasion Research: A Critical Appraisal and Theoretical Model." *Journal of Economic Psychology,* 8:215-235

White, J. & R. Humeniuk (1994). *Alcohol Misuse and Violence: Exploring the Relationship.* Canberra: Australian Government Publishing Service.

Whitehead, J.T. & S.P. Lab (1996). *Juvenile Justice: An Introduction,* Second Edition. Cincinnati, OH: Anderson Publishing Co.

Whitehead, J.T. & R.H. Langworthy (1989). "Gun Ownership and Willingness to Shoot: A Clarification of Current Controversies." *Justice Quarterly,* 6:263-282.

Wilcox, S. (1973). "The Geography of Robbery." In *The Prevention and Control of Robbery,* vol. 3. Davis, CA: The Center of Administration of Justice, University of California at Davis.

Wilkins, D.L. (1996). "The Spatial and Temporal Distribution of Crime on a University Campus: A 'Hot Spots' Analysis." Unpublished master thesis. Department of Justice Sciences, University of Alabama at Birmingham.

Wilson, J.Q. (1985). *Thinking About Crime,* Revised Edition. New York, NY: Vintage Books.

Wilson, J.Q. (1975). *Thinking About Crime.* New York, NY: Basic Books.

Wilson, J.Q. & R.J. Herrnstein (1985). *Crime and Human Nature.* New York, NY: Simon and Schuster.

Wilson, J.Q. & G. Kelling (1982, Mar.). "Broken Windows: The Police and Neighborhood Safety." *Atlantic Monthly,* 29-38.

Wilson, R. (1963). *Difficult Housing Estates.* Tavistock Pamphlet #5. London: Tavistock Publications.

Wilson, W.J. (1987). *The Truly Disadvantaged*. Chicago, IL: University of Chicago Press.

Wormser, R.A. (1962). *The Story of the Law*. New York, NY: Simon and Schuster.

Wortley, R. (1986). "Neutralizing Moral Constraint." *Australian and New Zealand Journal of Criminology,* 19:251-258.

Yin, P. (1980). "Fear of Crime Among the Elderly: Some Issues and Suggestions." *Social Problems,* 27:492-504.

Zimring, F. (1994). Quoted in *New York Times,* August 27:A6.

Index

About the Authors

Patricia L. Brantingham, A.B., Barnard College; M.A., Fordham; M.S. and Ph.D., Florida State. An urban planner by training, Brantingham is Professor of Criminology and Director of the Institute for Canadian Urban Research Studies at Simon Fraser University. She served as Director of Programme Evaluation at the Department of Justice Canada from 1985 through 1988. Brantingham has been involved in the development and application of principles of environmental criminology and situational crime prevention for more than two decades. She worked with the Royal Canadian Mounted Police in the development of its standard training course on crime prevention through environmental design (CPTED), and has recently worked with the Architectural Institute of British Columbia and the City of Vancouver in development of an environmental criminology course for architects and urban planners. Brantingham serves on the editorial boards of many professional and scholarly journals, including the *Journal of Research in Crime*. She is the author or editor of 24 books and scientific monographs and more than 100 articles and scientific papers. Recent books of interest include: *Environmental Criminology* (1991) and *Patterns in Crime* (1984). Recent research has looked at the patterns of crime at shopping malls and on transit systems, the distribution of crimes on road networks, and the location of crime in complex urban ecologies.

Paul J. Brantingham, A.B. and J.D., Columbia; Dip. Crim., Cambridge. A lawyer and criminologist by training, Brantingham is Professor of Criminology at Simon Fraser University. He was Associate Dean of the Faculty of Interdisciplinary at Simon Fraser during the early 1980s and served as Director of the Simon Fraser Centre for Canadian Studies during 1992. He is author or editor of more than 20 books and scientific monographs, and more than 100 articles and scientific papers. His best known books include: *Juvenile Justice Philosophy* (1978), and *Environmental Criminology* (1991) and *Patterns in Crime* (1984) both co-authored with Patricia Brantingham. Brantingham has been involved in crime analysis and crime prevention research for more than 25 years. Recent research has included study of victimization on university campuses, study of the geography of persistent offending, and study of crime in complex urban ecologies.

Richard D. Clark, Ph.D. (Criminal Justice), SUNY—Albany. He is currently an Assistant Professor in Sociology at John Carroll University. His research interests include families and delinquency, school crime, and reactions to victimization. Clark is presently engaged in research assessing the extent and impact of harassment received by grassroots environmental activists.

Ronald V. Clarke, Dean of the School of Criminal Justice, Rutgers University. His graduate degrees are in Psychology from the University of London. He has held faculty appointments in criminal justice at the University at Albany and at Temple University, and has been a Visiting Fellow at the National Police Research Unit in Australia and the U.S. National Institute of Justice. He was formerly Director of the British government's criminological department, the Home Office Research and Planning Unit. Clarke is founding editor of *Crime Prevention Studies* and is a regular guest editor for *Security Journal*. He is author or co-author of more than 130 books, monographs, and papers, including: *The Reasoning Criminal* (1986, with Derek Cornish); *Situational Crime Prevention: Successful Case Studies* (1992); *Routine Activity and Rational Choice* and *Business and Crime Prevention* (respectively 1993 and 1997, with Marcus Felson).

Francis T. Cullen, Distinguished Research Professor in the Department of Criminal Justice at the University of Cincinnati, where he also holds a joint appointment in Sociology. He is author of *Rethinking Crime and Deviance Theory*, co-author of *Reaffirming Rehabilitation, Corporate Crime Under Attack, Criminological Theory*, and *Criminology*, and co-editor of *Contemporary Criminological Theory*. Cullen has served as President of the Academy of Criminal Justice Sciences and as editor of *Justice Quarterly* and the *Journal of Crime and Justice*.

Marcus Felson, B.A., University of Chicago; Ph.D., University of Michigan. Professor at the Rutgers University of Criminal Justice. He has served as Professor at the University of Southern California and the University of Illinois. His books include: *Crime and Everyday Life: Insights and Implications for Society; Routine Activity and Rational Choice: Advances in Criminological Theory* (with Ronald V. Clarke); *Business and Crime* (with Ronald V. Clarke, forthcoming); and *Crime Prevention through Real Estate Management and Development* (with Rick Peiser, forthcoming). Felson has also written approximately 70 professional papers, including "Redesigning Hell: Preventing Crime and Disorder at the Port Authority Bus Terminal."

Jennifer L. Ferguson, doctoral student in the School of Justice Studies, Arizona State University. She has been involved in various evaluations, including an evaluation of CSAP-funded community partnership and an evaluation of

Arizona's welfare program. Ferguson's research interests center around the issue of citizen participation in collective crime prevention efforts.

Bonnie S. Fisher, Associate Professor in the Department of Political Science at the University of Cincinnati. She is the co-editor of *Campus Crime: Legal, Social, and Policy Implications*. She has written articles that appear in *Crime and Delinquency*, the *ANNALS*, the *Journal of Contemporary Criminal Justice*, and *Research in Crime and Delinquency* that examine the extent and nature of crime against college students and their fear of crime. Fisher is currently examining the extent and nature of sexual victimization among college women thanks to a grant funded by the National Institute of Justice.

Ross Homel, Foundation Professor of Justice Administration at Griffith University, and part-time Commissioner of the Queensland Criminal Justice Commission. His Ph.D. is in Behavioural Sciences from Macquarie University, and resulted in the publication in the United States of *Policing and Punishing the Drinking Driver* (1988). Homel's research interests include: the prevention of crime, violence, corruption, and traffic injuries; the effects of legal sanctions on criminal behaviour; criminal justice processes including police enforcement and court sentencing; alcohol, drugs, and crime; theories of the criminal justice system; and statistical methods in the social sciences. Since moving to Griffith University in 1992, Homel has continued his research into the prevention of alcohol-related violence, with particular reference to the use of safety action programs implemented through community development methods at the local level.

Tim Hope, Ph.D. (Sociology), University of London. He is Reader in Criminology, Keele University and Director of the Economic and Social Research Council Crime and Social Order Research Programme. Previously he worked at the Universities of Manchester and Missouri—St. Louis and was principal research officer for crime prevention at the Home Office Research and Planning Unit, London. He has researched and published on communities and crime, crime prevention, environmental criminology, and victimology, including work on the British Crime Survey. Hope has also designed and directed major evaluation research on community crime prevention interventions. His publications include: *Coping with Burglary* (1984), *Implementing Crime Prevention Measures* (1986), *Communities and Crime Reduction* (1988), and *Crime Prevention and Community Safety* (forthcoming).

Steven P. Lab holds a Ph.D. in Criminology from Florida State University and is presently Professor and Director of Criminal Justice at Bowling Green State University. He is the author of *Crime Prevention: Approaches, Practices and Evaluations*, Third Edition (1997); *Juvenile Justice: An Introduction*, Second

Edition (with J.T. Whitehead, 1996); *Victimology* (with W.G. Doerner, 1995); and numerous articles. His current research work focuses on crime, victimization, and crime preventive activity in secondary school settings.

Paul J. Lavrakas, Professor of Communication and Journalism in the College of Social Behavioral Sciences at The Ohio State University and Director of the OSU's new survey research center. Prior to 1996/1997 academic year, he was Professor of Communications Studies, Journalism, Statistics, and Urban Affairs at Northwestern University. In 1982, he founded the Northwestern University Survey Laboratory and served as its director through the summer of 1996. Since the early 1980s, a main focus of his scholarship and teaching has been on survey research methods. He is the editor of two books on election polls and the news media: *Polling and Presidential Election Coverage* (Lavrakas & Holley, 1991) and *Presidential Polls and the News Media* (Lavrakas, Traugott & Miller, 1995). He also is co-author of *The Voter's Guide to Election Polls* (Traugott & Lavrakas, 1996). Lavrakas regularly serves as a consultant to federal and other governmental agencies, and to private sector organizations. He was the 1994-1995 President of the Midwest Association of Public Opinion Research and currently serves as Chair of AAPOR's Conference Operations Committee.

Chunmeng Lu, Ph.D. (Political Science), University of Cincinnati. He is currently an Associate Professor at the Shih Chien College, Kaohsiung Campus in Taiwan. His primary research interests are public policy analysis and research methodology. He is working on several papers that originated from his dissertation that examines the organizational compliance behavior with a regulatory policy.

Dennis Palumbo, Regents' Professor of Justice Studies at Arizona State University. He has published books, chapters in books, and articles in criminal justice, evaluation, public policy, public administration, statistics, and American politics. He was founding editor and editor of the *Policy Studies Review* for 10 years. His most recent publication was an evaluation of the Gang Resistance Education and Training Program (GREAT) with Jennifer Fergerson, in *Evaluation Review*. Palumbo is currently involved in an evaluation of the Community Partnership of Phoenix.

John J. Sloan III, Associate Professor of Criminal Justice and Sociology at the University of Alabama at Birmingham, where he is also Director of Graduate Studies in Criminal Justice. A sociologist by training, his research interests include fear of crime, victimization, the police, and criminological theory. His most recent research has focused on crime, fear of crime, and perceived risk of victimization on college and university campuses. Sloan is co-editor (with Bonnie S. Fisher) of *Campus Crime: Legal, Social, and Policy Perspectives.*

Judy Stein, doctoral candidate in the School of Justice Studies, Arizona State University. She has conducted evaluation research for the G.R.E.A.T. Program, Project Intervention, and The Phoenix Community Partnership. Stein's major research interests include: policing, domestic violence, and capital punishment.

Ralph B. Taylor, Ph.D. (Social Psychology), Johns Hopkins University. He is currently on the faculty of Criminal Justice at Temple University. He has held positions at Virginia Tech (Psychology), and Johns Hopkins University (Psychology, Center for Metropolitan Planning and Research). His research has been funded by the National Institute of Mental Health, the National Science Foundation, and the National Institute of Justice. His work has appeared in many journals including: *Urban Affairs Quarterly, Social Problems, American Journal of Community Psychology, Journal of Criminal Law and Criminology, Sociological Forum, Environment and Behavior, Journal of Personality and Social Psychology, Journal of Applied Social Psychology, Journal of Research in Crime and Delinquency,* and *Criminology.* He is the author of *Research Methods in Criminal Justice* (1993) and *Human Territorial Functioning* (1988), and the editor of *Urban Neighborhoods* (1986). Taylor will be a Senior Visiting Fellow at the National Institute of Justice during 1997.